THE

BIG

ASK

THE

UNLOCK the POSSIBILITIES

BIG

in YOUR WORK, LIFE & DREAMS

ASK

with COURAGEOUS REQUESTS*

 *Opportunities, Exceptions, Help, Support, Advice, Second Chances, Feedback, Clarity, Connection*

PAUL QUINN

The Big Ask

The big ask: Unlock the possibilities in your work, life & dreams with coura-geous requests / Paul Quinn.
Publisher: Quinn Spire LLC. Printed in the U.S.
Motivational | Self-Help | Communication Skills | Success in Business | Success in Life

ISBN: 979-8-218-51727-4 (paperback)
ISBN: 979-8-218-51728-1 (epub)

Proofreading: Connie Eyer
Layout design: Olivia Hammerman
Cover design: Colin Denney
Model illustration: Cliff Questel
Author Photo: Alan Luntz

This book is set in Adobe Caslon Pro and Zeitung Pro.

www.quinnspire.net
www.bigaskbook.com

This book is for everyone who hesitates to,
doesn't know how to,
or never thinks to,
ask.

CONTENTS

INTRODUCTION

I MAY NOT KNOW YOU PERSONALLY, BUT I KNOW THERE are things you want to have, know, or experience that would enrich your personal or work life, whether for the moment or the long term. Some of these desires you could fulfill with no help from anyone. But some will not come about without others' consent or participation. If you are to succeed you must ask.

The story I'm about to share broke all the rules for me when I heard it 25 years ago. It was the story that got me thinking that, more than a mere transaction or means to an end, asking was a life skill, one I'd mostly overlooked. It suggested, too, that asking was an outlook. A mindset. A way of living from an expanded sense of possibility.

One summer evening my then-neighbors Mike and Mona, a couple in their late-30s, sat on the front porch of their beautiful Edwardian home enjoying the cool lake breezes when another couple of about the same age, Peter and Pamela, came strolling along. (The couples' real names aren't as cute; I'm ensuring their privacy.) Though strangers to the homeowners, Peter and Pamela stopped on the walkway and called to them across the flawless lawn.

"We love your house! We've walked through the neighborhood many times and always stop to admire it."

Mike and Mona soaked in the compliments.

After a few more pleasantries, Peter and Pamela came right out with it: "Would you consider selling it to us?"

Not a question one expects. Who asks to buy a house from the sidewalk, let alone moments after hello?

What made the ask even more surprising was that Mike and Mona had only *that week* discussed selling the house, a fact unknown to Peter and Pamela, but extraordinary timing, nonetheless. The couples exchanged phone numbers, and a deal was quickly made to sell direct, an advantage for both parties. A few months later, Peter and Pamela settled in as the happy new owners.

The story, as it quickly spread around the neighborhood, gave me mixed feelings. On the one hand, Peter and Pamela's dazzling ask made me feel as if all my life I'd been watering the lawn with a squirt gun, doing things the hard way. When had I *ever* had that kind of imagination for solutions? When had I ever asked that big? Not only would it have never occurred to me to make such a request, but I would've hesitated to ask even if I'd had the notion.

And yet, it also got me curious: what if an ask is an affirmation of the deepest kind, a way of saying yes to life by pursuing its possibilities? This book is partly an answer to that question, even if it can only be answered by experience, by our willingness to engage more fully with the world, and to ask.

But I'm getting ahead of myself. Definitions first. By *ask* I mean a request or inquiry on behalf of yourself, another person, or many people, whether spontaneous or planned, formal or informal, verbal or written. It could be a bid for a higher wage, a must-have object, steadfast emotional support, laser clarity, or an exception to the rule. It might be a request for a helping hand, a life-changing opportunity, or a plea for a second chance after you blew it the first time.

To ask is to speak up for what you want. It is an act of assertion, as is "speaking up" in general, although making yourself heard is not always an ask.

So, what is a Big Ask?

It's one that feels big to you. The size is defined by the courage or conviction it takes to voice it and the value you place on getting it. That might be asking an investor for a million dollars or a friend to listen without interrupting.

Big asks are often turning points. The request may seem small to onlookers, but for you it marks a shift in your relationship to yourself, to others, or to your life as a whole. A big ask is like the sudden spike in a brainwave scan that tells you *this* moment is not like the others. And when you succeed, the relief, gratitude, or confidence you feel may outshine the external rewards of getting what you asked.

This book invites you to consider a wider view of what is possible for yourself. It challenges you to identify those attitudes you've developed around asking and receiving that work against getting what you want in life, personally or professionally. You'll see, for example, that asking for opportunities or help is not a substitute for self-reliance or hard work but an act of initiative, a decision to move through life more efficiently and resourcefully.

You'll discover tools and strategies you can use *today* to improve your chances of getting what you ask, no matter whom you're asking. And you'll see how a request or inquiry, sometimes just one, can change an outcome for the moment or a lifetime, as it did for the more than 80 people who share their illuminating stories in these pages.

Incidentally, while this book includes wisdom from the worlds of sales and negotiation, it does not purport to be a how-to in either specialty. There are thousands of books published on those topics. But there are surprisingly few about asking as the key to an engaged and fruitful life.

* * *

Although my six decades have given me many "aha's" into the behavior of humans (being one myself), I'm not a psychologist or sociologist. Rather, I make the case for asking through the expertise and testimonials of the storytellers, recent studies from social psychology, my personal insights, experiences, and passion for the topic, and good old common sense.

In my professional life, I've asked a lot. After getting my bachelors in theatre I spent a few years working as an actor in Chicago. As a career, acting is one continuous hustle for work; as a craft, it trains you to ask yourself, "What does my character want more than anything else, and how does he try to get it?"—a question worth asking for all of us, the main characters in our own life stories.

I left acting to write multimedia training and marketing materials for everything from hi-tech and retail to manufacturing and fitness. Meeting each new client meant doing deep-dives with experts on subjects I often knew nothing about (like the time I had to ask a Silicon Valley client, "What's a server?").

In seven years as head of client coaching at Unipro Marketing Services in Chicago, then the second largest tradeshow marketing company in North America, I teamed up with our in-house sales pros to lead seminars for Xerox, Panasonic, Maritz, Ameritech, Sabreliner Aviation, and other clients on how to ask questions to engage, qualify, and turn their prospects into customers at exhibitions. ("Can I help you?" risked 40 lashes.)

I've written executive speeches, coached law students on delivering opening statements in mock trials, and co-produced corporate events, all of which gave me the privilege of working with some extraordinarily talented people. Today I continue my work as a presentation coach helping leaders create and deliver business and educational presentations that their audiences understand, feel, and act upon—a well-formed ask.

Outside the business suit, I've long pursued my interest in the intuitive and spiritual dimensions of what it means to be human.

I've been with the love of my life, Rich, for almost 40 years and married for nine of them. I enjoy good times with friends, writing my blog, and idealizing but not committing to dog ownership. (Though who knows—I could be throwing a ball to a rescue mutt by the time you read this.)

As for *my* biggest ask? You're holding it. Asking hundreds of people, from all walks of life, "What's the biggest thing you've asked for and received?" has been humbling and illuminating. It's given me the privilege of being a witness to the beauty of humanity; our inner-most strivings and dreams, sometimes within our grasp, sometimes just outside it. Above all, the experiences people shared with me for *The Big Ask* have deepened my appreciation for our capacity to be transformed, like Scrooge renewed, by the power of a dared ask or changed perspective.

Most asks escape our notice, but others may call upon untapped reserves of courage and creativity if not generous measures of self-trust, self-permission, and hope. As you read the stories, I hope you feel the same sense of possibility the storytellers felt and create similar, or even better, outcomes for yourself.

So, what would you like to have? To do? To know?

What ask would change everything for you?

And what will it take for you to ask?

HOW TO READ AND USE THIS BOOK

THE CHALLENGES AND BENEFITS OF ASKING ARE universal, as are the diverse voices within this book—people of different ages, color, nationalities, professions, economic spectrums, levels of achievement, etc. I encourage you to read all their stories, not just those specific to your work or personal interests. Why? Because *every* story has the potential to unlock something in you: a different perspective, a new strategy, an unexpected correlation to your own life. Any of these stories could be the one that inspires you to ask for something you wouldn't have asked as boldly or skillfully (or at all) before reading it.

The stories were told to me directly through recorded interviews that I later transcribed, edited, and had checked by the storyteller for accuracy. Occasionally you'll see quotation marks around names ("Mortimer") meaning I've changed the name to protect their privacy. Incidentally, the question I asked after each interview—"Who do you know who might enjoy sharing stories or insights for the book?"—enabled me to meet many of the remarkable people featured here, people I never would've met without asking for referrals.

If you're a flipper, you're probably not reading this sentence because you've jumped to Chapter 12 (without any thought to my feelings in the matter!). But I recommend you read at least the first seven chapters in sequence. They're the foundation, and I don't want you to miss how they interconnect.

Lastly, the book invites you to look at your own beliefs and behaviors around asking, so that you can make choices more aligned with getting what you want. Consider using the questions that pop up in each chapter as prompts for self-reflection and journaling—both of which take some investment, so take your time with the book. Read a chapter or two and then play with the kids. Have an apple. Shear the sheep. And come back to *The Big Ask* refreshed.

CHAPTER ONE

WHY ASK?

You create your opportunities by asking for them.
—SHAKTI GAWAIN, writer

PEOPLE SAY YES. AND THEY SAY IT MORE OFTEN THAN you might expect. In studies conducted for over a decade at Cornell University, students approached strangers and made small requests. The young researchers were tasked to find out: would people agree to fill out surveys or mail letters or count beans in a jar—just because they were asked?

In every year of the study, the student-experimenters were surprised that the rate of compliance was nearly *double* what they'd predicted.[1] Despite their misgivings, twice as many people said yes to their requests. (Though I, for one, wouldn't count beans without at least the promise of a bright red sucker for my efforts.)

And it's not just behavioral experimenters who ask and get. Pew Research Center reported that 66% of job candidates got better starting salaries after asking for more.[2] Fundraisers who secure a visit with a potential donor have an 85% chance of getting the gift.[3] High school students who ask their counselors about college financial aid are 28% more likely to get the aid than those who don't consult counselors.[4] If the math is any indication, asking pays off.

My friends Tom and Tina Albright went to a game at Fenway Park but got there too late to be among the first 10,000 attendees to receive free Boston Red Sox beach towels. The family seated next to them, a couple and their college-age son, had three of the towels. Around the ninth inning, the family got up to leave. "Excuse me," Tom said to them, "we came in late and were just curious if we could possibly have one of the beach towels?"

The couple declined the request. "We accepted that, of course," Tom told me, "and they walked away."

About five minutes later, the man came back with a rolled-up beach towel. "We only need two," he told Tom and Tina, "you guys can have one." And with that, he handed them the coveted plush towel with the Red Sox logo on a navy background.

We'll never know what made the family decide to "throw in the towel" after initially rejecting the request. But in her book, *You Have More Influence Than You Think: How We Underestimate Our Power of Persuasion and Why It Matters*, Vanessa Bohns reports that people "agree because they feel guilty or uncomfortable saying 'no,' because they want to feel like good people, because they want to look like good people, because it pains them to see someone else suffer, or out of genuine empathy and a desire to do something good."[5]

Sure, tender motivations like those might compel someone to give us a beach towel. But people need big incentives to grant a truly *big* ask, right?

On the contrary. Dr. Bohns says that generous responses tend to increase rather than diminish with the size of the ask. In other words, I'll feel like a good person for agreeing to help you assemble an IKEA bookshelf. But if you ask me to help you build a whole library of them, I'll feel like a superhero for saying yes. When we rise to the request, our level of positive self-regard rises proportionately (provided we don't feel like pushovers).

And if you're concerned that people will resent you for asking, you've got it wrong. According to social psychologist Dr. Heidi Grant, helpers "tend to like the people whom they help *more*, not less, after helping them."[6] So, if I give you a hand, it makes me feel good about myself—more generous, competent, engaged—and, by extension, I feel good about *you* for giving me the opportunity to feel good about myself.

The ask might even create a bond. A few winters ago, a neighbor I didn't know asked if I'd jump her car battery. I did and felt like I'd saved the day. Endorphins were released. I felt needed, more a part of my community. And that simple assist became the basis for our neighborly waves and hellos ever since.

Reciprocity Reigns

It's also reassuring to note that we earthlings are wired for consent from a faith in reciprocity. Dr. Robert Cialdini, an internationally recognized expert on the psychology of persuasion, names our sense of obligation to return favors as one of his six principles of social influence.[7] Reciprocity is so ingrained in us, he finds, that it's been shown to work regardless of whether the giver and receiver even *like* each other. That's because reciprocity tends to be more transactional than personal.

For example, have you ever felt the nagging need to repay favors? When you finally reciprocate, you may find less pleasure in pleasing the person than in the relief of the repayment. The "debt" paid, you're free to mentally move on with a clean slate.

Candice DeLong understands the power of reciprocity. The true crime podcaster and retired FBI agent once gave advice to a young agent who was trying to get pertinent information from a woman who knew the suspect in a murder case. Candice told her protégé, "After your first meeting, send her flowers with a note saying, 'Thank you for your time.' You just might be surprised."

The young agent did as Candice suggested and was shocked that the recipient not only supplied the requested information but volunteered leads that tied the suspect to past crimes. What made the informant so willing to talk? Candice concludes, "No one had ever sent her flowers before." [8]

Crimefighting aside, helping each other can be an impersonal but meaningful opportunity to *pay forward* the kindnesses and goodwill one receives from life. The thought takes hold: *It's a joy to give when I have received so much.* Or, as St. Thomas Aquinas more lyrically stated it, "It is the nature of goodness to pour itself out."

Of course, some requests are a holy pain in the ass. They rope us in when we'd rather be left to graze. But we might take some satisfaction, if not in helping, then in *having helped,* and enjoy the opportunity to rack up those karmic points. And human nature being what it is, we can be reasonably assured that the asker will help us out in return. Because more often than we might expect, people say yes.

A Life-Changing Exception

Twelve years ago, when I first started talking to people about my idea for this book, I met up with Russell Leander, a psychotherapist, educator, and artist in Chicago, our mutual hometown. But the inspiring story he shared with me is not about his profession. It's about asking, against all odds, for an exception. It's also about following a dream on only the thinnest thread of possibility.

At 19, after a post-high school "gap year" of jobs digging ditches in the Arizona desert and folding underwear, I realized that I'd better go to college, or the gap year might become a gap life. I applied to several colleges, all of which turned me down for the same reason: I never officially graduated from high school.

For my last attempt, I pulled on a tie and drove three and a half hours in summer in a car with no air conditioning to Northern Arizona University (NAU), where I'd made an appointment on rather vague terms with Joseph Rolle, dean of admissions. His secretary led me into a darkly paneled room where the austere, white-haired Mr. Rolle sat behind his desk in a gray suit.

I pleaded my case, telling him that despite not fulfilling my high school requirements I wanted to be of service in my life and become a special education art teacher. Attending NAU would start me on that path. Peering out from heavily lidded eyes he said, "I'll give you one semester to prove you can do this." And, with one stroke of his pen, I was in. My parents paid the tuition.

Asking has helped shape the better parts of me, given me a positive view of humanity and inspired me to pay it forward. Five years ago, I decided to find Mr. Rolle's descendants and write them a letter to honor him, to thank him, posthumously, for the opportunity he gave me that resulted in my degree and 25 gratifying years in human services. To my delight, my research revealed he was still alive, 93 years old, and living in Flagstaff. I wrote the letter to him personally.

A few weeks later, I received a letter from his wife. She had read him my letter and related that even in his much-diminished state, he managed a smile. I learned that he died two weeks later. As a lost young man I had asked for an exception, and Joseph Rolle gave me one that changed my life.[10]

Asking for exceptions (a theme of many stories here) is like feeling around for hidden panels in seemingly solid walls. Tap here, press there. Suddenly, a secret passage appears. We're in! But the one rule in asking for exceptions is that we must commit to being exceptional in exercising the opportunity given. We'll owe it to the people who believed in us and bent the rules on our behalf.

What walls might open for you, what pathways revealed, if you asked for an exception?

> Only those who ask for more can get more
> and only those who know there is more, ask.
> —ALAN COHEN, teacher and author

More Good Reasons to Ask

The obvious gain from asking is *getting*. It's why we do it. But there are rewards that transcend the transaction. Asking empowers us, frees us from regret, and inspires others by our example.

Empowerment

For those who hold back, asking works like a defibrillator. Just the act of making your needs known, out loud, gives you a jumpstart. Asking is an act of self-determination. It affirms what's important to you and your readiness to receive it. In stating clearly what you want you waste no time wishing, wondering, or worrying. You shift from doubter to decider, from dreamer to doer. You have agency.

Asking both empowers you and makes you vulnerable. You're empowered by asserting your needs or desires, and vulnerable because you can't control the response you get. But by asking you're essentially declaring to yourself,

I know what I want. I'm worthy of the ask and know I can get it. I communicate it clearly and with respect for the person I'm asking. And I do right with what I am given.

"No" may be hard to hear, of course, but it gives us something, too—valuable feedback as to where we stand in relation to getting what we want. And that's something we didn't have before we asked. We're free, then, to accept the no and move on, redirect our approach, or ask someone else in the hope of a better answer (like we did when asking Dad after Mom said no, or the other way around).

Freedom from Regret

In the short documentary film *Ten Meter Tower*,[9] wary-looking individuals contemplate diving from a platform into a shimmering blue pool 32 feet below. The people are real, as is the terror on their faces. As you might expect, some leap. Most leave. And barely a word is spoken.

Like the divers, mulling over an ask can find us trembling at the very edge of our doubts: *Who am I to ask for this? How would I survive rejection? What if I get what I ask for but then fail?* When the risk seems too great, we scramble off the diving board. But the relief is temporary. Over time, those rattling voices of regret get louder.

Why didn't I ask for help in school?
Why didn't I ask for the sale?
Why didn't I ask to be included in the fun?
I wish I could go back in time and ask her out!

Regrets drive our fists into pillows at three in the morning. But asking keeps us current, with less to drag us back to the past. It connects us to what we want and very often to who we *are*. If reading this book brings up regrets about your past failures to speak up, don't despair. Today is yours. It's not too late to start asking.

Inspiring Others

When you receive what you asked for and tell others about it, you plant in them the seeds of possibility. You give them hope. The story of your bold or creative request could move people to follow your example and become, like the stories in this book, proof of what can happen if only we ask.

A Pivotal Question

Dr. Michelle L. Buck is clinical professor of leadership at Kellogg School of Management at Northwestern University. Her work has been published in academic journals as well as in *Fast Company*, *The Hill*, and *Psychology Today*. As an educator and consultant, her stated commitment is to "inspire and empower others to unleash new possibilities for themselves, for others, and the communities in which they find themselves." Judging from her story, she walks the talk.

In 2010, I was moderating a panel of speakers for a university conference. One of the speakers, Dale Dawson, was a former CEO who was on the presidential advisory council for the president of Rwanda, helping the post genocide transformation of the country. I was intrigued by the media reports about all the transformation occurring in Rwanda, because my rational brain couldn't understand the genocide nor the rapid rate of change in its aftermath.

But the focus of the panel discussion was not on Rwanda, which is why it seemed like synchronicity to discover that Dale was playing a key role in that country. I wanted to understand more. Even though I advise people to speak up, I'm not necessarily good at asking for everything that I want or need myself. I pulled him aside for a moment and asked if sometime after the conference I could ask him about what was happening in Rwanda. It felt like a big ask because he was busy, I was busy, and the subject was not part of the work we were there to do.

I expected we'd plan to meet over coffee or something. But Dale asked, "Rather than me tell you about Rwanda, why not just come with me on my next trip there and observe?" Intuition told me this was a life opportunity that I couldn't pass by.

Six months later I went to Rwanda.

To see the genocide memorial and hear the stories of the people who survived changed my life in so many ways. While there, I was thinking, *I teach students on leadership, and leaders want to know about change and transformation, and this is the best case study imaginable.* It became my dream to someday bring students there.

Three-and-a half years later, I took 30 MBA students to Rwanda. They listened, learned, met with entrepreneurs and government leaders, and I was able to arrange a private meeting for all of us with President Kagame. Many of them told me it changed their lives as well. And being leaders, I knew they would take what they learned and could go out and impact others.

I had a life-changing moment during my first visit to the genocide memorial in Kigali. I was visiting a gallery with life-sized photos and descriptions of children killed in the genocide. These children did not have a chance to grow up as adults, to live the rest of their lives. I was deeply touched and inspired by the profound privilege of my life, and a desire and commitment and sense of responsibility to use my life in a meaningful way. To this day, I think of the children in Rwanda who did not have a chance to grow up, and I am inspired to live my own life with gratitude and a commitment to use my opportunities, my strengths and my work in a way that serves others.

I had not wanted to disturb Dale Dawson by asking him, "Could I learn a little bit more about what's happening in Rwanda?" And yet that question, and Dale's generosity, led to experiences that have profoundly impacted my life and created learning opportunities for others as well. We never know what might be possible if we follow our curiosity and ask a question.

By following our inquisitive nature, we open ourselves to discover connections to ideas, people, and experiences we never imagined. If you allowed your natural curiosity to flourish, what might become more alive in you? Where might that interest lead you? And who might you ask to help show you the way?

What Are We Afraid Of?

When I was writing this book somebody asked me, with a snarky *Gotcha!* tone, "Yeah, but what if *everybody* asked for what they wanted?"—as if I'd overlooked an obvious flaw in the premise. Today I wish I'd asked him, "What's concerning to you about that?" or "So, what's the worst that could happen?" But instead, I told him he had little need to worry because, of the hundreds of people I'd asked, "What were your biggest asks in life?", most were unable to recall any and admitted to hating asking in general. Judging from his silence, I'd reassured him that society was safe from collapse.

When I ask people their reasons for not asking for things like help, support, exceptions, or opportunities, the answers are predictable:

- Fear of looking inept, weak, or "needy"
- Concern about seeming selfish or opportunistic
- Feeling unworthy of the ask
- Not wanting to be a bother or feel indebted
- Worry that requests could turn into confrontations
- Dread of disappointment and rejection

Any ask we perceive as a risk—to our desired outcome, our self-image, our relationship to the person we're asking—can scare us into pulling the reins. These fears grip all of us. If you thought you were weird or alone in this, take heart. You're not.

There are two reasons for not asking I hear most often. The first, which isn't on the list above, is innocently simple: it rarely occurs to people to ask. Who can't relate to that? Who would *know* that many banks will refund ATM fees charged by competing banks, or that surgical teams will speak affirmations while you're under anesthesia ("You're doing great and will enjoy a swift recovery")—just for asking? I was 50 before I learned that hotels would give me a free toothbrush if I left mine at home (for keeps, not a loaner!).

The second big reason people hold back is the fear of being told no. And yet, as we heard from the experts, people are generally motivated to say yes. To put this into perspective, here's Apple founder, Steve Jobs:

> Now, I've actually always found something to be very true, which is most people don't get those experiences because they never ask. I've never found anybody who didn't want to help me when I've asked them for help … I've never found anyone who's said no or hung up the phone when I called—I just asked.
>
> And when people ask me, I try to be as responsive, to pay that debt of gratitude back. Most people never pick up the phone and call, most people never ask. And that's what

separates, sometimes, the people that do things from the people that just dream about them.

Ok, so maybe we shouldn't be surprised that nobody said no to STEVE JOBS (though in fairness, he was speaking of his early years). But to his point: doers must ask. And when they do, things get interesting.

Asking Apple

Sometimes a single ask changes everything, as it did for Russell Leander and Dr. Michelle L. Buck. At other times it takes a whole chain of asks to reach our goals. Such is the case in the next story, set in the Netherlands. If you're not a technophile, rest assured there's no jargon to clog its inspiring message. And the storyteller's remarkable make-or-break moment is a virtual master class in self-trust.

In 2010, self-described "ideas guy" Michel Elings was having a drink in the town of Bussum with travel writer and photographer Jochem Wijnands when Michel asked the kind of question idea guys love: What if? "What if," Michel asked Jochem, "we build a magazine based on all the old travel articles that you have … provide those in English for a worldwide audience … and the iPad is the new channel to bring the magazine to the world?"

The question ultimately drove them to create TRVL, the first iPad-exclusive magazine. By 2012, it was voted best iPad magazine and the highest rated on iTunes, with 1.5 million readers—a grounded answer to a lofty "What if."

TRVL's success earned Michel a VIP ticket to the 2012 Worldwide Developers Conference in San Francisco, the biggest Apple conference in the world (and number one cause of techie hyperventilation). Even more exciting was that Apple planned to showcase TRVL magazine about their innovative use of Apple's platform (along with stories from other start-ups) in a video lead-in to CEO Tim Cook's keynote.

Among the 5,000 people pouring into the Moscone Center on the opening day of the conference, was Michel, who slipped into a seat in the VIP section just six rows behind the Apple senior team.

> I was sitting between the CTOs of Facebook and Pinterest. And I thought, *Holy shit, I'm in San Francisco with a VIP ticket! We're in the video! All my dreams have come true!* I thought that was it. When the conference ended, everyone started to leave the auditorium and I was following them, looking at all these backs drifting away. Then I looked back toward the stage and saw all the Apple executives mingling there.

One of the mingling executives he spotted was Eddy Cue, Apple's senior vice president of services. Michel knew that Cue was a dealmaker who played a major role in developing iTunes and the App Store. And he instantly realized this could be his moment to capture Cue's attention with the promise of a new software Michel and his team were developing, one that would enable *anyone* to publish magazines on iPads. "I thought, this is my only chance in life I will ever get so close to such influential people," Michel told me.

His next moment was almost cinematic, so let's picture it as a scene in a movie. A drone shot shows 5,000 bodies funneling out the exit while, at the opposite end, a tiny group clumps together at the stage. Suddenly, a lone figure breaks off from the departing masses. The music turns momentous as the figure moves steadily, purposefully toward the small group at the stage.

> **I changed my direction from going out to going in.** I think I was the only external person in the group. Eddy Cue was talking with someone else. But at one point he

looked at me and I said, "Hey, we were in the video!" He said, "Congratulations." And I said, "Listen, we are making something far bigger than the TRVL magazine you saw in the video—we are building the software you guys forgot to make."

An irresistible overture. Cue handed Michel his business card and told him to send an email.

It was a pivotal moment for everything. And things went really fast after that. I had my calendar booked with massive numbers of appointments with people from Apple [to demo the new, self-publishing software], but in the first meeting they already knew that I talked with Eddy Cue. I started asking for pretty much everything and got it, lots of marketing and promotion advice.

Fast-forward to 2013, the year Michel and his team launched Prss, the very platform he'd promised to Eddie Cue would enable anyone to publish an iPad-compatible magazine. It turned out that Apple liked Prss. So much, in fact, that they acquired it and made it the foundation for Apple News.

"It was insane," Michel told me. "The whole process was just unbelievable. Our whole team, about 16 people at that point, got jobs at Apple. We started working on Apple News. A number of folks from the team are still working there."

Michel and his team not only asked "What If," resulting in two innovative products, but made a habit of requesting advice, opportunities, referrals, and feedback. But what stands out for me is Michel's fateful decision to approach the executives rather than join the mass exit: "I changed my direction from going out to going in."[11]

Move your thoughts and your feet in the direction of your dreams. As it did for a lost young man asking for college admission, a professor asking about Rwanda, and a tech entrepreneur asking for the world, life just might hand you the Golden Ticket.

Three Keys to a Successful Ask

What do you want? An exception to the rules? More days working from home? A colleague to recommend your services? Help moving a piano up a narrow staircase? In every effective ask there are three core elements:

Desire: You know what you want, and you want it enough to ask. (Chapter 2)

Belief: You believe it's ok to ask for what you want, that you're worthy of it, and that it's possible to get it—or are willing to challenge your *dis*belief and ask anyway. (Chapters 3–5)

Skill: You ask in ways that people feel comfortable giving what you want. And when stakes are high, you create a strategy to be most persuasive. Presentation counts. (Chapters 6–7)

Desire, Belief, and Skill are interdependent components. A compelling Desire with a strong Belief but poor Skill guarantees frustration. Desire without Belief can weaken an ask, even with effective Skills. And a room-temperature Desire won't even get your ask off the couch.

Does that mean that a request fueled with optimum Desire, Belief, and Skill *guarantees* the outcome you want? If only! There are just too many variables in human interactions. You may never know the reasons behind yes or no. It could be who, how, when, or where you asked, or your physical resemblance to somebody's best friend or hated ex. But the very uncertainty of outcomes makes the case for learning to ask effectively. When you do, you increase the chances of unlocking life-changing possibilities for yourself or others.

And who doesn't want that?

Nee heb je, ja kun krijgen.
—Dutch expression ("No is a given until you ask")

CHAPTER TWO

WHAT DO YOU WANT?

If you don't know what you want,
you will probably never get it.
—OLIVER WENDELL HOLMES, U.S. Supreme Court

"BY THE WAY, I'M LEAVING THE COMPANY IN THE FALL to start law school," my young client informed me after a presentation coaching. Congratulations would have been in order had I not caught the flatness in his voice and the crease in his brow. I expressed surprise at his decision to move from sales to law and asked what drew him to it. "I don't really want it," he replied with a forced chuckle, "but my parents are pushing for it and they're paying for it, so ..."

I didn't stay in touch with the young man, but I strongly doubt "Attorney" appears after his name today. That path wasn't his.

Craving a parent's approval has, for better or worse, driven many people to succeed. But in his case there seemed to be no clear desire or drive at all, only a lack of personal will and a fear of rocking Mom and Dad's boat.

This chapter is about becoming clear about what you want or need. By *want* I mean anything you'd like to be, do, or have but which, when compared to a need, you could tolerate living without it. A *need* may be a survival essential, such as food, water, safety, and sense of belonging, or an intense want: the yearning for meaning and fulfillment in your life, in ways particular to you. The difference between wants and needs, then, is a matter of degree, like one person who thinks it might be fun to ride a horse and another who feels only half alive if not astride an Appaloosa. In this book, the words *wants* and *needs* are used interchangeably.

Goals are commitments for which you are accountable to yourself or others to achieve within timelines. And then there are dreams, those heart-sparked desires that you either enjoy as fantasies or pursue as goals.

Beyond superficial requests, knowing what you want, need, or strive to achieve gives you a leg up on life. Decisions get easier. There are no lesser options, no false alternatives to pull you in other directions. And that laser clarity gives you a sense of purpose that can make you more persuasive. Bonus: others sense your confidence and commitment and *want* to give you the green light.

We all desire that certainty. And yet, being part of the human comedy is being oblivious to our own feelings and needs. For example, have you ever found yourself thinking, *Whew, it's hot in here!* and only then realized that *for the last hour* you'd been sweating like an ironworker? It's easy to become so used to an unpleasant situation that you stop noticing its impact. But the moment you become *aware* of the discomfort—in this case, the droplets pooling in your pits—you're able to identify what you might prefer instead.

Suddenly options abound. You can open the window or turn down the thermostat or ask that it be turned down or bring in a fan or remove some clothing or change rooms. You have choices that weren't apparent before the point of awareness, the moment you felt the heat.

Sometimes, though, someone steps in to hold up a mirror. They show us the wants we failed to see, those desires "hiding in plain sight." When I asked for examples, these next two storytellers raised their hands.

Clearing the Air. *Jennifer Gladston Butler is a writer, painter, and author who lived for many years in London and now calls New York home.*

John Roger, the head of my church, was giving a talk in London, and afterward, I approached and asked his advice. "J-R, I have tried to give up smoking 40 times. I've tried everything but nothing works. What can I do?" He looked at me. Grinned.

"Jennifer, do you *want* to give up smoking?"

I looked at him like a ghost. 'I don't know. Everyone tells me it's bad for my health. It stinks. It's expensive. Nobody ever asked me that!'

"Well, *I'm* asking you. Do you *want* to give up smoking?"

His simple question profoundly clarified my intention. I had lied to myself, broken my word to myself, but somehow his question resonated within my core: To Thine Own Self Be True.

"Yes, J-R, I want to quit."

I never had another cigarette after that.

Nobody Asked Me. *D. C. Anderson is a New York–based actor and recording artist.*

Sometimes I revisit a recording of mine. Let it play through. Of course, there are always cringes and 'what was I thinking's,' but I let those pass. We are all in process. And writing and recording has been mine since the late Kris Pruett came to a concert of mine and asked me, "Why aren't you recording?"

"No one has asked me," was my innocent (and ridiculous if his facial expression was any indication) answer.

"Book a recording studio and DO IT!" he said. The next day I did so and never looked back, released from the idea that the fulfillment of dreams had to come from external and approving sources.

Brian Little knows the power of questions to heighten self-awareness and spur change. As vice president and global head of corporate human resources for Intel, he conducts career development, mentoring, and coaching sessions in which he invariably asks the question, What do you really want? "When I ask that question," Brian explained, "ninety percent of the time somebody says some version of 'I'm not sure.' Or they're vague—'I *might* want this, I *could* do that.' Even if they have it inside them, something prevents them from clearly saying it."

For most of us, he told me, "Understanding what you want is difficult because so many other people *tell* us what we should want, whether it's our parents, siblings, spouse, friends, society, television. But you've got to put all that aside and deep down know yourself well enough to say, *What do I want?* If you can answer that, you're probably going to be pretty happy and successful. And even if you don't make that goal per se, the journey itself is valuable."

Brian Little calls out the pressure of being told what we should want as an obstacle to knowing what we truly want. To that I'll throw in three more obstacles: distraction, not wanting to know what we want, and focusing on what we don't want. Let's lift the hood on each and see what's going on.

Obstacle #1: I'm Distracted

The inscription on the ancient temple of Delphi, "Know Thyself," might have beckoned the ancient Greeks to look within, but they didn't have multiple seasons of *True Detective* to keep up with.

A steady diet of digital distractions drowns out introspection. We look at screens an average of 8.5 hours a day. We check our phones 205 times a day, the first glance before getting out of bed. After a full day's work there are the kids and errands, the bill-paying, the worrying. Add to that the strain of trying to be and do what others expect of us. Without finding time for stillness and reflection, it's easy to lose sight of what's going on "in here," our feelings and needs—the keys to our very aliveness.

Obstacle #2: I Don't Want to Know What I Want

As soon as we name what we want, the ball is in our court to do something about it. We'll feel the pressure to take action, to *ask* something of ourselves if not of others. But we may be unwilling to make that commitment.

Getting honest about what we want means evaluating whether we have the courage, devotion, skills, or resources to get it. We'll also need to ask, *Am I worthy of it? Do I believe it's possible to get it?* Any doubts around these questions could send us slamming on the brakes. And if we don't take responsibility for our own failure to act, we'll look for someone to blame: "I'd be a huge success today if it weren't for YOU!"

For all these troubling reasons, not examining what we want can seem the safest choice.

Obstacle #3: I Focus on What I *Don't* Want

I don't want to be stuck working here another three years.
I don't want a relationship like my last one.
I don't want to always have to do what *they* want.

Affirming the negative is like telling the GPS, "I don't want to go to the airport." Unless we know what we want and say it aloud, we won't get far. And saying what we don't want invites misunderstandings. In the past, when I ordered coffee at drive-throughs, I'd say, "No sugar." Despite the explicit request, all too often I'd get a sweet surprise in my java. After many disappointments it occurred to me that maybe just the *mention* of sugar brought confusion. Now, instead of "no sugar," it's "cream only," and my coffee comes the way I want it.

Wants and don't-wants don't mix. When you stop focusing on what you don't want and focus on what you do want, you'll get much further in life.

Which of those obstacles get in the way of knowing what you want? No pressure, but the engine is running, and the GPS awaits your destination.

Anything But This!

At times it feels liberating to scream NO, NOT THIS! about some unwanted situation. There's power in a forceful negation. We're claiming our truth and drawing a line in the sand. We may not know what we want, but we sure as hell know what we *don't* want. And that's a good place to start (but not to end up in).

Not sure what you want? Then start with what you don't want. Contemplate the questions below. Name your discontents. Go ahead—wring out the sponge!

What limits or frustrates you in your personal or work life? Where in your life do you complain or grumble instead of asking for what you want? What conditions continue because you haven't spoken up? On a sheet of paper or in your journal, write them in the left column below, adding as many items as you need.

I DON'T WANT	I WANT

Next, revisit your answers. But this time, explore the flipside. Ask yourself, "What are the *positively stated wants* (potential asks) hidden in my discontents?" Write down your corresponding wants in the right column. For example:

I don't want a desk job |
I want employment that keeps me outdoors, at home, or on my feet.

I don't want to badger the kids to pick up after themselves |
I want to learn effective ways to negotiate family responsibilities.

I don't want to continue shrinking in fear from the world |
I want to explore ways to confidently engage with people and the community.

When you catch yourself in the Not-This! habit (and you will), don't beat yourself up about it. Just begin the next breath with what you *do* want. It's only when you know what you want that you can take steps to get it. And that might require an ask or two. By my count, there are four options for handling discontent:

1. **Do nothing** and continue to suffer.

2. **Change your perspective** to intentionally and peacefully accept the situation as it is, as best you can.

3. **Take action to change it** through an ask, a creative plan, negotiation, third-party intervention, political action, developing new skills or relationships, etc.

4. **Walk away from it** (if that's an option).

Our next two storytellers got results from Option #3. They knew what they wanted and took action to get it.

Ask for Compensation. *Jennifer Loftus lives in Maui and teaches voice, piano, and movement classes.*

During a window installation in my home, the installers stopped working when they discovered that insulate for two of the windows was missing and would have to be ordered. The work was then rescheduled for 8:00 a.m. one morning the following week. When on that day an hour went by and the workers hadn't arrived, I called the company but got their voicemail. When I reached the secretary at 10:00 a.m., she said the workers had a schedule mix-up and wouldn't be coming.

I told her I'd arranged to be home at 8:00, waited two hours, and that in my professional life my time was (then) worth $50 an hour. I asked to be compensated with a $100 credit of some sort, whether credit on the bill, a check, or gift card. The secretary was taken aback but made a few phone calls. The installation was rescheduled, began on time, and I received a $100 Visa gift card. I'd simply asked. It was really that simple.

Ask to Learn. *Kieran Meeke is a journalist who has explored more than 100 countries, lived in eight, and currently resides in Kerry, Ireland.*

I'm obsessed with horses. I had a friend in Africa, Micky, a London-Irish bookmaker who kept some thoroughbreds for the racetrack. He was a former professional jockey. I asked Micky if he would teach me to ride. I was 35. I'd never ridden before.

Micky put me in the ring on one of his horses and eventually I was riding out with him to train and exercise the horses, three a day at weekends. We often rode in a game reserve, among herds of wild animals. So, I became a very experienced rider. I was so, so lucky. It was the right ask, right time. Because of that, I've been able to work as a stockman [cowboy] in Australia, ride with the Bedouin in Jordan, and enjoy week-long pack trips in the Canadian Rockies. I even rode the Pony Express across America—a re-ride of the original route.

So, What Do You Want?

Some need to hear this: there's no shame in wanting. Unless your wants infringe on the rights or well-being of others, there's no need to rationalize, defend, or apologize for them. There are some choices you make in life that only you can understand, which can never be explained to anyone's satisfaction but your own. Want what you want and ask.

Which of the categories below trigger desires (immediate or long-range) you have at work, home, school, in relationships, community, or other areas? Come back to the list later if you wish (perhaps as an extended journaling exercise). I've provided sample wants/asks to spur your thinking in each category.

Cooperation: compliance, agreement, teamwork
Ask neighbors to point security lights away from our windows

Help: assistance, favors, intervention, rescue
Ask for professional help in coping with my loss

Support: encouragement, validation, endorsement, emotional backup
Ask Skylar for pep talk before I visit the relatives

Guidance: advice, insight, counsel, mentoring
Ask Mel how I can be most effective in this new environment

Commitment: investment, consistency, dependability, priority
Ask Aiden to make our family dinners a priority

Collaboration/Partnership: allies, synergy, interdependence, trust
Ask R.W. if we can join forces for mutual wins

Opportunities: consent, permission, exceptions
Sell boss on letting me join transition team in Toronto

Financial Support: loans, grants, scholarships, donations
Consult counselor about scholarships I may not know about

Compensation: raises, benefits, bonuses, equity
Ask for a raise that reflects the value I bring to the business

Extras: perks, privileges, freebies
Ask company to cover fees for my personal hygiene coach

Integrity: fairness, accountability, truth, reciprocity, justice
Ask Boris to show the same honesty and transparency he expects of us

Harmony: understanding, empathy, forgiveness, problem-solving, unity
Ask M.J. if we can try to patch things up and move forward

Respect: consideration, courtesy, kindness
Ask Stanley to be kinder to my sister Blanche

Intimacy: attention, caring, listening, touch, reciprocity, trust, openness
Ask Carla to hold me close tonight without the TV on

Fun: joy, play, spontaneity, excitement, gifts, adventure
Invite Nick to get his skates out and join me on the ice tomorrow

Recognition: acknowledgment, validation, visibility, rewards
Ask Neal to acknowledge my team's efforts

Input: ideas, expertise, problem-solving, projections
Ask my students what questions should be on their exam and why

Feedback: impressions, opinions, assessments, ratings
Ask Paul for one thing I can do to improve the presentation I gave

Information: facts, data, clarification, updates, details, plans, expectations
Ask resort to explain "management not responsible for reptiles entering guest sleeping quarters"

Efficiency: processes, workflows, schedules, conveniences
Propose reduction of our complicated 6-step process to 3 simple ones

Creativity: artistic expression, innovation, reinvention
Ask team to brainstorm their wildest ideas for reinvigorating the business

Freedom: autonomy, self-determination, separation, space
Ask for more decision-making authority in the field

Safety: well-being, protection, boundaries, rescue
Ask in advance for escort to my car after the party

Closure: decision, resolution, endings
Ask Kirby to repay the money I loaned him two years ago

Did you identify a few wants? Did they stir up a sense of possibility? A feeling of hope? Or did you write them off as impossible? In Chapters 3–5, we'll look at the effect of beliefs on asking—and how "impossible" might be a belief worth challenging.

> What are you not asking for that if you asked for it
> would give you all of you?
> —GARY M. DOUGLAS, author and speaker

Settling for Less?

In negotiations, parties come prepared knowing three things: their starting point, where they aspire to end up, and the least they'll accept (their bottom line). There's little profit in pursuing the *least* acceptable outcome. Only aspirations have the power to bring the parties to the table.

But many of us focus only on the bottom line in life. We go after the least we'll accept. Why is that? The usual suspects: inability to imagine a better result; believing ourselves unworthy of what we want; or flat-out pessimism. (As a friend's Russian wife once argued, "Optimism is just a lack of information!")

Valerie Jones advises people not to invest in low expectations. As president of Valerie M. Jones Associates, she educates her clients, students, and audiences on successful nonprofit fundraising and board development. Through the years, she has often observed that many of the people she mentors and advises set their sights too low when pursuing careers. Her expertise is fundraising, but her advice applies to opportunities in any field.

> Why would you apply for jobs that are just "available" and not start networking with the places you love and are really excited about? Why would you settle for *this* when you haven't even tried for your heart's desire? Maybe you won't get your first choice, or your second, but you'll be networking with people who can help you later. Even if you get your third choice, that's better than starting with your tenth. Or worse, just starting with the jobs on offer.[2]

To Valerie Jones' point, why not make a beeline for the work, experience, or adventure you want? Why not pursue the aspiration instead of the bottom line? Why not ask big rather than settle for less?

Ambitious Ask. *Marty Gilbert is founder and CEO of the NorthShore Networking Group, a Chicago-area job search networking and coaching organization.*

After 15 years with Motorola, I began looking for opportunities to work at a small or mid-sized company. I found a firm that was looking for a vice president of marketing, a position well-aligned with my background. The company provided the data and analytics for major professional sporting events, which had always been an interest of mine. I applied for the job.

After several rounds of interviews, the company narrowed the search down to me and one other person.

Naturally I was disappointed when the CEO, who had been part of the interview process, informed me they had chosen the other candidate. I asked him what had led to that decision.

"Given your background," he said, "we felt you could do a lot more than marketing for the company and would probably get bored."

"I don't disagree," I replied. "But if at any point you are no longer interested in running this company, let me know— because the job I'm really interested in is YOURS and I would like to be first in line should you wish to make that kind of a change."

I had basically just asked for his job because I knew I could make a strong impact in that position.

About six weeks later the CEO called and said, "You planted a very interesting seed. Why don't you come back, and we can talk about this?" In the meeting that followed, he shared with me that he wanted to pursue his real passion, writing software, rather than running the entire company of more than 300 people. As it turned out, my ask had been the catalyst that put both of us closer to where we wanted to be. I served as chief executive officer for three years.

Marty Gilbert's story reminds me of the one I shared in the Introduction, about the couple who asked the homeowners for their house. Both asks were well-timed, unexpected, and resulted in contracts that made everybody happy. Some requests are mutually beneficial. But we don't know that until we ask.

Most people go about day-to-day life thinking
they're acting on what they want, when in reality they're
acting on their expectations.
—JENNICE VILHAUER, social psychologist

How Much Do You Want It?

I once had the privilege of spending two insightful days in a seminar with G. Dan Lumpkin, who's spent more than 45 years giving them. When Dan was in the 7th grade, he overcame a learning disability with the help of a teacher whom he describes as a "leg up" person, one who sees and nurtures the potential in others. As a Certified Management Consultant (CMC), certified counselor, and president of Lumpkin & Associates, Dan has been that "leg up" for clients worldwide seeking his expertise in organizational, personal, and professional development. From his office in Fairhope, Alabama, he talked with me about the two most important questions we can ask ourselves.

> I practice as a consultant exactly the way I did as a therapist. The most important question I can ever ask a client is, What do you want to have happen? The reason people don't get what they want in life is because they don't know the answer to that question or even think to ask it.
>
> And the second most important question is, What are you willing to do to get it? How badly do you want it? When I was seeing patients, my strategy was always helping them learn, to make a plan. I'd say to them, If *this* is what you want to have happen and *this* is what you're willing to do to get it, between now and the next time I see you, you will have done these things, right?
>
> But if they came back and said they didn't do what they said they were going to do, then they must have a really good

excuse, or changed their priorities, or didn't really want it badly enough to ask for it or change their behavior to get it. Or they lacked courage. We have to turn our wishes and desires into *behaviors*.

I think when people don't ask, they should explore the reasons they're not willing to do that. Some of them are just comfortable sitting back wanting and not acting. But until you move from just thinking about things to actually doing them, you can't change your life.[3]

Dreaming can inspire and motivate you. But desire without action is a car without an engine. Asking sets things in motion, inviting opportunities, resources, and support into your life. What do you want? Do you want it enough to pursue it? To ask for it?

Everyone Said No

Brian Little, whom you met earlier in this chapter, is vice president and global head of corporate human resources for Intel. His leadership was recently recognized by the magazine *HRO Today*, which named him its for-profit Chief Human Resources Officer of the Year. But his professional development began much earlier, far from the corporate settings in which he'd one day make his mark.

I grew up in Peoria, Illinois, a hardworking blue-collar city. People didn't really ask that much. It was kind of the opposite—put your head down, work hard, do your best, and maybe someone will notice you.

But I was fortunate to have some role models that were different. I had my older brother, James, a very confident guy. And he would help me find things to do that put me out of my comfort zone. Big brothers do that—*Let 'em sweat a little bit!*

I was 13 when I went to my dad one day and said, "Hey, I'd love to have some Converse shoes!"

And he said, "Sounds great. You should go out and buy them."

It was clear he wasn't going to buy them for me, because he figured I didn't need another pair. My brother told me I should go out and get a job, but I said I don't know if I can get a job at 13. And he said, "Well, make one for yourself."

So, late that summer I went out to try to get opportunities to cut neighbors' yards. My father was a big yard-cutter type guy. Our lawn was always immaculate. It looked like a golf course. So, I picked up on how to do that from him, and he allowed me to use the equipment. I knocked on a whole bunch of doors that summer, but I was a horrible salesperson.

Every single person told me no.

My brother teased me like there was no tomorrow: "You need to practice or give it up!" That motivated me to practice for the next summer. I got in the mirror. Practiced my pitch. And he'd come by from time to time and say, "That's awful, you're still gonna be broke!" Until one day he said, "You know … you're actually getting a little better."

When the next summer came, I went out early because I wanted to be first. I decided to go to a neighborhood that was bigger than ours. And the first house I saw had a big lawn. It was an unusually hot day, and the woman of the house was outside looking at her husband who was trying to get the lawnmower started and he was sweating bullets. They both looked miserable. And I walked up to her and said, "How would you like to have your summer back?"

She said, "What?"

I said, "Your summer, wouldn't you like to have it back? I can take care of this lawn and I guarantee that you're gonna love it or it's free." She looked at her husband and said, "Great! When can you start?"

I started that day.

I kept getting more lawns and got to the point where I had *too many* lawns. Then I hired some of my friends, subcontracting to them. I remember riding my bike over to the sporting goods store. I didn't really like the guy who owned it (he didn't like kids very much). I pointed to the Converse shoes I wanted, and he brought them over.

And then something clicked inside my head. I said, "You know what? I want *every color*."

It was collection day, so I pulled out all this money—a ton of cash—put it on the table, and said, "And send them to my house, because I'm on a bike."

Later, this truck rolled up to the house and delivered all these shoes!

Before I'd approached that first couple, I had five or six ready quips I was going to use. Some were really corny. But the effectiveness was in the delivery, not just the words themselves.

By asking, I was able to build a little confidence. It made me feel like I had more control, and that's what it comes down to for me: Do I want to be controlled or have control? There are so many things that control our lives—we're on the clock, we've got to do this and that—and at times we don't feel we have any freedom at all. But that summer I learned I could create my own space. And it helped me become more confident in asking for what I wanted.

As a young entrepreneur, Brian Little devised a question few could ignore and asked his way to a successful lawn-care business (and a veritable rainbow of Converse shoes, delivered as requested). I asked his advice for asking successfully.

> When asking *What do I really want?* we need to be thoughtful and introspective. It's not about getting what you want at the expense of other people, because that will eventually turn on you and hurt you. It's getting what you want in a way that helps or inspires or engages others too. That's going to help you get what you want faster.[4]

Clarity about what you want, and the commitment to act on it, is #1 in the Desire-Belief-Skill foundation. But as you'll discover in the next three chapters, what you *think* about what you want may be more consequential than your desire for it. It's time to put the spotlight on the triple components of affirmative Belief: believing that it's ok to ask, that you're worthy of asking, and that it's possible to get it.

> To hell with circumstances—I create opportunities.
> —BRUCE LEE

CHAPTER THREE

IS IT OK TO ASK?

Do not go through life like a leaf blown from
here to there believing whatever you are told.
—SOCRATES

ONCE, WHEN A FLIGHT ATTENDANT OFFERED ME A packet of peanuts, I asked for two. The passengers next to me, a couple in their thirties, turned their heads, eyebrows skyward, as if I'd asked for the entire snack cart. As the attendant leaned in with the two tiny bags, the couple's eyes followed the peanuts passing from her hand to mine. I saw resentment in their faces. Envy. "Hey!" they silently screamed, "He asked for more peanuts *and got away with it!*"

As my seatmates munched their single bags and I, transgressor and glutton, gorged myself on two, the absurdity struck me. If you won't ask for peanuts, what *will* you ask for?

On the surface, asking is a no-brainer. You make a request and wait for the response. And yet, your attitudes and behaviors related to asking—what and whom you ask (or don't ask), how you go about it, and how you feel doing it—are determined by a whole network of influences, including your:

- family and cultural rules and values
- gender conditioning
- attitude about your feelings, wants, and needs
- beliefs about your self-worth
- level of assertiveness
- attitudes toward power and authority figures
- capacity for imagination and hope
- beliefs about what is possible
- comfort with intimacy
- religious faith

Gradually these influences become part of your identity, the person you believe yourself to be. Although you're not always conscious of these influences, they combine to inform the "rules" about what you feel is ok to ask for and what is not. Some people, for example, have no problem asking on behalf of others. They'll happily request donations to their favorite charities or ask management for an employee game room but will haul heavy boxes into their attic two weeks after back surgery rather than ask a friend to help.

How might cultural norms establish rules for asking? The story that follows, from Jim Lew, the son of Chinese parents, gives us a clue. Jim is a former teacher, psychotherapist, trainer, and public speaker. Although his story is culturally specific, notice if there are parallels to your own acquired beliefs.

My parents immigrated to the U.S. from the Pearl River Delta region in China. When I was a kid, we lived in Wichita. There was a Chinese lady who lived a few houses down and I remember sitting in her living room. I saw a jar of candy on her coffee table and said, "Can I have a piece of candy?" Well, my mother was immediately "Oh my god!" and "How dare you!" You see, asking in the Chinese culture is not approved of. And the lady chuckled and said, "Of course you can have a piece of candy."

Decades later, when I was in my 30s or 40s, we all took a trip to San Francisco. The neighbor lady had moved there so we thought we'd visit her. When we walked in, the first thing she said was, "Oh, there's the kid that asked for candy!" So that's the position of asking in the Chinese culture—the kid who asked for candy was remembered *decades* later.

It's a real strong cultural thing: you wait until your time. That's how you respect the culture. When you're ready for things, people will tell you. But don't ask. And that includes your power as a person in the community. You humbly work hard, and you wait for somebody to offer you something or to give you a job, or whatever, but you're not expected to ask.

I remember from my education and often in my work somebody saying, "Well, who wants to take the lead on this?" And some white person would raise their hand and say, "I want it." And I would be qualified and want it too, but I just didn't feel it was right for me to stick up my hand and grab for it. So, somebody else would get it. And I'd get that tight feeling in my throat. Because it was really something that I *wanted*.[1]

I'm willing to bet that, even if you are not of Chinese descent, you too have waited to be offered something you wanted badly rather than asked for it. When were you, as Jim Lew was, qualified but reluctant to raise your hand and say, "I want it?" In what ways are you *still waiting* to be noticed, to be asked?

Blessings or Baggage?

We carry into adulthood our family and cultural views about asking just as surely as those passed down to us about money, sex, and religion. Some of us learned early that asking anything beyond "How are you?" is prying. Others got the message that asking and demanding are the same: *"I need you* to lend me $20." Many were taught that it's nobler to struggle alone or suffer in silence than ask for help. New York-based psychotherapist Rachel Sussman told me that the assumptions we learned to make as children are sometimes hard to shake:

> Sometimes you had a parent or sibling in your family of origin you couldn't speak to effectively, or your needs weren't met in that relationship. So, you come to assume your needs aren't going to be met in other relationships either. And if you assume your needs aren't going to be met, you're not going to ask.

Our inherited attitudes (about anything) are typically a blend of blessings and baggage; and only through experience and reflection can we sort out for ourselves which is which. Let's look at a few more examples of how early family dynamics influence our adult views about asking.

Show Up for Me. *Diana Mudenda is a DEIB (Diversity, Equity, Inclusion, Belonging) consultant.*

I grew up in a very privileged household in Zambia. Both my parents worked a lot. I was the oldest and had to be the support structure for myself and my three siblings. I got used to being the person taking care of everyone else, which meant not asking for my needs to be met. I've always had a lot of pride in being a very, very self-sufficient person, but sometimes hyper-independence is just a way to have protections and stay isolated.

As a giver and recovering people-pleaser, I'm now asking for reciprocity. I'm getting better at having conversations where I say, *I need you to show up for me in these ways.* You have to allow people the opportunity to show up for you in the ways that you show up for them. That's how you become an advocate for yourself.

Ask at Your Own Risk. *Benjamin Dahlbeck is a writer and playwright in Atlanta, Georgia.*

In my family, one did not ask for things. Asking for help, or for anything, was a very risky exercise, for several reasons. It meant you were weak, you had a need, a vulnerability that could be exploited. It showed you cared about something, which could then be taken away.

I asked for a stuffed toy rabbit one Easter when I was four or five. I received it and was ecstatic, but on Easter Sunday my father was in a drunken rage about something and threatened to take all the toys and candy I got and burn them in the backyard. I hid the rabbit under the sofa and did not retrieve it for two weeks until I was sure my father had forgotten about it.

Asking also allowed the other person to have something to hold over you with no expiration date and no proportional reciprocation—"Ten years ago you asked for an apple and I gave it to you; therefore you owe me a kidney." The toxic message was, "Who was I to think I was important enough, deserving enough, or just plain worthy enough to actually receive what I was asking for?"

Perhaps this is why as an adult I have ended up with a lot of friends who are assertive about asking. Some of my most healing moments have been when I asked these friends for help and they charged in like the First Cavalry and got things done while I stood off to the side like a good Southern child of an alcoholic, quiet and unobtrusive, happy but secretly embarrassed that my needs were being met.

Let Him Ask. *Kathe Mull is a theatre professional in New York City.*

I was doing a show in New York working with Dennis Paver, an extremely talented hat maker. He was sitting at his counter one day, putting a beautiful, plumed, blue-spangled hat on a sock puppet. My son, Mac, then two years old, was with me and he *loved* puppets. When he saw what Dennis was working on, his eyes got really big. He walked up to Dennis and said, "I want one of those."

I jumped in and said, "Mac, you can't do that, you can't just ask for …"—and Dennis interrupted. "Hold it!" he said, firmly but kindly. "It's taken me 50 years to figure out how to ask for what I want. Let him ask. I'll decide to say yes or no, but let your son ask." And I said all right.

Growing up as I did, a middle child in a family of seven, you were either given or you weren't (and most of the time you weren't) but you didn't ask. So, when Dennis said that, it was a pivotal moment for me as a new parent. I thought, well, why *wouldn't* a two-year old ask for something they passionately love? I am not going to squash this little guy's ask.

For the rest of his life, I allowed Mac to ask, even for the most extraordinary things. He'd say he wanted to write to the White House or invent something, and I would just say, All you can do is ask; let's do the research. Who do we know who can possibly give you what you want? Some of those things just passed by the wayside. But the permission to ask fed his imagination and gave him encouragement. (And Dennis did make a puppet for him, complete with a blue-spangled hat!)

How about *your* family? What was ok to ask, and what was not? Which of those family rules or attitudes determine your behaviors today?

What about gender? How might it influence what you do or don't ask? We all know the templates. Males are raised to compete, take risks, be self-sufficient, and hide vulnerability. Females are taught to be collaborative, unfailingly polite, and attentive to others' feelings and needs above their own. These gender norms become the way we perceive and do just about everything, including questions and requests. But how might these learned behaviors prevent us from getting what we want?

What Women Don't Ask

Women who conform to their gender norms may not ask for professional opportunities. They may find themselves fighting to be heard in meetings. And as parents and caretakers, they may find it difficult to ask for their needs to be met. These three outcomes, respectively, reflect the experiences of our next three storytellers.

Waiting My Turn. Darci Nalepa Elam is an actor who has performed on many stages in Chicago including Steppenwolf Theatre Company, Northlight Theatre, and The Gift Theatre Company. She was featured in the film *Henry Gamble's Birthday Party* and has appeared on NBC's *Chicago Fire*, Amazon's *Patriot*, and Showtime's *Shameless*. Darci lives in Nashville, Tennessee with her husband and two sons.

A prestigious Chicago theatre company asked me to participate in the reading of a play they would soon be producing. Although I read the part well and was right for several of the roles in my age group, I had assumed the theatre would invite me to audition if they wanted me in the actual show. When no invitation came, I didn't ask to audition. I didn't let them know I wanted that opportunity.

I'm a different person today, but at the time I was wrapped up in being a "good girl," waiting my turn, and playing by what I imagined the rules to be.

Many "good girls" who grew up "waiting their turn" struggle against the belief that it's arrogant or selfish to promote themselves. Sociolinguist Dr. Deborah Tannen notes, "Whatever the motivation, women are less likely than men to have learned to blow their own horn. And they are more likely than men to believe that if they do so, they won't be liked."[2]

Fighting to be Heard. Hadley Jaeger, a self-described avid reader, animal lover, and outdoorswoman, is employed in public works on the Oregon coast. Her story is not about asking, specifically, but the more fundamental challenge many women face in speaking up and being heard in mostly male environments.

In my previous job in manufacturing, I found it difficult to speak up. I had ideas and perspectives to share, but I was 25, the only woman in the room, and could tell my male coworkers didn't consider I had anything important to say. They inherently didn't think I had to offer the same value as they did.

In that environment, I felt like I had to wait to be asked or wait for silence before I could quickly interject. But I gradually realized that the only way there could be space for myself in the conversation was for me to make my own space by being loud and interrupting like everyone else.

I don't think trying to assert myself in that way made them respect me more, but at that point I didn't care what they thought of me. I would not have gotten what I needed as the sales department rep had I not fought to be heard just like the rest of them. But having to fight was discouraging. It made me less inclined to work there, and I no longer do.

Studies by Dr. Tannen have shown that men are conditioned to communicate in ways that boost their visibility and status, jostling for wins, whereas women are taught to be cooperative, not call attention to themselves, and take turns speaking and listening.[3] The frequent result is that women don't get heard in meetings, and perceptions get fixed: men interpret women's apparent sideline-sitting as a lack of confidence, and women see men's dominance as a dismissal of the women in the room. Given the layers of complexity in *any* communication, however, there may be accuracy and misunderstanding in both perceptions.

Everyone Else First. When New Yorker Kathe Mull met theatre costume designer Machine Dazzle, she told him, "I don't know who you are, but I want to work with you." It was the bold ask that set everything in motion. In the four years since that ask, Kathe has been thrilled to serve as wardrobe supervisor in shows domestically and abroad featuring hundreds of the designer's costume pieces. But asking did not always come easily to her.

> Culturally we women are not taught to ask for what we want. We're taught to live for other people. I had jobs, raised two boys, was the primary breadwinner, and never considered what I wanted. To be honest, I didn't even know that wanting something for myself was an option.

It wasn't until my children were raised and I became single that I thought, *Well, what do I want and how do I ask for that?* And so, I started, gently at first, asking for things. And I was very surprised that ninety percent of the time I was given what I asked for. I'm now taking steps to be responsible for my own path and happiness, which is joyful and terrifying.

If women don't know that wanting something for themselves is an option, they won't ask. In an article in *Psychology Today*, psychotherapist and interfaith minister Nancy Colier said, "We [women] are deeply conditioned to … do without, and find our nourishment in giving rather than receiving. We learn, early on, that it's not okay to ask or dare insist that our needs be taken care of." [4]

Might Kathe Mull's evolution from "my needs are unimportant" to asking, be a natural outcome of becoming a little older and wiser? Nancy Colier thinks so. "As we grow and evolve," she writes, "many of us learn how to tap into, identify, respect, and ask for what we need."

What Men Don't Ask

The Behavior for Boys instruction booklet hasn't changed much over the years. Men today are as likely as their grandfathers were to avoid asking if they think it could make them look weak or incompetent. But male silence has its costs. The next three stories reveal how the reluctance to ask can sabotage men in travel, leadership, and most gravely, mental health.

Real Men Don't Ask. Growing up as the son of an Air Force pilot, Jon Ziomek cultivated a love of travel. Later, his careers as a *Chicago Sun-Times* reporter and an assistant dean and associate professor at Northwestern University's Medill School of Journalism deepened his respect for the rigorous pursuit of facts. For the past seven years, he has combined his twin passions—keeping others informed and travel—as an information desk volunteer at Chicago's O'Hare International Airport.

There's the old notion of men not asking for directions when they're lost. But I see that a lot at O'Hare. I'll see a family, they're looking around for the right sign, and the guy is talking to himself, *Where is baggage claim?* And it's the woman who will say, "Let's cut through this!" and come up to me and ask. It's far less often that the guy does that. He's thinking, *Hey, my self-worth is on the line here if I can't figure this out on my own.*

In Tel Aviv, I went to a museum and thought by looking at a map I could figure out how to walk back to my hotel. There are no straight streets in those old cities, and it was clear after about 30 minutes of walking that I was far off. So, there I was, doing what I see guys doing at the airport, and told myself, *Jon, this is stupid!* And then I asked for directions.

I think back to my childhood when we'd be on one of our many Sunday drives. My father was good about directions and locations, but if he got uncertain, my mother was usually the first one to say, "Let's stop and ask someone." So, I probably got that reluctance from him. I do think it's tied up with gender identity, that the man is supposed to know this stuff. Maybe in modern society that's changing. I hope so.

Jon Ziomek's experience confirms the stereotype that men would rather die than ask for directions. Before the face-saving advent of GPS, I, too, dreaded asking directions—not out of pride, but because as soon as my guides used words like "north, east, west, and south" they might as well have been talking to a housecat. GPS is my dashboard Jesus. Our "men are supposed to know this stuff" theme continues in the next story.

A Slippery Pole. Allan Biggar is founder of Allan Biggar & Company Limited, a business strategy and branding firm. He is a former managing director (London) of the global public relations and communications PR firm Burson-Marsteller, who later became chairman of its global corporate and financial practice.

> Boys are brought up and educated to be strong and tough. Men find it very difficult to ask for help or information because there's a presumption that you're supposed to *know*, and if you don't that's perceived to be a sign of weakness. So, men don't ask.
>
> I've seen that in business where the male CEO who's climbed the slippery pole to that position is expected to know the answer, expected to know what to do, and believes that he's expected to *be* that. He's therefore often completely blind to what's going on and doesn't want to ask. I think part of the problem of asking in general is a perception that asking is weak, when asking is in fact strong.[5]

Allan Biggar offers the scenario of a CEO afraid to ask questions that could reveal his uncertainty or ignorance. While that's a problem for the leader, imagine the negative impacts on a company that must contend with the uninformed decisions of an ask-averse leader. On the other hand, imagine the *gains* for companies whose leaders ask for and listen to the ideas and needs of staff, customers, and other stakeholders. Asking *is* leadership. We'll touch on this theme again in Chapter 13.

End of His Rope. It was sometime during his fourth and final incarceration for crimes ranging from burglary, assault, armed robbery, and drug dealing, that Dave Dahl decided he could no longer suffer alone, silently, in shame. Speaking from his home in Portland, Oregon, he told me of the ask he had long avoided but which would ultimately change his life—inside and out.

I was 38 years old when I finally figured out that asking for help could be a good thing. It was maybe the eleventh or twelfth year of my total 15 years in prison. I'd spent a lot of sleepless nights obsessing about suicide, and I came to the end of my rope. I was like, I can't do this anymore.

In prison you have an opportunity to put in a "kite," a written request to the authorities. I wrote that I needed to speak to someone in mental health. It took me years to make that decision because I didn't have the humility, and it's the last thing you want to do as a prisoner, tell on yourself. Another factor that kept me from asking for help was that people would *see* that I had asked for help. You don't want to have everybody looking at you like some weak bastard or whatever. But when I dropped that paper into the little box, it was such a relief. Best thing I ever did.

Once I got on the meds for my depression, I didn't care what anybody thought. I owned it. Everything started to change. I don't know how much of it had to do with the meds or the fact that I got into a computer drafting class around the same time, or just that I had made this surrender. It was the first time in my life I felt really good about myself. And from that point on I was a freight train. I was unstoppable.

I believe you need to see yourself as you are and accept it and realize that there's a lot of crap out there that makes you feel that you have to be something you're not. The absolute best advice I can tell anybody, is ask for help when you need it.

Born into a family of bakers, Dave Dahl went on to co-found Dave's Killer Bread in 2005. The company employed over 300 people, nearly one-third of which were ex-felons (the ultimate "pay it forward"). In 2015, the company was acquired by Flower Foods for $275 million.

The men in these three stories challenge the lone-wolf notion that the only achievements that count are those won by solo struggle. They demonstrate that asking can move a person more efficiently toward a goal. Asking for directions, advice, and help isn't cheating. Nor is it weak. And even my manliest readers will agree that asking sometimes takes *guts* (or parts more southerly).

Especially in matters of mental health, seeking help is critical. Men are statistically less likely than women to get help in handling anxiety and depression, and our prized masculine ability to bottle-up emotions makes us three times more likely to die by suicide. But as Dave Dahl discovered, if we ask for help, the "end of the rope" can become the one we grab to climb up into the boat.

To Ask or Not to Ask?

When is asking a detriment? When might it be better, if possible, *not* to ask?

When experience tells you the person in question would try to shame you for asking or, just as oppressive, give you what you want and never let you forget it. The same distance is due those who would expect some unethical or creepy compensation in exchange for helping you. Better, then, to ask someone else or find another way to get it. Because nobody should be held hostage to an ask.

Another reason you might choose to abstain from asking is when it conflicts with your principles, such as:

I won't ask for what I can easily do for myself.

I won't ask for anything that I wouldn't do for others.
I won't ask people to do things that would be a genuine hardship for them.

Brian Vandenbroucke, a career entrepreneur living in the Dominican Republic, puts limits around his requests as a consumer. While visiting Guatemala, he met a man selling alpaca blankets made from the llamas he raised. "I was struck by the beauty and craftsmanship of the blankets," Brian said. "As an entrepreneur myself, I was equally impressed by how well organized his family business was. I selected a particularly stunning blanket and paid him what he asked, about $200."

"It wasn't long before someone said to me, 'Oh, you idiot, you got so ripped off! They have a low cost of living—you should've asked for a third of that price!' But it was worth $200 to me. Sure, back home I've asked for discounts for various commodity items because I know the games of markup and margin. But the artist who spends his life creating and perfecting his craft, I can't devalue it. If something is worth it, I don't dicker. And I never get ripped off."

Choosing not to ask can be an act of integrity, the honoring of one's personal codes of conduct. And yet, the timeless call to "Know Thyself" invites us to be curious, at least, about our motivations: *What do I refuse or struggle to ask, and why? What, if anything, do I feel unworthy of asking or receiving?* In the next chapter, we'll look at how beliefs about our worthiness bring us closer to what we want or keep it forever out of reach.

If you are reluctant to ask the way, you will be lost.
—Malayan proverb

CHAPTER FOUR

ARE YOU WORTHY OF THE ASK?

Self-love, my liege, is not so vile a sin as self-neglecting.
—WILLIAM SHAKESPEARE

"I WAS 35-YEARS OLD AND WENT TO A SKI SHOP IN South Pasadena," said Greg King, a freelance writer and video producer. "That's where I saw the most beautiful woman, a salesperson who worked there. She was gorgeous and very friendly. I really wanted to ask her out but thought *Who am I to ask, she'll probably turn me down*. I left and felt frustrated that I hadn't asked her out for lunch or even coffee."

"For quite a few months, I regretted not asking," Greg said, "and would occasionally drive by the store, trying to get up the nerve to go back inside. I finally did go into the ski shop one day, but she wasn't there. It was a missed opportunity in my life."

This chapter challenges the boundaries we create from our beliefs about the things we don't feel worthy or qualified to ask.

Meribeth Kisner was a veteran of several professional dance and theatre companies when she founded Chi-Town Jazz Dance, a Chicago-based touring troupe. Under her artistic and business direction, Chi-Town performed 30–50 concert dates a year, which she attests was a better-than-average success rate for a dance company.

Despite Chi-Town's achievements, money was scarce. Looking back, three decades later, on the company's 11 seasons, Meribeth said, "I was so grateful for the breadcrumbs that came our way that I didn't see the big opportunities. I was surrounded by people who came to see our shows every year. They were people who had money and resources to share, but I didn't ask. I never asked for a Board of Directors. I figured, why would a board want to give their time to a little company like ours? So, I never asked. Instead, I was just holding onto the little crumbs we got, saying, hey, we're still afloat!"

The years have given her perspective. "As artistic director, I was good as ever," Meribeth said, "but if you don't feel worthy you won't even see the possibilities there for you."

Permission begins with self-permission. Without your own consent you won't ask. And to ask you must feel worthy. You must believe in your value as a human being, as a person equal to the joy or fulfillment the ask could bring. Yet such fundamental self-regard is not a given. Many who were shattered by physical, emotional, or sexual abuse, or who suffer from addiction, struggle with self-worth. This is why the road to recovery so often begins with reclaiming without question one's essential value.

It is only from a foundation of self-worth that we can permit ourselves to seek wholeness, draw appropriate boundaries, and create a healthy vision for our lives. It is only when we decide that we matter that we can relax into being seen, heard, and included. And it is only when we claim ourselves to be worthwhile that we can ask without shame and open our hands to the good that is available to us.

Shamed for Needing?

Many of us judge ourselves for having these inconveniences called *needs*. And the judgment starts early. Some children are shamed for seeking comfort—"Don't come crying to me just because you had a bad day!"—or for wanting things—"You dare ask for a toy when we're behind in the rent?" In an adult ashamed to ask there often lives a child who learned that emotional survival meant pretending their feelings and needs were not important, and so never voiced them: *I'll be safe if I'm very good and stay very quiet and don't ask for anything.* A woman I interviewed explained what it was like having to hide her needs at an early age.

> My mother was schizophrenic. My siblings and I were her targets, but I was the major target. There was a lot of physical and emotional abuse. I found the best way to cope was to be invisible. Duck and cover. To survive, I had to not draw attention to myself. And that certainly meant not asking for anything.

In unsafe homes, many find safety in silence. It's an extreme example but a relatable one. Because regardless of our upbringing, most of us had needs of some sort—Attention! Approval! Encouragement! Security! Structure! Truth!—that we hid, if not for fear of punishment, then of losing a parent's love. The question to ask ourselves now is, *What needs am I still hiding today for fear of 'causing trouble' or seeming 'needy' if I voice them?*

"Needy" once meant poverty. "Give to the needy." Today we use it derisively for anyone who chronically (or even momentarily) seeks attention, reassurance, or help. But as every good therapist will tell us, what some call neediness may simply be basic human needs that no one should be denied.

We closed the last chapter with the idea that our principles may inform our decisions about what *not* to ask. And yet, we owe it to ourselves to be sure that those decisions are coming from genuine, high-minded principles and not from a feeling of unworthiness cowering in the crawlspace. One way to find out is to ask yourself, *What do I refuse or struggle to ask? How do I respond when things are offered to me unasked?* A few red flags:

Support: feeling shame when asking for or receiving help or support

Money: undercharging for your services or never asking for a raise

Gifts: feeling unable to graciously accept gifts expected or otherwise

Romance: not feeling attractive or interesting enough to ask for or accept dates

Sexuality: deciding that your physical desires matter less than your partner's or that your age or body type make you unworthy of pleasure

Any of those red flags belong to you? If so, notice if "doing without" has become a badge of pride. Does letting your needs go unmet make you feel humble? Disciplined? Selfless? Manly? Spiritual?

How might these self-denials affect your emotional, physical, or financial health—or your ability to get things done? French philosopher Simone Weil advised honesty in this. "The danger," she said, "is not that the soul should doubt whether there is any bread, but that by a lie, it should persuade itself that it is not hungry."

What did you once deny yourself that you now freely ask for? What do you continue to deny yourself because you're not asking? What if you asked for it before you turn the page?

> You cannot give to people what they are
> incapable of receiving.
> —AGATHA CHRISTIE, mystery writer

Giving *A+* / Receiving *F*

If you've ever felt the undertow of unworthiness, you know what it's like to believe you're unfit to have certain things, much less ask for them. And if you don't ask but are given them anyway, it's as if the unworthiness doubles down. You lose the gift card or "forget" to follow up with the gallery owner who expressed interest in your work. Self-sabotage is an effective way to drive away love or success when you feel unworthy.

And yet, even when we *do* ask, some of us are terrible receivers. We drive the giver crazy with our apologies or take such a controlling hand in *how* they help us that they regret having said yes. Maybe we even snap at our helpers for being witness to the "shame" of our needing them. The role of giver suits us fine (after all, we're in charge), but receiver needs work.

If you often do for others yet refuse to ask or allow them to help you, you pave the way for power imbalances in those relationships. One-sided giving has a controlling effect that leaves recipients feeling indebted and resentful. Deny them the opportunity to give back and you rob them of self-expression. Worse, you send the message that what they have to offer us has no value to you. Learning to receive with grace and ease, on the other hand, is a gift we give ourselves and the giver.

A widely circulated internet quote, attributed to Islamic scholar Ali al-Jifri, beautifully captures this idea:

> I heard my mother asking our neighbor for some salt. I asked her why she was asking them as we have salt at home. She replied, "It's because they are always asking us for things; they are poor. So, I thought I'd ask them something small from them so as not to burden them, but at the same time make them feel as if we need them too. That way it'll be easier for them to ask us for anything they need from us."

Worth It

Several years ago I was scheduled to lead a breakout session at a conference. Mine was one of three breakfast seminars attendees could opt to attend. The day before the event, I set out to find my assigned presentation room in the hotel, the invitingly named "Lounge," only to discover that it was ... the bar. Small. Dark. Big TV on the wall. Little tables with drink specials on tent cards. I'm no snob, but nothing about it was remotely suitable for the presentation I was there to give.

Now, you're probably thinking that I immediately hunted down the event manager and asked for a better location, right? Why, no. I stood there in dismay imagining reasons, all of them humiliating, for getting such a lousy location. *The conference team doesn't value my presentation. They don't think I'll have much of a turnout. Maybe I somehow offended the organizer. Blah, blah, blah.*

Moments later, a slightly more encouraging voice urged me to not take the room assignment personally. *They must've run out of rooms. C'mon, Paul—a true pro would make the best of this situation. Deal with the hand you're dealt!*

That spin felt a little better than the first, but not much. When it finally occurred to me to *ask* the conference organizer for a better room—an evolutionary leap from scales to backbone—a reasonable-sounding voice warned, *She's going to say exactly what you expect, that if another room were available they wouldn't have given you this one*—which was followed by a saintly appeal to compassion, *Why add to her headaches?*

What I was doing, of course, was talking myself out of asking rather than risk an answer that might confirm the reasons I feared and leave me in shaming defeat. But the alternative—welcoming attendees to a fun presentation in a dark, cramped space—was unacceptable. I had to ask.

I approached the harried-looking event manager with calm concern.

"I'm unhappy with my breakout location. I want to inspire the attendees, but the bar is dimly lit and the size really limits the number of participants." Then, mustering a show of certainty that something could be worked out, I asked, "Would you look into finding a bigger or brighter location for us?"

With a look of anguish, she apologized for the inadequacy of the space and without a single "but" promised to investigate alternatives.

She made good on that promise. The next morning, I happily greeted a few dozen attendees in a spacious room bright with sunshine pouring through floor-to-ceiling windows. Don't know how she wrangled it. Don't care. But rather than surrender to my excuses, I'd asked. As if I mattered. As if my attendees mattered. As if the problem would be handled. As if good things could happen. And it literally let the light in.

You Just Didn't Ask. *Karen Vaccaro is an actor who has appeared in numerous television, film, and theatre productions.*

In non-Equity [non-union] theatres actors sometimes work without pay. Many years ago, I was one of them. I had won a couple of Joseph Jefferson Awards, which recognizes excellence in Chicago theatre including non-Equity actors like myself at the time. I was doing great, so when a non-Equity theatre asked me to do one of their shows, I said, "Sure, but I want to get paid."

Nobody was getting paid at the time. You just didn't ask. The theatre told me they'd think about it and get back to me.

A few days later, the artistic director called me in and stuck a cash roll of $300 in my hand saying, "You can't tell anybody else about this." And I didn't. The show demanded a six-week commitment, so the $300, even decades ago, was merely a token. Still, they could've found another actor to work for free, and didn't, which I saw as a validation of my talent. More importantly, my asking for payment had felt like an affirmation of my self-worth at a time when I had little, which is something I'm proud of to this day.

Heart's Desire. *Muriel Patay is a licensed clinical social worker with a practice in Evanston, Illinois.*

When I was a child, my two siblings and I didn't dare ask for things. Birthdays were not celebrated. There was no cake, no gifts, no special treatment. My parents argued a lot about money. The running theme was that there was not enough, and that we were barely getting by. So, it was an unwritten rule that you didn't ask for things.

Being a therapist, I've had a lot of healing around the things I missed in my childhood. I don't carry pain about it anymore, though I did for a long time. Maybe it's partly because of the appeasement I learned back then, but I've always been pretty accommodating and mostly feel OK about that. I hardly ever push for my will.

Except for the time I became aware of the Australian Labradoodle.

To have an Australian Labradoodle became my heart's desire. The greatness of my longing surprised me, made me feel very small, like a little girl. I set out to learn about the breed and regularly showed the adorable pictures to my husband—but the "oodle" part was a big turnoff to him, as our previous dogs had been burly German shepherds and labs. The breed was expensive, too. Grudgingly, my husband agreed to come with me to meet a breeder's Labradoodle but left unimpressed.

Normally I would have backed down and given up, but this dog was the longing of my heart.

One day I came to him and said, "I know you don't want this kind of dog, and that my choice seems irrational given my obsession and the expense. But I want it more than anything. And if we get the dog, I need you to be on board with the decision and not resent it."

A week later he said ok.

Madeline has now been with us for 11 years. She's a lovely dog, even if she does prefer George who is quite indulgent in all the attention he gives her! I'd had to implore him to agree to the dog, but in that moment, I felt I was speaking for my own inner child who had never felt worthy of asking for what she wanted.

Self-worth comes from one thing—
thinking that you are worthy.
—WAYNE DYER, psychologist

Are You Qualified to Ask?

So far, we've looked at worthiness as a birthright: our right to occupy space, be counted, have a shot at happiness, and ask for what we need or want. We're all worthy! Hurrah! High fives and fist pumps!

Not to spoil the party, but we also need to examine worthiness through a narrower lens, as something *earned*. There's no way around it: asking for certain things takes qualifications. Standards must be met. If you ask for someone's trust, you've got to be trustworthy. If you ask for a job as a paramedic, you need training and the ability to stay vertical at the sight of blood. You can ask for the honor of creating your friends' wedding cake, but you'll owe it to the couple and their guests to have a knack for baking.

In 2013, Vanderbilt University student Michael Pollack was among hundreds attending a campus question and answer session with music legend Billy Joel. A YouTube video captures the moment when Michael, from the audience, says to his hero in a hesitant voice, "My favorite song of yours is *New York State of Mind*." He tells the superstar of his good fortune to have played the song many times in New York City with Joel's longtime saxophonist, Richie Cannata.

"And I was wondering if I could play it with you," Michael asks. "I would accompany you, that is."

Joel pauses a moment.

"Ok."

The audience goes wild as Michael walks to the stage and takes a seat at the piano. Moments later Billy Joel is singing his signature song to the student's superb accompaniment. Their musical rapport is so tight, you'd swear the two had gigged together for years.[1]

Michael Pollack earned his big moment not because he's a nice guy but because he was qualified for the opportunity asked for. Qualifications count.

Except when they don't. Because "qualified" can mean either proven or potential ability. We'll look at the potential part next.

Are You Not Qualified?

Have you ever decided not to ask or apply for an opportunity because you thought you were unqualified (unworthy of it) ... only to learn the person who got it was no more—or even less—qualified than yourself? It's the reason I'm going to partly pull the rug out from under the "qualifications" argument I just made. Because our beliefs about what it takes to be qualified may be way off base.

The truth is that we disqualify ourselves too quickly and without investigation. Nowhere is this more evident than in job searches. Women's leadership expert Tara Mohr asked women and men (mostly American professionals) if they ever chose not to apply for jobs because they didn't meet all the qualifications. Of more than 1,000 respondents, nearly one-quarter of them (23.5%) said yes, that they presumed the "who should apply" guidelines were non-negotiable. Notably more women (15.0%) than men (8.5%) saw the guidelines as gospel and wrote themselves off as candidates.[2]

That sort of assumption would limit any of us. But why such a gender gap?

Mohr says that women, socialized since childhood to be rule-followers, are more likely than men to believe that job qualifications are firmly fixed. As a result, many women won't apply for jobs [or ask for promotions] unless convinced they meet every bullet point in the criteria. Sure, employers prefer hiring people with fewer training needs. And women and men with scant experience in a field are smart to avoid applying for jobs that expect them to "hit the ground running." But the power of a cover letter that emphasizes the ways one *is* qualified, such as having the right disposition and transferable skills, shouldn't be underestimated.

Not every opportunity demands we come to it with full command and credentials. Some qualifications are carved in stone. Others are paper-thin. To know the difference, we've got to ask.[3]

Or better yet, apply first and ask questions later.

I've witnessed this practice many times in my professional life. As a freelance writer, I was part of many creative production teams invariably headed by charismatic dynamos. When our clients would ask, in so many words, "Can you give us the moon?" our fearless leaders would answer, "And the stars!"—though they had no clue at that moment how we'd pull it off. But as your own experiences may have taught you, sometimes there's no surer path to solutions than pledging to provide them.

Writer Frank O'Connor captured that can-do spirit in a scene in his memoir. As a young boy, he adventures with his pals through the Irish countryside where they encounter a wall that appears too high to climb. The determined lads respond to the challenge by throwing their caps over the wall, thus committing themselves to find a way over it. And they do.

Perfectionists may scoff, but there are times when being "qualified" is just the willingness to take an opportunity seriously and give it our all. Before you dismiss yourself as unqualified (and therefore feel unworthy of asking), consider whether this might be a chance to learn as you go. If it is, go ahead. Take off your hat. And throw it over the wall.

If you wait until you know everything it's too late.
—WARREN BUFFETT, investor and philanthropist

Unqualified Successes

Let's hear from a few "unqualified" folks whose initiative and requests opened doors others might've assumed were locked.

Willing to Gamble. *Suzann Marsh Look is an instructional designer, crafter, and crafting technology coach in Grand Junction, Colorado.*

I had long been working in the fundraising world and decided it would be great to get into event planning, but didn't know how to go about it. I don't recall the event I attended, but it was there that I saw Eleanor Woods, who was then the president of one of the most successful event-planning businesses in Chicago.

I introduced myself to her as a fundraising professional who was eager to switch careers. I said, "I know it's a big career change, but this is something I want to do, and I would really like the opportunity to talk with you." She took my phone number and a few days later called to invite me to her office.

"I know it's a gamble," I said within moments of our meeting, "but I'd really like the chance to show you what I can do." It was a big ask for me because I had hardly any experience in this realm. I did feel, though, that I had a natural affinity for the work, and wanted to convince her of that.

Her answer came in the form of an assignment, a mock proposal for a catered corporate party, complete with entertainment. She gave me a "budget" and I soon came back with a creative theme, logistical plan, and cost estimates. In the end, she hired me, not just for my work on the proposal, but because I think she saw a little of herself in me. That ask was a huge step in my life and the key to everything that followed.

Incidentally, statements like, "I know it's a gamble" or "I know it's a long shot", can unwisely call attention to the difficulty of a request and blow your chances. On the other hand, such comments show empathy. You're taking the decision maker's perspective. You're letting them know you're a reasonable person who understands that your request is unusual, that it may not be easy for them to agree to it. By doing so, you're building rapport by saying something they can agree with upfront. And that could yield a yes.

The Right Stuff. *Corey Washington is a marketing professional and entrepreneur in Marietta, Georgia.*

I was in my seventh year working on the project management team managing clinical trials at Covance, now part of Labcorp, a pharmaceutical contract research organization. My schedule was packed working full-time while going to school for a marketing degree. Around that time, I asked myself, *How do I start looking for work at a marketing technology company when I'm still in school and have no marketing background?*

A solution came to me in the form of another question: *What if I stay here and ask for an internship with the marketing team?*

Internships were very uncommon at the company then. But I identified the person to contact and sent an email that told them I was a marketing major, was excited by the marketing team's objectives and challenges, and how my skill set as a strategic project manager would be of value to them. I included the names of a few executives as internal references, gave my hourly rate, and asked if they'd be open to the idea of an internship that I could do in the evenings.

They loved my proposal, not just because I would be cheaper than a typical intern (which I was!) but because when we met, they liked how I presented the creative and strategic thinking behind the projects I was doing. That internship opened the door to another big ask that led to my developing and managing a global training program for a web-based tool that is still in place today, 10 years later.

Corey Washington has advice for anyone looking for new opportunities. "A lot of times," he said, "people don't want to apply for *this* or ask for *that* because they don't have this exact title or aren't in that department. You may have less experience than someone else, but if you have the passion to learn something and can show transferable skills that can be tailored to their needs, go for it."

Figure It Out Later. *Don Lessem, president and CEO of animatronic dinosaur enterprise Dino Don, Inc., has created and hosted documentaries on dinosaurs for the Discovery Channel and NOVA.*

When I was advising on the movie *Jurassic Park*, I knew they were trying to make an entertaining movie, but it was really annoying to me when they didn't get the science and facts right, which to me are gospel. I had access to Steven Spielberg and told him I wanted to make an exhibition about everything that was factually wrong with the movie and that we'd give all the money to paleontological research. And he said sure.

I knew nothing about the exhibit business, but I had access to the thing people would really want—the sets and props from the movie. This turned out to be the best way to educate people, because the public was *so* interested in the movie and I could layer onto that some understanding of the science that *wasn't* applied in it. It became to this day the most attended traveling exhibit in the history of natural science.

So, if I was hesitant because I didn't know anything about making an exhibit—which I didn't then—it would never have happened. Figure it out later.[4]

Don Lessem figured it out. In Chapter 6, you'll discover another ambitious ask Don made in an unforgettable appearance on *Shark Tank*.

Is there an opportunity you'd like to pursue but have disqualified yourself? How do you define "qualified" in this case, and what would it take to become qualified? Do you need to be 100% right for it, or do you already have the "right stuff"? What would it take for you to ask for it?

Do You Deserve It?

There's nothing like the satisfaction of telling ourselves, about some hoped-for reward, "I deserve it!"—and no quicker way to cheer on a friend than assuring them, "You deserve it!" "Deserve" is so validating, so energizing, that we use it expansively, claiming we deserve a doting partner, a third cocktail, or a job offer over equally qualified contenders.

And yet, I suspect there is more in life of which we are worthy than legitimately deserving. That's why I recommend reserving *deserve* for matters of true merit (pulling the sword out of the stone, for example, makes you rightful ruler of England, no questions asked). But if there's something you're reluctant to ask for because you can't in good faith claim to *deserve* it, swap it for *worthy*. Ask yourself, "Am I *worthy* of it?" Small shift, big difference.

Another overused but misunderstood word is *entitled*. Are you entitled to what you ask for? That is, is it yours by right of a law, contract, or agreement—like legal settlements, Social Security payments, and refunds for undelivered pizzas? Or are you entitled to it because it's a moral imperative, like fairness and civility? Clarify for yourself what you mean (and expect) by *deserve* and *entitled*. Even Michael Pollack wasn't entitled to play for Billy Joel, though his musical backstory proved to Joel he was qualified and therefore worthy of the ask.

Finally, let's not confuse *entitled* with the obnoxious "attitude of entitlement." By that I mean the parent who demands the teacher change a C to an A because their child is a talented athlete or needs the higher grade to avert an anxiety attack. Or the driver who when the light turns green flips a finger at the honking cars behind him while he finishes texting. Understanding what we are and are not entitled to keeps our feet in the ground and our heads out of our backsides. It compels us to respect the rights and boundaries of other people, making us better neighbors, citizens, and leaders. In doing so, we create the kind of world we all deserve to live in.

> It is not the correct thing to take offence if a neighbor states civilly that he would prefer your children should cease from breaking his windows.
> —FLORENCE HOWE HALL,
> The Correct Thing in Good Society, 1902

Are You Congruent?

If you feel hesitant to ask for something, ask yourself: *Do I believe I'm worthy of it? Qualified for it? Capable of doing well with what I'd receive?* If you answer no to any of these—or say yes but *feel* no—you probably won't ask. If you ask anyway, your doubts could leak through and makes it easier for the decision makers to say no.

Nothing kills an ask quicker than coming at it as if you've already lost. When people smell doubt, you can just about kiss your ask goodbye. Which raises the question: is it even possible to get a yes if you don't feel worthy of the ask?

Sure. Nothing beats head-to-toe confidence, of course. But a bit of playacting can be an effective way to challenge your *dis*belief by tossing your hat in the ring (or over the wall) and asking anyway. Take the example of Cynthia Barnes. Years before she founded the National Association of Women Sales Professionals or delivered sales training to more than 500 companies, she faced a crisis of disbelief.

> When I first started coaching and consulting business owners on how to amplify their message, I went to a coach. And he said, "If you're going to be a coach, you need to multiple your prices by about 10." I said, "What! There's no way anybody's going to pay that!" The mere thought of me 10x'ing my price made my stomach clench, my palms sweat, and I broke out into a nice sheen—the glazed donut look on my forehead!
>
> But I did it anyway. I went to my would-be client and set out the deliverables and said this is how much the investment is going to be per month, minimum six-month agreement.
>
> And I stopped talking.
>
> And I stopped breathing.
>
> And they said, "Give us a moment, we're going to think about it." So, I walked out, shut the door, and almost hyperventilated. And they came back out and said, "We're ready for you." I went back in the room prepared for them to say that's really expensive and we're not paying that.
>
> And they said, "Ok!"
>
> From that moment on it was no problem asking for that. But I had to do it the first time in order to believe that, yes, people *will* pay that and, yes, they think I'm worth that. I had asked almost as a façade because I really didn't believe

people would pay it. But, as [author] Amy Cuddy says, we should fake it until we *become* it.[5]

Cynthia Barnes didn't believe she was worth the rate increase. And she didn't believe her clients would pay it. A double whammy. But she "borrowed" her coach's belief and, hoping her "faux" didn't show, asked anyway. The success of that first request made it easier for her to believe in herself, which made subsequent asks easier.

Even if we don't believe we're worthy or that yes is possible, often all we need is that initial yes to change our notions about both. In the next chapter, we'll explore the freedom that comes when we stop assuming "it's not possible" and embrace a broader spectrum of potential.

> Too many people overvalue
> what they are not and undervalue what they are.
> —MALCOLM FORBES, entrepreneur and politician

CHAPTER FIVE

IS *YES* POSSIBLE?

We have more possibilities available
in each moment than we realize.
—THICH NHAT HANH, Buddhist monk

CHAPTER THREE ASKED WHETHER YOU BELIEVE IT'S
ok to ask. Chapter Four asked if you believe you're worthy of
asking. This chapter asks if you believe it's possible to get what
you want.

The three intersect. If you don't believe you're worthy you probably won't believe it's ok to ask or that getting it is possible. Or
you might think, *I'm worthy!* yet believe that getting it would be
impossible for you (or for anyone). But the question before you is
twofold: Do you believe it's *possible* to get what you ask, and if you
don't believe it's possible, are you willing to challenge your *dis*belief
and ask anyway?

View from the Mountain

One summer, Scott Martin and his friend Marie flew from New York to Peru for their ultimate destination, Machu Picchu. In Cusco, they planned to take the train that every year takes thousands of visitors to the legendary Incan site. But when their private tour guide greeted them, it was with profuse apologies.

They would not be able to go to Machu Picchu, she explained, because a mudslide had completely smothered large sections of the track. Nothing and nobody could get through. Despite Scott and Marie's dreams of ascending the summit, Mother Nature, it seemed, had eliminated that possibility overnight.

And yet, as certain as the tour guide seemed about the impossibility of passage, Scott was just as certain there had to be a way. "The possibility of impossibility didn't even occur to me," Scott told me. "I implored her to find a way because Machu Picchu had been our whole reason for flying 3700 miles. I didn't know how, but I had absolute conviction we'd get there somehow."

"I don't know what strings she pulled, but a few hours later we were climbing aboard a huge, noisy, military-style helicopter. There we were, with about eight other tourists, flying over the Andes."

The train to Machu Picchu would've taken them four hours each way, but the copter brought them near the foot of the mountain in about 30 minutes. Landing in a clearing in a rainforest, they walked along the railroad tracks to a shanty town, boarded a bus that took them halfway up the mountain, and completed the ascent on foot. There at last they stood, exhilarated, at the entrance to Machu Picchu—and nearly had the place to themselves.

"I'm not the kind of person who would've said, Oh, darn, the train's not in service and I'm so disappointed," said Scott. "My method is to pursue something with surety, and it quite often works out. And I got a full refund for our train tickets."

* * *

Good story, isn't it? What would *you* have done in that situation? Would you have assumed, as Scott did, that there had to be another way? Or would you have surrendered to the idea that the mudslide meant "no go" and ordered a margarita? There's no right answer (but one of them may be harder to admit to!).

A major barrier to asking, and thus to receiving, is putting limits on what you believe is possible. If you don't believe you can reach your "Machu Pichu," you won't ask for it. As the saying goes, "You can't create what you can't imagine." Many of us don't ask for a very dull reason: we never even consider that things could be different than they are now. The rules may appear so solid, the traditions so established, our habits of thinking so fixed, that the possibility of "another way" doesn't even cross our minds.

Whenever we decide, consciously or not, "It's just the way it is," there's no incentive to imagine or ask. It can even seem cruel to hope for things we don't believe could happen. Yan Lianke, a writer whose prolific work is largely banned in his native China, contends that, "Someone who has spent years in a dark cell is bound to be grateful if a window in his cell is unshuttered and some light is allowed in. Would he dare ask for the prison gate to be opened for him?"[1]

Our asks are the size of our imagination and hopes, no more, no less. And hope begins with the question, What if?

From Why to What If

"Why do we follow work processes that slow down productivity?" "Why do I sabotage my goals?" "Why must families in this prosperous city go hungry?" We often ask *why* in frustration. And having vented, we move on, only to fire off the same *why*'s again and again.

But when we ask *why* not just from disappointment but genuine curiosity, we free up energy to understand the problem. The curious *why* sends us digging for reasons, causes, motives. Of course, digging carries risk. Intentionally or not, we might get too close to a guarded truth that exposes an elephant in the room.

In *A More Beautiful Question: The Power of Inquiry to Spark Breakthrough Ideas*, author Warren Berger observes, "A good way to become unpopular in a business meeting is to ask, 'Why are we doing this?'—even though the question may be entirely justified. It often takes a thick-skinned outsider to be willing to even try." To the author's point, if you've ever asked a question that challenged "the way things are," you know it can take as much if not more courage to ask a pointed question than to make a big request.

But, for the curious-minded, the problem-solvers, the innovators and dreamers, the natural inclination is to ask, "Now that I/we understand the *why*, must I/we just accept it? *What if* there's an alternative that's better (smarter, healthier, easier, fairer, more effective, original, sustainable, etc.)? And what might that look like?"

"What if?", that deceptively airy query, has a way of blowing through routine, rigid ways of thinking. The question engages the imagination, the uniquely human faculty whereby we may envision a future that does not yet exist. It shifts our focus from what is to what could be. Perhaps no other question so immediately challenges the limits of our perception.

What if there's a more original way to do x?
What if we could both get what we want out of this vacation?
What if we could offer the same services more cheaply than competitors?
What if I could tell the truth and not lose what I have?
What if we combined this with that?

"What if?" Just speaking the question prompts a pulsing sense of possibility. You'll recall that it was a compelling "What if" that pushed entrepreneur Michel Elings and his team to invent a software the world hadn't seen. "What if" frees the mind to vault over current limits and imagine the outrageous or the ideal (which may be one and the same). We can then advance these emerging ideas by asking, "How could it actually work?" or "What would it take to make it happen?" Even answers not fully formed may point to a trail worth following, a path toward hope.

Just Imagine. John Livesay is a sales expert and keynote speaker on sales, marketing, and negotiation. Throughout his 20-year career in media sales at Condé Nast, John worked across all 22 brands in the corporate division, earning recognition as Salesperson of the Year. The author of four books and host of The Successful Pitch podcast, John tells a story in his keynotes about the time he asked "What if" on behalf of the fashion magazine *W*.

> Speedo was in my territory. And I said, "Hey, I see that you have a new line of sportswear coming out. Would you advertise that in my fashion magazine?" And they said, "No, we're going to run in a fitness magazine. And I said two magic words: What if?
>
> When you get an objection and you say "What if" to your customers, you get them to start imagining a new possibility. For example, you might say, "Well, what if I could show you a way that you could be more efficient and more profitable and maybe even have time to go fishing or take a vacation?"
>
> So, in this case I said to Speedo, "What if we treated your sportswear like it was high fashion, and we could have a fashion show around the hotel swimming pool and Michael Phelps (who was on their payroll during the Olympics) could show up? I bet we'd get a lot of publicity. They loved

the idea, and I not only got the sale but also met Michael Phelps—which, as a former lifeguard and competitive swimmer myself, was a thrill!

What If I Could Have It All?

Just a few years out of college, and about three years into her job as a landscape architect in Denver, Colorado, Elena Scott became increasingly dissatisfied with her salary. She noticed she was doing more advanced work than others at her age and job level. Her workday began at 7:30 every morning, and evening meetings often meant not getting home until after 9:00 p.m. Elena thought she deserved more than the $40,000 she was getting. The approach of her annual review signaled an opportunity for change.

> I decided to ask for a $20,000 raise. I didn't know how much anybody else was making, whether they were making less or a lot more. And I was afraid. What if they tell me I'm not worth it?

Did you catch that? Elena used "What if" to contemplate worst-case scenarios. It *is* a useful question in contingency planning, but too often we use it to talk ourselves out of going for what we want. Fortunately for Elena, she caught her error and rebooted …

> But I talked positively to myself, telling myself I deserved it. I used to run track in State championships, where I learned that just because you're nervous doesn't mean you're not going to go for it. During my review, I provided details about my long hours and responsibly managing million-dollar projects for the company's high-profile clients. I asked for the additional $20,000, and I got it.

Smartly, Elena overrode her worried *What If they tell me I'm not worth it* with self-talk that brought authority to her ask. Notice her use of a more empowered "What If" in the second half of her story.

A few years after that I faced a difficult decision. Should I continue with my job? Or should I marry my partner, Mike, live with him in his home—one hour away, in the mountains—and start over in a new job? After agonizing over the decision, it suddenly occurred to me that **I had considered only the problems and not the possibilities.** I started asking myself, *What if I could keep my job AND live with Mike in the mountains?* That question got me thinking. I told my employers I could set up a small office near my new home and create a local presence for the company, expanding its opportunities. Once again, they said yes.

Elena Scott is now a principal and partner with Norris Design, the very firm in which she'd asked for a raise nearly 20 years earlier. She, her husband Mike, and their two children live in the mountains. "I've been able to have it all," she said. "Whenever I've convinced myself of some limitation, I ask, 'What *else* could be true?' Like asking 'What if,' it's a question that invites you to consider new perspectives."

Preparing to ask for a raise? See my recommendations at https://tinyurl.com/ce93rzde.

Ask to Shadow. *Dr. Dylan Fogel operates a dental practice in Oshkosh, Wisconsin.*

I was 24 and working as a high school special education

teacher and coaching basketball when I began considering a career change. I'd always wondered, *What would it be like to work in the health profession?* It occurred to me one day to ask my assistant coach, a successful dentist, if I could observe him at work sometime, and he said yes.

I spent the day shadowing him for nearly 12 hours. Watching him help and counsel patients, and seeing the contribution he made to his community, was inspiring to me. And it gave me the direct experience of what it would be like working in that kind of environment. I could see myself doing it. It was the ask that put me on my career path.

> I could use a miracle today. You look like the sort of person
> that can make miracles happen.
> —author Caroline Myss quoting a friend's successful ask

Assume It's Possible

Asking, especially for something that seems out of reach, puts to the test our capacity to imagine, believe in, and move toward a reality beyond the present one. The moment we ask, we invest in something larger and more sustaining than our doubts and fears. We take part in *creating* our lives, not merely reacting to circumstances.

Patricia Peters had recently completed her bachelor's in psychology/addictions and saw a notice for the opening of a new counseling center. She realized the counseling center could give her a base to see clients and decided to investigate. Yet even her close friends cautioned her, "You don't have a license, Patricia—you're setting yourself up for disappointment." But she was determined to ask. She walked into the center and asked to speak with the supervising psychiatrist.

I showed her my resume and said this is who I am, this is what I want to learn, and this is what I have to offer. And yet, I still didn't know how I could practice there, or anywhere, without a license.

The psychiatrist told me she could see that I was teachable and then gave me some life-changing news. Indiana law, at the time, permitted counselors with bachelor's degrees, like me, to have a private counseling practice *provided they were under the supervision of a psychiatrist*, like her.

Had I not asked for the appointment, I would not have known about the law. I would not have wound up having my own office at the center for my private practice, nor the psychiatrist as a mentor, nor the support I enjoyed from the center's many therapists and psychologists with whom I worked during those five years.

Patricia Peters assumed possibility and asked without first trying to figure out *how* it could happen. Scott Martin assumed there was a way to get to Machu Pichu and left the details to the tour guide. Cynthia Barnes didn't believe it was possible to get 10x her fee but was willing to let her clients decide that.

When we say, "I don't see how it's possible to get what I want," it's true: *we* can't see it. But others might see solutions we don't. And we won't know what those possibilities are unless we ask and let people use their expertise, problem-solving, or connections on our behalf. If you've been on the helper end of such a request, you know what a pleasure it is to bring the magic, to pull a rabbit out of a hat for someone convinced it was empty.

Dr. Janyce Agruss told me about an unforgettable "What if" (or as she put it, "Wouldn't it be nice?") that rocked her world. She's a longtime faculty member at Chicago's Rush University College of Nursing where she's played a key role in the development of its Family Nurse Practitioner program. As an undergraduate, however, the profession in which she would one day distinguish herself seemed a lifetime away.

As I neared the end of my bachelor's program, I was anxious to be done with school and get my career going. A fellow student and I had a conversation about wouldn't it be nice to finish early? But the only way to do that would've been to take a particular class we needed over the summer, and the school had never offered it then.

We could've just taken it for granted that you take classes according to the school's schedule, because that's how it's done. I don't know what gave us the gumption, but we figured it wouldn't hurt to ask for an exception. All they could do was say no. So, we went and asked a senior administrator if they could offer the class that summer so that we could graduate in March instead of June.

A very short time later the College replied to us that, yes, we could do this. We don't know what made them decide this, but we were thrilled. I can't even remember if there were other students in the class, but my classmate and I took the course that summer, which put us on track to graduate a quarter earlier than the rest of the class.

Now, that was definitely a "wow." But it got even better. A whole outcome we didn't ask for or expect was that, out of our class of 80 students, the university created a graduation ceremony just for the two of us! The dean and a few faculty members presided in a ceremony in the College of Nursing lounge. It was beautiful and so memorable because it was so intimate and there were no restrictions as to how many of our family members could attend.

Even thinking about it now, it's all pretty remarkable. And, after we graduated, we learned that the university started regularly offering more summer courses.

Not only did Janyce Agruss get a class that wasn't offered, but the college threw in a private graduation ceremony for good measure—the very definition of "an embarrassment of riches." Let's look at a few more surprising examples of what can happen when we assume possibility.

A Few Favors. *Manny Veiga is a marketing professional in Boston.*

Several years ago, my wife, Krystle, and I wanted to move to a larger apartment in the same building, but the one we wanted needed some *major* improvements. Our landlord is set in her ways and needs a lot of convincing before she moves on any requests, let alone big changes to the property. We assumed she'd prefer to find a tenant to rent the unit as-is, without any investment on her part.

Despite our hesitations, I gave her a call. I explained our interest in the larger apartment and then asked her for a "few favors" including installing new carpeting in the bedroom and living room, replacing the entire flooring in the sunroom, upgrading the kitchen and bathroom sinks and a portion of the counter, and permitting us to repaint the sunroom and kitchen. Almost an entire renovation.

To my surprise, she wound up agreeing to each one of our requests, proof that she was far more open-minded than I had imagined her to be. Our end of the bargain was to pay for the paint, one-quarter of the carpeting costs, and fifty bucks more in rent. And though we had already requested so much of her, there was one final ask: would she reconsider her "No Dogs" rule?

For the next several years we lived happily, with Baker the Chihuahua, in our larger, much-improved apartment!

Let It Rain. *Robert Griffin is president of a financial strategies firm in Evanston, Illinois.*

After I retired, an old colleague of mine asked me to become a "rainmaker" partner in his business, which focuses on estate planning and charitable giving. In that role, I would introduce him to high-net-worth individuals, and we would split commissions on any business that came out of those relationships.

A former client of mine fit the profile for my friend's business. However, I was very reluctant to approach her since at our last meeting, she had emphatically assured me that her estate planning had recently been executed thoroughly by her attorneys and accountants. The message was loud and clear that the chances of her needing anything at this point were extremely unlikely indeed. I was concerned that if I called again, she'd think I hadn't listened the first time and I'd look unprofessional and lose her trust. In my business, trust is everything.

But I believed in my own judgment and my friend's expertise. With that, I summoned the courage to call her and ask that she meet my friend. I reminded her that I was aware that her estate planning was fully in order, but that my friend might have an idea or two that might further benefit her. Though somewhat reluctantly, she agreed, and we scheduled an appointment.

During the first half-hour of the meeting, my consultant friend discovered an opportunity to reduce the client's income and estate taxes considerably. We had several subsequent meetings with her that resulted in my receiving over $100,000 in commission—all because I had challenged my assumptions and overcome my hesitancy to ask for the appointment.

When you assume possibility, you free yourself to act. You ignore well-meaning friends who tell you that asking would be a waste of your time. You ask school administrators to add classes, landlords for upgrades, and clients for just one more meeting. What possibility are *you* ready to assume?

> So many things are possible as long as
> you don't know they are impossible.
> —MILDRED D. TAYLOR, novelist

Act as If

At the end of the last chapter, Cynthia Barnes told of the time she didn't believe herself worthy of asking 10x her coaching fees nor that her clients would pay it. But she made a "Hail Mary pass" and asked anyway (when it works, it works). So, how do you move from faking a show of worthiness and possibility, to truly believing it?

You *Act as If* you believe it. As if you already have what you want. As if you already are who and where you want to be. It's not a new idea. Twenty-five hundred years ago Guatama Buddha observed, "What we think, we become." To that, neuroscience has added only footnotes.

There are many things we don't yet know about the subconscious mind. But we do know that "it believes" whatever we consistently tell it through our thoughts, words, and feelings. We also know that those deeply stored beliefs inform our expectations, which in turn determine our actions and experiences—in sum, our reality.

That's a troubling logic if we've racked up a hoard of self-limiting beliefs. According to the National Science Foundation, 80% of our thoughts (the things we tell ourselves and the internal images we create) are negative and 95% are repetitive.[2] How dreary is that?

Our fears and doubts become so familiar that we don't even notice how firmly they've taken root in our identity.

But the "believing mind" principle can work in our favor if we feed ourselves thoughts that match up with what we want to be, do, or have. The impressionable subconscious mind then becomes an ally rather than a saboteur. And a happy alignment between conscious choice and unconscious belief is the very aim of the empowerment practice known as Act as If.

For Jeffrey Breslow, working in the world of hospital supplies paid the bills but couldn't compete with his dream of becoming a professional game designer. For two years he tried to get an interview at Marvin Glass & Associates, a leading toy and game design and engineering firm in Chicago. When he finally got invited to interview, he realized he would need to ask for money.

> In 1967, I was making $5,000 a year [1967 U.S. median household income was $7200] in my job at American Hospital Supply when I prepared for my interview with Marvin Glass. I wanted to ask for $10,000 a year. I don't know how I came up with that number. I had no idea what he paid anybody else. I didn't even know what I'd be *doing* there.
>
> But to me $10,000 a year was a lot of money. Twice what I was making. So, I rehearsed it. I looked at myself in the mirror and said, "Ten-thousand dollars." I tried to get it out as naturally as I could, that this is what I'm worth. And I pumped myself up—"I'M GOING TO GET THIS JOB!"
>
> I walked into the interview feeling very positive. I gave a five-minute presentation, and Glass asked me to come work for him as a toy designer. He asked how much money I wanted. I knew I had to look him in the eye when I asked for the ten-thousand dollars. It was the big ask and I had prepared for it.

He said, "That's a lot of money for a kid your age."

I said, "Mr. Glass, I'm worth it."

And he said, "Ok. You got the job."

Eighteen months later I was made a partner in the business.

Jeffrey Breslow's creative ideas and winning interview got him the contract. But his practice of Act as If—in which he repeatedly and wholeheartedly affirmed his worthiness of the $10k and that the job was *already his*—undoubtedly boosted the belief he needed to make a believer of Marvin Glass.

Incidentally, we're not talking about some magical, New Age process here. You already Act as If, every day. Whatever you happen to believe, about anything, you Act as If it's so. So, why not choose beliefs that support the vision of what you want to be, do, and have?

What would you tell yourself if you believed you already are who you want to be, or already have what you seek? What changes would you make in your life? How would you treat yourself and others? How would you dress? What goals would you set? What risks would you take?

The *act* in Act as If is not self-deception but self-mastery. In the words of one of the most successful actors of our time, Sir Anthony Hopkins, "Whatever you want to do, believe it, believe it, believe it. Even if you don't believe it, play the game of belief. Act as if you believe. That is power."[3] To be clear, Hopkins is not speaking here about the make-believe of the actor's craft but the decision to live a more empowered life.

As I noted at the start of the chapter, we'll put the brakes on asking if we believe we're unworthy or that it's impossible to get what we want. And the first step to change those limiting beliefs is to realize we have them (like the time I caught myself ready to accept the hotel bar location rather than ask for a better room). Once aware, we can reach for tools that help us replace our confining beliefs with ones that instill a sense of possibility and purpose. Act as If is one such tool, as are positive affirmations and visualizations (two subjects I've written about in my blog[4]).

Ultimately, the purpose of Act as If is not just to build a new belief but to create an *intention*. Because when you intend something, you don't just wish for it, you expect it. Like Captain Jean-Luc Picard of *Star Trek*, you give the (internal) command to "Make it so."

> If you want a quality, Act as If you already had it.
> —ALFRED ADLER, psychologist

Hope: The Heart of the Ask

Ask "What If?" Assume possibility. Act as If.

What do these three good habits have in common? They are conduits of hope. Asking creates space for solutions, for alternative futures. There is no asking *without* hope, for both breathe life into the possibility, if not the determination, that things will get better.

And yet, who doesn't struggle with hope? There are times when the gap between what we want and what *is*—personally or collectively—seems unbridgeable. Too frequently we use our precious imaginations to obsess over worst-case scenarios. Or we hobble our hopes to preemptively ward off the fear of disappointment, convincing ourselves, often with little investigation, that having what we want is impossible (and so why ask, why attempt?). It's an oppressive outlook that organizations and governments run by tyrants instill to ensure complacency: kill people's hope and they won't push for change.

But we need hope. In his TEDx Oklahoma City talk, "The Science and Power of Hope," Dr. Chan Hellman reports that "Over two-thousand published studies tell us that hope is one of the single best predictors of well-being across the life span."[5] Hope is both a cause and a result of our resilience. Psychiatrist Dr. Karl Menninger called it "the indispensable flame." We feel its warmth most intensely when guided by a faith in our direction. Or we may feel it in a broader way, as a belief that something better is possible for our loved ones, our community, the world.

Our next story is about a woman who kept that "indispensable flame" alive despite seemingly impossible odds.

Is There Any Way?

Jan Woodhouse worked toward her Doctor of Education degree, intermittently, for six years. At age 63, she was close to completing her doctorate. So close, in fact, that all that remained was to make some final chapter revisions and undergo the oral defense, in which she would need to face the faculty's most challenging questions about her dissertation.

In 2004, she began suffering a series of aches and pains. By the following year, the breast cancer she had beat 12 years earlier reappeared, invading her bones. Medicines delayed its effects enabling Jan to enjoy an active life teaching, writing, and traveling.

But now, five years later, her condition had worsened. On a beautiful day in June, a frail and exhausted Jan lay in a hospital bed. Next to her, a hospice worker counseled her about end-of-life matters.

"Jan, do you know you're dying?"

Her response was firm. "No way I'm going to die. I've got to get my dissertation done."

"She was in denial about the seriousness of her condition," said Cliff, Jan's partner of 31 years. When Cliff or other family members tried to bring Jan gently to a place of acceptance, her response was the same: She was not going to leave. Not with her doctorate so nearly within reach.

David, a cousin of Jan's and a physician, recognized the hopelessness of her prognosis yet saw the determination in her eyes. He took Cliff outside the hospital room and, once out of Jan's earshot, urged him to call the university and ask if they could give Jan her doctorate *now.*

It was an idea Cliff had already been considering. Yet as a former college professor himself, Cliff knew this was no simple request. He would need to ask Jan's dissertation chairman. The chairman, in turn, would need to get approval from her dissertation committee, the Dean of the College of Education, and the Dean of the Graduate School. Plus, they would have to agree to waive the university's mandatory oral defense requirement.

Cliff knew the complexities. And he knew he had to ask.

He called the dissertation chairman, a man he had heard Jan speak about many times with fondness and respect. "Jan is in the hospital, and I don't think she's going to make it. Is there any way she could get her degree?"

The chairman took a deep breath. "I'll work on it." He then added his private support, promising Cliff that if the request were approved, he would personally see that the few required revisions were made in the final chapter of Jan's dissertation. Cliff made no mention of the conversation to Jan and heard nothing more from the chairman.

Five days later, at the hospital, as Jan's family quietly chatted at her bedside, an unexpected visitor knocked at the door. Cliff and Jan's eyes brightened as the dissertation chairman approached, a big smile on his face. Struggling to maintain an unbroken voice, he announced that Jan would receive her Doctor of Education degree. "The whole family was crying," Cliff recalled, "but mostly tears of happiness."

A short while later, several nurses, tipped off to the news, entered humming the graduation march and carrying a small cake with "Congratulations, Jan!" on top. One of them had fashioned an impromptu mortarboard of black construction paper and placed it on Jan's head. The ceremony continued as the nurses playfully bopped latex glove "balloons" into Jan's bed. Meanwhile, two nurses strung a hastily created banner on the wall that announced in bold letters, "DR. JANICE WOODHOUSE." Jan beamed throughout the hubbub. As Cliff later noted, for the first time since being admitted to the hospital she looked relaxed and at peace.

Four days later, Jan quietly passed away. "She had four days as Dr. Jan Woodhouse," Cliff told me, "and she worked a long time for that. Getting her doctorate probably allowed her the sense of closure she needed without fighting it."

Cliff had asked on Jan's behalf. That ask, in turn, triggered a chain of asks at the university. And by holding fast to her dream, even to the last, Jan had never stopped asking.

We're all just walking each other home.
—RAM DASS, writer and teacher

CHAPTER SIX

HOW EFFECTIVELY DO YOU ASK?

Communication works for those who work at it.
—JOHN POWELL, film composer

YOU'RE CLEAR ABOUT WHAT YOU WANT. YOU BELIEVE it's ok to ask for it, that you're worthy of it, and that it's possible to get it (or you're willing to challenge your *dis*belief by asking anyway). You're ready to ask, right?

For some asks, maybe. But if your request is sensitive, or complex, or you've got only one shot at it, off-the-cuff won't do. You'll need to decide the best approach for the ask and how best to deliver it.

In this chapter, we progress from Know Thyself to Know Thy Audience, those with the power to say yes or no. You'll discover the five-part Big Ask Plan and its seven related (but optional) tools, to make your next request as compelling as possible.

The Big Ask Plan
ASK THE RIGHT PERSON
PROJECT THE RIGHT ATTITUDE
STATE YOUR NEED CLEARLY
    Give Reasons
    Provide Facts
    Express the Importance to You
    Sell the Vision
TAKE THEIR PERSPECTIVE
    Tell How They'll Benefit
    Appeal to Their Values
    Make the Ask Conditional
MAKE "THANKS" MATTER

Ask the Right Person

In two-parent households, kids learn fast which parent will be more sympathetic to which requests. And that instinct for efficiency—finding the people who'll say yes—never stops being an asset in life. I once found a refrigerator I wanted on the Sears website. But the price shown on the product page was $145 more than the same item featured on the homepage. I called Sears. The rep acknowledged the error. He explained that the lower figure was a sale price that had ended the previous day, but that he couldn't give me the lower price.

"I *understand* that the store made a mistake posting both prices," I said, "but does it seem fair to you that the customer should pay the higher of the two listed prices?" Yet neither he nor his supervisor, who was brought in to rule on the matter, thought the price contradiction should tilt in my favor. (The irony: I'd written over 40 training videos for Sears, including an award-winning one on how the stores could prevent and handle price inconsistencies!)

A few minutes later I called again. Different rep, same runaround.

I probably could've gotten the answer I wanted had I tried reaching the supervisor's boss. But it was a Saturday, and I decided I might get faster results by making my case at the store directly. I made the 15-minute drive to Sears, headed to Appliances, and casually pointed out the price discrepancy to the salesperson. She grimaced. "A hundred and forty-five dollars is a big difference! Our mistake. We'll give you the lower price."

Ask the one who'll say yes, even if it takes a few tries to find them. If you already know who they are, find out what you can about their criteria for consent and approvals, and the interests that drive their decisions; it'll make it easier to make your case with confidence (more on this later). That's exactly what the couple in our next story did, and in quite a spectacular way.

Targeting a Shark

In 2020, at the height of the COVID-19 pandemic, Don Lessem and Valerie Jones drove from their home in Philadelphia to Las Vegas and walked onto the famously intimidating set of ABC-TV's *Shark Tank*. Their objective: ask $500,000 for a 10% stake in Dino Don, Inc., their $1.8M animatronic dinosaur business.

Beneath the gaze of a pair of life-sized, moving, roaring dinosaurs, Don and Valerie shared their vision to help zoos and museums recover lost attendance—"and make millions of kids happy"—by expanding the company's rental platform to make dinosaurs available to more venues. Don reported that the presence of the dinosaurs increased attendance 15 to 50% and would bring in $10 million to Dino Don, Inc. over the next five years.

Their "target Shark" was billionaire investor Mark Cuban. Why Cuban? I asked the couple about their strategy.

"We learned that 80% of the deals he [Cuban] agrees to on air he actually closes," Don told me, "so we knew that's the guy we would want to do business with. Plus, the rest of them don't do anything in entertainment."

Valerie explained that the Sharks "all have business models they're competent in and add value to. [Shark panelist] Daymond John even said he really loved our project but didn't see where he could add value. It's not his game, whereas Mark Cuban is a partner in 2929 Entertainment, the biggest global monster of all integrated entertainment, and owns the Dallas Mavericks, so he understands the entertainment business."

Fortunately for Don and Valerie, the presentation attracted their chosen Shark. Cuban offered the husband-and-wife team their requested half-million, for a 25% stake in the company, which they quickly accepted. But what made the couple's presentation truly unforgettable (apart from the dinosaurs) was the showstopping closing moment.

"We want you to know how much we believe in you," Don told Cuban. And at that point he and Valerie turned in unison to reveal the message, "We love you Mark Cuban," printed on the backs of their t-shirts. The force of Cuban's laughter slammed him into the side of his chair. It remains one of the most unforgettable moments on the show.

When I asked Mark Cuban about his reaction to Don and Valerie's t-shirt reveal, he replied in an email: "It was hysterical. Obviously, I had no idea it was coming. It surprised the heck out of me and I loved it. I also love working with them. They are fun and as you might expect, lovingly quirky!"

Don Lessem and Valerie Jones did their homework. They targeted the right person. They asked for backing from the man whose name was literally on their backs. And they walked out of the "tank" with a T-Rex-size investment.[1]

Aim higher. In business, Valerie Jones recommends aiming high on the organizational chart when asking for buy-in. "There are lots of 'no' people," she says. "Perhaps only one person has the authority to say yes. Sometimes you're just wasting your time unless you go to the top."

Whatever the arena for your ask (business, school, government, etc.), find out who has the authority to say yes. Based on what you discover or can reasonably deduce about the decision maker, let that inform the *attitude* you bring to the ask, which we'll explore next.

Project the Right Attitude

An effective request shows respect for the decision maker; anything less is a demand. There are no limits to what we can ask and receive from a foundation of respect. It's an attitude. Respect says, *I see you as a person, not just a means to an end.* And empathy, an expression of respect, says, *I care about the impact of my request on you.*

"Attitude" is the whole effect: the mood or feeling that beams through your choice of words, tone of voice, facial expressions, energy level, posture, gestures, and feelings about yourself and the person you're asking. As leadership expert John C. Maxwell noted, "People may hear your words, but they feel your attitude." Attitude speaks louder than words.

So, is there a "right" attitude? Yes—the one that's right for the purpose of your ask and the person you're asking. An attitude that says, "I'm getting what I want," as if the outcome is already decided, could offend a person who expects deference but impress one who enjoys a show of bravado. Here, appeasement gets the nod; there, audacity. But if you're asking for an opportunity to prove your capabilities, an attitude that says "I'm confident and capable" is your best bet.

Lilly Harris is a farmer and project manager in Portland, Oregon. "Most of the jobs I've had I've pretty much asked for," she says. In our conversation, she spoke about the flexible attitudes she's brought to her job searches.

I was 22 and had just moved to Portland. I had a really crappy job at a bagel shop and saw this French restaurant was going to be opening near my house. One day I decided to put on a nice outfit and go down there. When I walked in, I told the manager, "I'm your new waitress!" He seemed surprised at my forthright manner and was a little confused—he thought I was already hired! We sat down and talked over my resume, and I started work there the next day.

Lilly's disarming mix of boldness and humor took her overnight from bagels to Boeuf Bourguignon. Many years and a few jobs later, she targeted a new career opportunity that required a very different attitude.

At 34, I was interested in getting a warehousing and operations position at a farm food delivery service in Portland. I sent a few emails to Carina, the woman who ran the business, but never got a reply. So, I went to an event where she was speaking.

Someone I knew in the audience asked me, "So, what do you want to do next? What's your next job move?" And I pointed out Carina and said, "I'm going to work for *her*."

At the end of the presentations, I approached Carina, introduced myself, and told her I had been emailing her and that I was really interested in her program and thought we should have a meeting. She was a little surprised, I think, by my directness, but she met with me a few weeks later and we had a good 90-minute conversation. I started soon after that as director of operations.

Had Lilly used the same strategy that got her the restaurant job and brightly announced to Carina, "I'm your new director of operations!" the conversation might've ended there. The right attitude is everything. A successful ask calls on us to intuitively "read the room" and adapt our approach to the people, mood, and situation as best we can.

Keep it upbeat. Some folks don't like to ask and say so: "I PRIDE myself on not having to ask ANYONE for ANYTHING, which is why I HATE having to ask you this, but …" Mistake! Ask with an attitude that enlists their support. Make them feel good about saying yes.

Show empathy. Empathy is being able to feel and understand someone's emotions regardless of our thoughts about the person. Put yourself in their shoes before you ask. What pressures are they under? What might be the impact of your request on them? Empathetic nods, like, "I know how busy you are"; "I realize this is last-minute"; or "I've been asking a lot of you lately" may be enough to acknowledge the potential imposition. But don't confuse such comments with the bad habit of apologizing before and after requests. Self-put-downs are not empathy (and they can be irritating).

Is it really empathy? Empathy is a beautiful thing. But if you're concerned, let's say, that asking the server to reheat your cold spaghetti would impose an unreasonable hardship on them, it could be feelings of unworthiness *masked* as empathy. If you're prone to people-pleasing, what you call "empathy" might just be worries that the server won't like you if you ask for a reheat. But we can be compassionate *and* assertive, and stronger for it.

What about *Please?* It's still the "magic word" that can make others more willing to comply (or feel less resentful about it). But unless it's said with a lilting tone of radiant goodwill, *please* can sound too emphatic, even pushy: "Leave my bag where it is, please" or "Would you please let me know when you're done with that?" But *how* we say anything makes a bigger impact than *what* we say. A politely worded request can come off harshly and one roughly blurted sparkle with charm.

State Your Need Clearly

I once had a manager who made clear verbal requests but vague written ones. In a single email she'd mention two male names and three different projects and direct me to "call *him* to discuss *it*." Or she'd write, "Send the client *everything* before noon," leaving me to wonder which of the dozens of project documents she had in mind. My replies to her many ambiguous messages typically began like this:

"I want to be sure I understand your request ..."

"When you said _____ did you mean _____?"

"You know me, I can always find a dozen ways to interpret anything! Ha-ha! But would you clarify what you mean by 'make the message clearer?'"

In fairness to my manager, she probably sent more emails in a day than she took breaths. Clarity took a backseat to speed. Most of us, I think, are guilty of this sort of "hazy ask," emailed or not. We assume that if we say what we want it'll be instantly clear to others, and if it isn't, well, surely, they'll ask for clarification. Can't you just smell the disappointment brewing in that assumption?

We suffer from the illusion of transparency, a cognitive bias that our intentions, feelings, and needs are as obvious to others as they are to us. (They're not!) If our request is unclear, we'll get only the listener's best-guess of what we asked for, if we get anything at all. And if they're worried that they'll sound stupid asking for clarification, it won't end well for anybody.

Chapter 2 was about identifying your wants clearly and positively for yourself. But when a want becomes an ask, the outcome rests on how effectively you make that want clear to others. Check the weather on your request: is it hazy or clear?

Hazy: "Honey, would you try to be a little more supportive of my accomplishments?"
Clear: "When I get a new client, it'd mean a lot to me if you'd give me a high-five or say, 'Great job!' or give me a big kiss. Would you do that for me?"

Hazy: "Rowan, thanks for letting me use you as a reference. If a prospective employer calls and asks about me, say nice things, ok?"
Clear: "It would help me if you'd let them know that ABC Corp. asked me to project-lead for those two years, and how you and I got deeper with EFG, Inc."

Hazy: "I guess it's cold and flu season again, huh?"
Clear: "I'm sorry you're sick, but for my protection would you mind sneezing into your sleeve?"

The next three examples feature authority figures. The speaker in each is giving a directive (command). Unlike asks, directives compel compliance. This is a book about asking, but because a lack of clarity can muddy a directive as much as it can an ask, I've included a few examples.

Hazy: "Make sure the branding video is a reasonable length."
Clear: "Cap the video at 90 seconds."

Hazy: "Put more substance in your book reports."
Clear: "I need you to give clear reasons for your opinions other than saying that something is 'awesome' or 'stupid.'"

Hazy: "I don't want you kids spending our entire vacation on your phones, is that clear?"
Clear: "I want all phones turned off when we're having our meals together or sitting around the campfire. That's family time, and it's important to me."

When and Why? Be clear about due dates and times. To boost compliance, say *why* you need it then. "I'll need the photo proofs by noon Wednesday so that I can review them on my flight that afternoon. Is that doable for you?"

Respect the exec. When making a request of an executive verbally or in writing, summarize the vital details upfront, such as: "I'm asking for _____ which will result in these benefits _____ for these stakeholders _____ and will roll out as follows _____."

> ***Own It.*** *Brian Little is vice president and global head of corporate human resources for Intel.*

In corporate language we're trained to say *we* all the time, even when we don't mean we. It's kind of like a reflex. But when you really want something, you say: *I want, I need,* or *I request; I'm asking you for* or *I would like you to.* That personalization of the *I* gets to the heart of it, and clarifies the request.

I learned over time that the more elusive language is around a request, the less likely the request would be done. In almost any city in the world, if you can master the language enough to say, *I want, I need,* or *I request,* others are more likely to do it. When people say, "I would like a favor," it's hard to say no. Even when they want to say no, people feel compelled to say yes because you've asked them directly. If they can figure out how to do it, they'll do it.

Are you ready to get even more explicit in your requests? Alrighty then. Let's look at four related-but-optional components of State Your Need Clearly:

State Your Need Clearly

☐ Give Reasons
☐ Provide Facts
☐ Express the Importance to You
☐ Sell the Vision

State Your Need Clearly: Give Reasons

"Please pass the salt" doesn't need a because, but some requests may not be clear, complete, or compelling without a *why*. Especially in a sensitive ask, the absence of a reason may appear baseless, too blunt, or presumptuous. And that can invite resistance.

Neighbor Smith: Neighbor, would you be willing to limit the leaf-blowing to evenings or weekends?

Neighbor Jones: It's a free country! I'll blow it when I want to!

Is Jones just a belligerent jackass? Maybe. But by adding a reason, Smith has a better chance of finding some peace.

Neighbor Smith: Neighbor, I work at home, and no matter where I am in the house the blower makes it hard to hear my clients on the phone. Would you be willing to limit the leaf-blowing to evenings or weekends?

Neighbor Jones: Happy to oblige! Better yet, I'll donate the blower to a resale shop. Damn thing's a public nuisance anyway.

(Ok, so it's a fantasy scenario. But Smith's reasons were hard to dismiss.)

Reasons legitimize your request by making it sound more reasonable. They also give the listener a basis on which to evaluate it, as in the examples below.

REQUEST	+REASONS
Boss, could you authorize me to approve merchandise returns?	... so that I can give our customers faster service and you wouldn't have to run to the front desk.
I'm asking for a 10% raise.	I brought in three new clients, have taken on most of Jana's duties since she left last year, and ...
Would you wash the dishes tonight?	The cat's on my lap.

Even if you are legitimately in charge, making requests in a bossy way—"Because I said so"—makes you a resentment magnet. But give a reason for the request and the listener feels respected. In the next examples, notice how blunt commands are softened by adding *why*:

COMMAND	+REASONS
Leave my bag where it is, please.	I still need to put a few more things in it.
Tommy, take your binoculars into the house.	The neighbors are having a cookout, and I'm concerned they'll think you're spying.

COMMAND	**+REASONS**
Be here 10 minutes early for the meeting tomorrow.	Because the CEO is very punctual and never forgets latecomers.

State Your Need Clearly
- ☑ Give Reasons
- ☐ Provide Facts
- ☐ Express the Importance to You
- ☐ Sell the Vision

State Your Need Clearly: **Provide Facts**

I once served as a juror in a civil trial concerning a driver who was slightly injured in a collision. Toward the end of the arguments, the plaintiff's attorney asked us to award his client several thousand dollars for "pain and suffering." Trouble was, he'd offered evidence of neither. Absent that proof, we, the jury, were conservative in his client's compensation: one dollar. Some requests don't persuade without facts or evidence.

Kathy Bond, a project manager in marketing communications and content production, recalled a time when a health-related ask hinged on her command of the facts. Kathy, who has diabetes, was once diagnosed with cancer. Her primary care doctor prescribed two medications to manage her blood sugar throughout her cancer treatments. When she became cancer-free, she met with the doctor to review her case. Her goal was to go back on the single diabetes medication she'd been on before her cancer diagnosis.

I told him I was very disturbed that I was still on the two diabetes medications with side effects that included weight gain when I was trying to lose weight. I asked him if two medications were still critical and he said yes, until my blood sugar levels got down to 6.0. I left his office upset that I was going to be stuck on both medications for a long time.

But my blood sugar continued to lower each time we tracked it. And I discovered, while looking through a record of my previous testing numbers, that the doctor had had me on a lower dose when my numbers were even higher than they were now.

I made an appointment to see him. I knew exactly what I was going to say and how to say it, yet I was still nervous about the possibility that he might continue to insist on the higher dosage. My strategy was to come off as a vibrant, healthy person, so I wore bright colors. I brought him fresh blueberries from the farmer's market. I walked in there determined that he was going to agree to my request.

I explained my reasons for asking for a single, low dose medication and cited the numbers supporting it. He looked at me. He looked at the data. "You're right," he said. And he wrote up the new prescription. When I walked out of there, I was proud and grateful that my determination paid off.

Kathy Bond knew the facts—and brought them. Making her entrance in brightly colored clothes with a gift of fruit likely helped set the stage for the doctor's positive expectations. [Her "costume" and "props" are classic examples of *priming*, in which the "audience" is exposed to effects designed to subtly influence their decisions.] Kathy summed up her experience:

People put doctors on pedestals and whatever the doctor says, goes. People don't ask them questions. They don't challenge them. And people don't always take charge of their own healing. If I hadn't done the research and asked my doctor for a change in my treatment, who knows how much longer I would've stayed on two side-effect-heavy medications?

Facts alone rarely convince; facts backed with *stories* win more hearts. Nevertheless, critical thinkers will expect to hear some evidence that supports your request. What facts (research, data, documentation, testimonials, photos, examples, comparisons, proven capabilities, etc.) do you need to make your request compelling? Come prepared to prove your case.

Talk Results. Is your request big or complex, such as a grant, loan, or project proposal? Then you'll want to be explicit not only about the reasons for asking but the *results* you plan to create with their permission or buy-in. How do you intend to carry it out? Who's on your team? How will you measure the success of your efforts? Show them how you intend to succeed with their support.

State Your Need Clearly
- ☑ Give Reasons
- ☑ Provide Facts
- ☐ Express the Importance to You
- ☐ Sell the Vision

State Your Need Clearly:
Express the Importance to You

Some asks, no matter how clearly stated and reasoned, are easy to dismiss. The decision maker may hear requests like yours all the time (and say "no" a lot). Or your request might push the limits of what they're willing to approve. In such cases, you need something more to move the needle in your favor. How can you boost your chances for consent, especially when the stakes are high?

You can make a personal appeal. Emotionally connect with your listener by expressing what their consent would *mean* to you and/ or others affected by your ask—and what it would be possible to do and feel as a result. Give your ask not just reasons but a sense of your emotional investment. Though you're not saying it directly, you're asking for their empathy.

If you've watched *Shark Tank* or *Dragon's Den*, you're familiar with the power of personal appeals to influence decisions. On these shows, entrepreneurs strive to create excitement about their products or services. Many tell inspiring backstories of how hard they worked to develop their ideas, the sacrifices made along the way, and what investor support would mean for them, their colleagues, and families. Even allowing for a degree of producer interference (it's television, after all), a good story can turn the investors from lukewarm to hot in their decision to make offers.

In her book, *A Big Life in Advertising*, Mary Wells Lawrence tells of securing legendary singer Frank Sinatra for her agency's hugely successful "I Love New York" TV campaign. But on the night of the shoot Sinatra, annoyed by delays to clear the street of gawking fans, insisted on doing only one take. As the cameras rolled, the legendary singer bumped into one of the dancers and blew the shot. With literally millions of production dollars at stake the director, Stan Dragoti, pleaded for another take.

Sinatra refused.

That's when Dragoti secretly signaled one of the most attractive dancers, who came up to Sinatra and said, "Oh, please, Frank, my mother will be watching. I told her I was making this shot with you and she is so thrilled."

"OK," said Frank. "I'll do it for you. For you and your mother!"[2]

The commercial was saved. Never underestimate the power of a personal appeal.

Consider, too, the example of "Chad," a young man who told me how financial issues had forced him to consider dropping out mid-semester in his second year at college. He asked school advisors what to do. They told him about school-sponsored grants but informed him he was too late to apply. One advisor suggested he apply anyway by writing an appeal letter but warned that he shouldn't get his hopes up.

Chad wrote the letter. He emphasized his good grades, how he couldn't turn to his family for money, had been turned down for financial assistance, and gotten burned from a private loan with high interest rates his first year.

> I also poured my heart out. I wrote about how eager I had been to get back to school, that I wanted to continue my education without interruption, and what it would mean to be the first one in my family to graduate from a university. I expressed my passion for my chosen major and how I was working in my field while in school. My letter was basically pleading. I didn't know when or if I'd get a reply and had very low expectations. Most students are in debt and schools don't just dish out money.
>
> A few weeks later the university informed me it would cover the entire outstanding balance of my year's tuition, about $14,000. It was like an overwhelming weight was suddenly off my shoulders. I'll never know for sure what made them decide in my favor, but when I spilled my guts to them, I meant it.

Chad's story proves two points: (1) there is no help without asking, and (2) authentic personal appeals can trigger empathy and open the safe.

Avoid using "benefit" to describe your potential gains. "Getting your support would benefit me immensely" smacks of self-reward that could turn people off. Instead, say what their consent will *help* or *enable* you to do (or help you do for others).

If you're not the expressive type, don't force it. There's nothing so un-convincing as hearing, "I'm passionate about …" from a poker-face. But no matter your communication style, commit 100% to your ask. If it's not coming across as important to you, it won't be important to them. In the words of D.H. Lawrence, "Be still when you have nothing to say. When genuine passion moves you, say what you've got to say, and say it hot."

Use personal appeals sparingly. "It would mean a lot to me" or "I would be so grateful" may be enough to get the support you seek. But tread lightly here. If your tone implies that declining your request would be a personal betrayal, your would-be helper could feel coerced and resentful. Avoid overusing feeling-based appeals. Keep your ask clean!

Don't make asking for a raise or promotion "personal." Provide mea-surable evidence of your great work rather than emphasize your great need. "The kids need braces, and I've promised them a pool this summer" won't bolster your case. Neither will "But I gave you that box of holiday cashews!" Keep it professional.

With any ask, let the people, stakes, and your best instincts inform whether or how to communicate the importance to you.

State Your Need Clearly
☑ Give Reasons
☑ Provide Facts
☑ Express the Importance to You
☐ Sell the Vision

State Your Need Clearly: Sell the Vision

Despite the budget strain, you want to excite your spouse about the possibilities of transforming a sorry patch of lawn into a spectacular rose garden.

You strive to inspire one-thousand 18-year-olds in an underrepresented school district to register to vote by organizing a series of get-out-the-vote events.[3]

You start an online fundraiser to raise a sunken passenger ship by asking, "If you could stand beneath the Titanic's propeller, would you?"[4]

A big dream needs a big ask, a platform to sell the big picture. But the vision must be compelling. It must be exciting or inspiring enough to capture people's imaginations and enlist their support or collaboration. What does your vision look like? Why is it important? Who would it benefit? What would it cost?

Robert M. Eschbach was mayor of Ottawa, Illinois, and a member of a planning committee for a downtown plaza that would feature a fountain and bronze statues commemorating the site of the first Lincoln-Douglas senatorial debate in 1858. But with a population of less than 20,000, Ottawa didn't have the money to bring the $450,000 project to completion. The committee realized it would need to seek donations from local citizens, and Robert knew he had to start asking.

I made an appointment to discuss the project with a local businessman who was known to be generous and had a soft spot for Ottawa. I gave him a short presentation on how the project would **improve the park, create an enduring symbol for the city, and inspire pride within the community**. I don't like asking, but after showing him the design renderings and models of the statues, I dove in and asked for $25,000.

At the time, I had never approached anybody for $25 let alone $25,000. That's why his "yes" was pretty mind blowing for me. I've since learned that it's sometimes easier to ask for big money, for big projects, than it is asking for small amounts, for small projects, because **people get excited about buying into a vision.**

Fortunately for Ottawa, the vision was sufficiently grand to garner larger cash gifts as well as city and grant monies. Three years after the first planning meeting, the Lincoln-Douglas Debate Plaza was installed in Washington Park. "The project taught me how to 'ask big' for contributions," Robert said, "which as mayor I had strived to do every day."

Tell a story. To enlist people in your vision or cause, help them *experience* it. Use vivid sensory language and visual aids. Give them a sense of what they'll see, hear, smell, taste, or touch in your realized vision. Make them feel it. Tell them success stories about people who had dreams like yours and succeeded. Engage their imagination through *What if* or *Picture this* language, such as:

"Picture this, honey: You and me on a safari in Botswana, eye to eye with a beautiful family of cheetahs just outside our vehicle. We're so close we can see their fur rippling as they walk, hear them purring as they breathe. And at night, you and I looking up at more stars than we've ever seen before …"

"How would you feel if you knew that your gift could help women living in extreme poverty grow their small businesses, provide for their families, send their children to school, and create jobs for their neighbors? How would it feel to know you were helping connect them to resources that would transform their lives and communities?"

"Imagine two students, right here in our district. One has learned to memorize facts; the other critical thinking skills—analysis, problem-solving, and deductive reasoning. Which student leaves our school more confident? More independent? More prepared for the future? And what would it take for us to become a school committed to developing critical thinkers?"

A big ask takes salesmanship. You need buy-in, the enthusiastic endorsement or collaboration of the people you're asking. And for that to happen, you'll need to pull in the full complement of skills already covered in this chapter plus some from the next section, *Take Their Perspective.*

State Your Need Clearly

- ☑ Give Reasons
- ☑ Provide Facts
- ☑ Express the Importance to You
- ☑ Sell the Vision

Take Their Perspective

The more you know about the person you're asking, the better your sense of the right attitude for the conversation. You might also be able to anticipate their likely response, and tailor your request accordingly. This dynamic is perfectly illustrated in an old story of two monks in a monastery. One monk approached the abbot and asked, "May I smoke while I pray?"

"Absolutely not!" his superior snapped. "It would be disrespectful."

A second monk, who'd observed the interaction, approached the abbot and asked, "May I pray while I smoke?"

"Why, yes," the abbot replied, "and what a fine example of devotion!"

The second monk gets the 'A.' He took the decision maker's perspective before he asked.

John Cummins sees perspective-taking as a fundamental communication skill. At 25, the native Australian was appointed as head of youth programs at Channel 4 TV UK, where he launched the careers of several of the UK's best known TV personalities. He later built and sold Hydra Associates, a leading media advisory company whose clients included Comcast and Time Warner, and became vice chairman of Hawkpoint, the investment bank that acquired it. I asked him about the importance of understanding the perspectives of key players in an ask.

> I learned early on that dealing with celebrities and difficult talent is very good training ground; I became hyper-empathic and aware (which certainly made it easier raising my children!). Everything is about empathy. The question I used to ask in TV is, "Who has to do *what* to make this happen, and what do they *care* about?"
>
> Whether you're trying to get an outside broadcast done at a difficult location or trying to sell a company, it's critical to know who the decision makers are, what's their agenda, what are they getting rewarded or punished on—and then work back from how to make what *you* want from them, work for them. And the clearer you are on the outcome the clearer you can be on the questions to get you to the outcome.
>
> The big projects are always like children's parties: no child leaves without a prize. But you have to know what they care about, so the prize is right for *them*.

"Everything is about empathy," John told me. His use of the word *empathy* seems to encompass not only compassion (discussed in Attitude a few pages back), but something that negotiation expert and author Chris Voss calls "tactical empathy." Here, one endeavors to understand the other's concerns not only to behave more compassionately toward them but to turn that knowledge to advantage.

Negotiations hinge on leverage. Each party has something the other wants and works toward mutual wins. In an ask, however, the listener (like the abbot in our parable) may hold *all* the power in the situation. They may have nothing to gain by saying yes and nothing to lose by saying no.

In such cases, it may not be enough to state what you want, why you want it, and what "yes" will mean for you. You may also need to take their perspective and, if possible, show them what might not otherwise be apparent to them: how your request is *aligned with their interests* and therefore to their advantage to say yes. And the interests of the decision maker boil down to three factors we'll cover next:

Take Their Perspective
☐ Tell How They'll Benefit
☐ Appeal to Their Values
☐ Make the Ask Conditional

Take Their Perspective: Tell How They'll Benefit

Benefits are the ways others profit from helping you. Benefits answer the typically unspoken question, "If I say yes, what's in it for me?" These benefits could be solid, such as returns on their investment, or intangible, such as the hero's rush they feel when their consent saves the day.

Benefits are perceived gains in ability, money, assets, reputation, security, wellness, and relationships—and, even more compelling—anything that *prevents the loss* of these things. We hate to lose what we already have and will fight to keep it. The examples below show requests (or lead-ins to requests) that convey the benefits that the asker knows are important to their audience.

Benefit: Productivity
"Boss, you've said that communication coaching would be too 'touchy feely' for a maverick like Bob, but his staff has the highest

rate of turnover. Could we revisit coaching as an option for him, so the company *doesn't fall short of the productivity goals you've set?"*

Benefit: Peace of Mind

"Mom and Dad, if you help me upgrade to a car with more safety features, I'll be more protected, and *you can feel more confident and less worried about me* on the road."

Benefit: Status

"As a Platinum Imperial Prime Priority Plus member, you would enjoy the exclusive privilege of sitting in the red-carpeted section of our bus terminal—accessible only with a golden key."

Of the three examples, Productivity is the only benefit that can be proven or measured. The value of the other two, Peace of Mind and Status, can't be calculated on spreadsheets. Yet all three examples share something in common with all benefits: an underlying appeal to the *feelings* that benefits generate. If it doesn't grab the decision maker in the heart, gut, or ego, it's not a benefit for them.

The benefit is not the "thing" itself; it's the contentment, confidence, pride, joy, hope, relief, well-being, pleasure, or avoidance of pain or loss that it brings us. When you consider your listener's (likely) perspective and then show them how they could benefit by giving you what you want, you make your request more persuasive.

What is your request, and how could the decision maker benefit by agreeing to it?

Take Their Perspective

- ☑ Tell How They'll Benefit
- ☐ Appeal to Their Values
- ☐ Make the Ask Conditional

Take Their Perspective: Appeal to Their Values

What if there's no disadvantage for them to say yes ... but no real benefit either? In the absence of benefits, you might choose to ask in a way that appeals to their values. Values are the principles that guide our decisions and affirm what we believe is most important in work, relationships, and life (even if our actions often contradict our values), such as:

Authenticity	Adaptability	Loyalty
Originality	Community	Independence
Candor	Harmony	Learning
Courage	Tradition	Reason
Discretion	Collaboration	Personal Growth
Accountability	Sportsmanship	Innovation
Fairness	Self-expression	Creativity
Efficiency	Persistence	Wisdom
Discipline	Passion	Risk-taking

Like benefits, values reward us emotionally. Just think about how good it feels when you behave in ways true to your values—accountability or fairness, for example—and how bad it feels when you don't. Our values are linked with our self-image and integrity. In the examples below, the askers appeal to the values *they know are important to their audience*, thereby enhancing the impact of the request (or inquiry, in the case of the third example).

Values: Honest, Authenticity
"I know you're also considering other consultants for your brand development, and you should know upfront that I'm a firm believer in 'telling it like it is,' which I realize not every client wants to hear."

Values: Persistence, Achievement

"I'm asking for your endorsement because I know you understand the importance of hard work, discipline, and sacrifice toward a goal, which are exactly what have brought me to this critical point in my career."

Values: Peace, Harmony

"How does holding onto your anger at your son create the family harmony you say is so important to you?"

What big ask are you contemplating? Based on what you know about the decision maker, what values are important to them? Relative to your request, how do your values align with theirs—and how will you communicate that?

Take Their Perspective
☑ Tell How They'll Benefit
☑ Appeal to Their Values
☐ Make the Ask Conditional

Take Their Perspective: Make the Ask Conditional

Take time to imagine or discover (if you don't already know) the listener's desires, goals, needs, beliefs, concerns, and principles. Once you connect the dots between what you want, what they value, and how they'll benefit from saying yes, you can create an outcome everybody feels good about. One way to get closer to that handshake is by making mutual wins a *condition* of your ask. A conditional or provisional request follows the If/then model: "If I do *x* would you do *y*?" or "Would you do *y* if I do *x*?"

"If I'm able to meet those goals sooner than expected, could we revisit my request for a raise?"

"Would you consider letting me have the clock if I promise to keep it in the family?"

"How about we try it my way and if it doesn't work better for both of us, we go back to your way?"

A conditional request isn't always 50-50. It may be an attempt to convince them that their cooperation would be great for you and, if not exactly an advantage for them, not a *dis*advantage either. Wayne Paprocki, a coach, trainer, and speaker in the areas of sales and negotiation, says, "If you ask for anything and say, 'Fair enough?' they're going to consider it. It's like sprinkling sugar at the end of a request. Everyone wants to be fair."

Conditional Refund. *Kathryn Hutchinson is an award-winning poet and editor-in-chief of a poetry journal.*

I started taking my son, Ramon, to movies when he was seven, never knowing if he could make it all the way through them. Because of his autism he had a tendency to be loud and have tantrums.

After the first time when he wanted to leave immediately after the previews (since he'd mowed through the popcorn), I felt like I'd wasted several dollars on tickets we didn't use. I've never been one to ask for special treatment or refunds, but the next few times we went to the movies I asked the ticket-sellers if I could get a refund if we didn't make it past 20 minutes. They always said yes, and I did take them up on it a couple of times!

Take Their Perspective
- ☑ Tell How They'll Benefit
- ☑ Appeal to Their Values
- ☑ Make the Ask Conditional

Make "Thanks" Matter

We are duty-bound to acknowledge every answered ask. A note or text. A phone call. A wave to the driver who's let us squeeze into their lane. Appreciation closes the loop: kindness given; kindness received. No loose ends. Everybody's happy.

A simple "Thanks!" may be enough. But a big ask deserves big appreciation, rich and meaningful. To convey that, tell the person what their help enabled you (or others) to *do*, and how you *felt* as a result. If appropriate, share a few warm words about them, to make it personal.

"Hey, Seth and Olivia, thanks to your help, I completed those data entries on time and got home at a decent hour. Grateful! You guys are the best. If I can ever return the favor, let me know."

"Jacob, I can't thank you enough for picking up Matthew and Nina from school yesterday. Knowing they were with you cut my stress—and theirs—in half. You saved the day for all of us. Thanks for being such an incredible neighbor."

Want to ignite more sparks with your romantic partner? The next time you thank them for an answered ask (or for anything), speak less about what their help enabled you to do—"I can now sleep in on weekends"—or how it made you feel—"It felt amazing", otherwise known as the *self-benefit* form of expressing gratitude.

Instead, make it all about them, known as *other-praising*—"Honey, I love how you understand even the little things that are important to me" or "You always know when I'm stressed and are so good at helping me laugh and relax." In one study involving young couples, the recipients who received other-praising statements from their partners reported feeling more loving toward them.[5] Have fun with this one!

Offer payment? For a favor? Never! At least not for someone you know. Payment can undermine the relationship ("Put your wallet away, Mother, I'm happy to wash your car"). It's at your discretion, of course, to give some token of appreciation *after* the help is given. Tip: gift cards are less crass than cash and harder to refuse.

Thank them in advance. The next time you call customer service to resolve a problem, set a tone of positive expectation early in the conversation—"I really appreciate that you're here to help me resolve this, Hector—thanks." That personal acknowledgement, and your pleasant expectation that it will indeed be resolved, could be enough to motivate the agent to work harder on your behalf.

Appreciation makes life richer. Richer still is thanking not only those who do as you ask but those who do what you *never* have to ask. Whose day would brighten with a word of gratitude from you? Bookmark this page and thank them now. (Go ahead. I'll wait!)

Big Ask Plan: Destined for Disney

We opened the chapter with a story of a big ask on *Shark Tank*. And we'll close with one dreamed up in a dorm and delivered at a kitchen table. The two stories may be worlds apart in scale, but both illustrate the importance of a strategy and core set of skills.

Rachel Katz was 18 years old and in the first semester of her freshman year at California State University Northridge (CSUN) working toward an animation degree when she applied to the Disney College Program, a paid internship in Orlando. Even though the Disney program complimented her major, Rachel knew that her parents—her mother in particular—wouldn't want her to delay her upcoming second semester at CSUN for five months in Disney's program.

Rachel thought through the situation strategically. She knew she wanted to come across with an **attitude** that said, "I'm serious, responsible, and passionate about this program." She considered her parents' likely **perspectives**: What would be their fears or concerns, and how would she effectively counter them? How might they **benefit** from her being in the program? And how best to communicate an ask and a **vision** of this size?

One night at school, Rachel poured it all into a PowerPoint presentation. She branded the slides with cheerful Disney imagery offset with no-nonsense titles: *Program Legitimacy. Why I Should Be in the Program. Housing.*

Several slides spelled out the benefits for her parents: the peace of mind they could enjoy knowing the campus safety measures; the thousands they would save in her housing and meal costs; assurance that their cash assistance would be limited to the round-trip airfare from LA to Orlando because all other expenses would be covered by her Disney wages.

A few days later, Rachel came home from school to present her case to her parents. "I was very nervous but thought *It's now or never.* I had them sit down at the kitchen table, and I talked them through my presentation."

Rachel's mother, Shelley, explained to me that she was skeptical but impressed with her daughter's carefully prepared arguments. "When my husband or I had questions, and we had a lot of them, Rachel had anticipated all of them: 'Well, I happen to have a slide on that, *click!*'"

Then came the final slide, a **personal appeal** entitled, *On a More Heartfelt Note.* It expressed **empathy** for her parents' feelings and emphasized self-confidence and self-reliance, **values** important to all three of them. Rachel read it aloud to her parents:

> I realize you wouldn't be just a quick drive away, and I'm not trying to leave you behind. But I believe this

is an instrumental part of my growing up, building my self-confidence and learning how to better take care of myself, so that in the future you won't have to worry as much about me and I can take better take care of you. I feel I am taking a strong step toward what I want to achieve in my career and in life. I hope you can support this. It means a lot to me.

"When it came to that moment in the slides," Shelley said, "I'm crying, my husband's crying, the dog's crying. But I still had to vet it, and that led me to *my* ask, which was to pick up the phone and call a former Disney executive I knew but, awkwardly, hadn't talked to in 20 years. And she said it was a great program."

Shelley gave Rachel her consent.

The second yes came from Disney, when Rachel got accepted into the program. A few months later, she flew to Orlando where she shadowed animators, learned 3-d modeling techniques, worked at Epcot, attended marketing seminars, and met executives and others working in the film animation industry. Rachel, who was 20 and in her junior year at CSUN when I interviewed her, reflected on the importance of asking.

Most people I know, when they have a big ask, get scared or nervous talking to authority figures like teachers, professors, parents, bosses. But you've got to prepare by doing your research on the topic and the person you'll be talking to and think through how they'll react. If I'd just said, 'Hey, Mom, I want to go to this program' without addressing her concerns and showing I was responsible, she'd have said flat out NO.

The Big Ask Plan

Ask the Right Person:

- Does the person I'm asking have the authority, experience, or resources to help me?

- Whose advice, buy-in, or endorsement might I need before I approach the decision maker?

- Do they already know what I want, or will my ask come as a surprise?

- Where and when might this person be most receptive to my request?

Project the Right Attitude:

- Based on what I know about the decision maker, what attitude should I bring to the ask?

- How do I want to be perceived, and what will help me create this perception?

- What pressures might the person be under that could affect their response, and will I choose to acknowledge that?

State Your Need Clearly:

- Is my request clear and unambiguous?

- What reasons, facts, or evidence could I provide that would make my request more compelling?

- What results would I create with their permission or buy-in? What specific steps would I take to get those results? How would I measure the success of my efforts?

- Would it be appropriate to make a personal appeal by expressing the importance of the request to me and/or others?

Take Their Perspective:

- Relative to my request, what purpose, interests, or goals do we have in common?

- What's in it for them to say yes? How would they benefit?

- How would consenting to my request align with their values?

- What constraints might keep them from saying yes?

- What concerns or questions might they raise and how would I answer (truthfully) to their satisfaction?

- Might a conditional request make it easier for them to say yes?

Make "Thanks" Matter

- How will I thank the person in a way that is meaningful to them?

- Where is my opportunity to give back to them or others?

You are 34 times more likely to get a yes in person than by email.[6] So, how can you make an emailed request effective when you can't be face to face? See my post at https://tinyurl .com/bdeybuz2.

In this chapter, we explored skills and strategies to make a big ask more compelling. In the next chapter, you'll discover options for making requests with varying degrees of directness using laser asks, lateral asks, or hints. And you'll be able to weigh the pros and cons of each before making an ask of any size.

Communication skills are the lifeblood of a successful life ... if you plan on spending any time there ...
—DOUG FIREBAUGH, author, trainer, speaker

CHAPTER SEVEN

LASER, LATERAL, OR HINT?

... oil your mind and your manners,
to give them the necessary suppleness and flexibility ...
—LORD CHESTERFIELD, British statesman

WHEN MIGHT IT BE TO YOUR ADVANTAGE TO MAKE blunt, soft, or indirect requests? I call these Laser Asks, Lateral Asks, and Hints. Each approach has its pros and cons based on your objectives and the person you're asking. But I ask that you regard these categories loosely. They're intended as a general awareness-builder rather than a linguistic model for analyzing communication. Let's test drive all three, one at a time.

Laser Asks

I once hired my friend Bill Bender, then a general contractor in Chicago, to do some renovations in my home office. As we discussed the project plans, his voice trailed off. Something at the top of my bookshelf had caught his attention. I looked up and saw he'd spotted a wooden carving of a hand, from India, its long fingers extending an ancient gesture of blessing. Bill was transfixed.

"I want that," he said quietly, decisively, not moving his eyes from it. His claim on the object was so spontaneous and disarming that I had to laugh. "It's yours, Bill!" He accepted it as directly as he'd asked for it: "Thank you."

Although Bill said only, "I want that," I correctly understood it to be an ask, not a demand. It's what I call a laser ask. Laser beams are narrow, sharply focused. They zero in on their target. A laser ask is similarly direct. It could be a pointed statement of desire as Bill's was, or an equally pointed question, such as, "May I have that wooden carving?"

By the same token, telling the boss "I'd like to work from home on Fridays" is less deferential than "Could I work from home on Fridays?" but both seek consent in a laser-like yes-or-no fashion (though a request of this importance would get more consideration in a longer conversation). Laser asks cut to the chase and signal your readiness for a quick, clear response. They're hard to misinterpret. They're almost impossible to ignore. And they may be the most expedient route to getting what you want.

The *I Want* statements in the left column and closed-ended questions in the right both seek consent in very direct (laser) ways:

LASER ASKS AS *I WANT* STATEMENTS	LASER ASKS AS CLOSE-ENDED QUESTIONS
"I want your honest opinion."	"Give me your honest opinion?"
"I'd like you to help me pick out a suit."	"Would you help me pick out a suit?"
"I want to kiss you."	"May I kiss you?"
"I'd like your support in my bid for the position."	"Will you support me in my bid for the position?"

Laser asks can also take the form of open-ended questions (who, what, where, when, how, why) when asking for information in equally direct ways:

Open-Ended Questions
"Why are we making this change?"
"What's keeping you from taking action?"
"How can I get my child into your school?"
"What went wrong with you and Max?"

The Downside of Laser Asks: Unless your face, posture, and vocal inflection say, "I will not take no for an answer!" a laser ask is not a demand. But a listener who expects a softer approach could perceive it as demanding. If you shoot an ask from a cannon at someone who expects it on a silver tray with flowers, it'll backfire. That's why it's useful to understand the tempering effects of lateral asks.

> I changed the way I asked for things in emails. I used to
> soften my requests with exclamation points and smiley faces.
> I still use please and thank you, but I don't waffle around
> because the point can get lost and the outcome muddled.
> —HADLEY JAEGER, public works employee

Lateral Asks

A laser ask is like making a beeline for the person, planting yourself squarely in front of them, looking them straight in the eye, and making a pointed request in few words. A lateral ask, in contrast, is less forward, less blunt. It's like casually strolling toward the person, at an angle, stopping at a respectful social distance, and then edging into your request. A lateral ask is tentative and accommodating—qualities that allow more "space" for the decision maker to consider their response.

Lateral asks are a way of saying, "I humbly acknowledge that my request could be awkward or inconvenient for you, but I hope to win you over with my respectful 'no-pressure' approach" (and that's saying a lot!). There's a deferential quality to lateral asks. That's why we may instinctively default to them when making requests of people who sign our checks, grade our exams, or set our curfew limits.

Here's a side-by-side comparison of the straightforward laser ask and its more cautious and formal counterpart, the lateral ask:

LASER ASK	LATERAL ASK
"Could I ride with you to campus?"	*"Would it be possible for me to* get a ride with you to campus?"
"Would you help me set up the garage sale this weekend?"	*"Might you be able to* help me set up the garage sale this weekend?"

LASER ASK	LATERAL ASK
"Could you help me with the sales reports tomorrow?"	*"I'm wondering if you might have time tomorrow to help me with the sales reports."*
"When will I know your decision?"	*"When do you think you could get back to me with your decision?"*

If the differences between the laser and lateral requests seem minor, read the examples aloud. You'll hear the gentler difference of the latter, which attempt to downplay expectation and minimize imposition. For situations in which a laser ask would seem too abrupt, a lateral ask can be a way to check the person's receptivity with an air of noncommittal inquiry. Lateral asks tend to sound more considerate than laser asks. And they use a little more "padding" to accomplish this.

As you'll see in the examples below, the lateral approach qualifies the request with words such as *if, possibly, maybe, perhaps, could, may, might, suppose,* and *consider,* to lessen the directness or force of the request.

The Language of Lateral Asks
I was wondering if
Would you mind if
Could you possibly
Could I ask you to
Do you think you might be able to
Would you see any problem if I were to
Would you consider
Would you be willing to
Is there a way for us to
How might I/we

How about if I/we
Is there any way you could
What's the chance that
What would you think if
How would you feel if
What are your thoughts about

Can you hear the tentative, searching tone in those examples?

"What's the chance?" At Chicago's Union Station, about an hour before our train departed for Portland, Oregon, I asked an Amtrak ticket agent, "What's the chance of getting a free upgrade from a roomette to a bedroom?" Pretty good, as it turned out. I got the upgrade. On his podcast, The School of Greatness, Lewis Howes said he asks the question "just to see if you can make something happen," such as, "What's the chance you can give me a discount on this? What's the chance you can get me in first class? What's the chance we can collaborate in a bigger way?"[1]

"You wouldn't happen to …?" In 2022, my friend Bob Griffin inquired about office rentals at a downtown commercial property on behalf of his wife, Meribeth, an aspiring novelist. He asked the building manager, "You wouldn't happen to have any office spaces for around $300 a month, would you?"—the very definition of a long-shot request. Astonishingly, the answer was yes. The 240-square-foot office had no windows and needed lots of work, but at that rate Meribeth was willing to make the effort.

Caveat: backpedaled inquiries that begin with "You wouldn't happen to …" or "I don't suppose you could …" are politely pressure-free but presume "no," so reserve them for low-importance requests.

Just for fun, here are a few variations of lateral asks that need their own categories:

Hedging: Um, maybe I could, like, I don't know, just sort of, like, you know, kind of tag along a little, or whatever?[2]

Placating: I just want to ask you something but it's honestly no big deal if you say no, in fact you probably *will* say no and that's completely OK, because …

Sweet talking: Would you be an angel and help me set the table?

Baby talking: Could me gets a itty bitty back wub? (Warning: could trigger gag reflex)

Appeasement Texting: Hi!!!!! ☺ Ok if I bring a friend????? ♡ ♥ ♡

Genuflecting: I beg your lordship's permission to enquire whether I might humbly request, should it not prove too great a burden, that I might have the honor of …

The downside of Lateral Asks: Just as laser asks may be too blunt for some situations, lateral asks may be too cautious or passive if the moment calls for directness. If you tend to tip-toe toward requests, exercise more assertiveness with laser asks.

> Your perfume is lovely, but it seems to be triggering my allergies. I'm sorry to ask, but would you be willing to leave it off at the office?
> —ALISON GREEN, author, Ask a Manager

Hints

My friend Connie Eyer told me about enjoying occasional visits from her neighbor's then-six-year-old daughter, Eden. The little girl would coyly ask, "Are you using that little stuffed animal?" or "Do you happen to have any more of those cookies?" Eden seemed to know that hinting was somehow more polite than asking directly for toys and treats. She also may have sensed that hinting helps both parties save face, by pretending the request isn't important—or isn't even a request at all—if the answer turns out to be no.

Another friend of mine, Bob Kucera, recently asked me, "How would you like to spend 90 minutes chatting with Judy [his wife] at the hospital on April 3rd while I have a minor procedure on my foot?"

I said, "Well, I always enjoy talking with Judy, but is she anxious about your surgery? Is that why she wants company?"

"She's not anxious about it."

"That's good. But still, she asked for my company?"

"She didn't ask. I just thought it might be nice."

A few moments later I "got it." Judy didn't drive, and Bob would be unable to drive after surgery. So, what he was really asking me was to drive them to the hospital, wait around, and drive them back. As a friend, I was happy to do it. But had I taken Bob's "invitation" at face value, I might've said, "If it's OK with you both, I'd rather meet for coffee sometime than hang out at the hospital!"

Hinting is a subtle, evasive, and sometimes playful way to ask. It *implies* our wants, and as ambiguously as we choose. A hint can be as discreet as a dinner guest drumming her fingernails on an empty wine glass in hope of a refill, or as sly as the flirty salesperson who lets it slip that they're newly single. Hints are also the "coded" language of family, friends, and coworkers attuned to each other's moods and needs: "When you get that look, Gary, I know you want a favor. What is it?"

Hinting

"Are those cupcakes as good as they look?"

"Boss, I heard our Tallahassee office just got raises."

"Ever give your employee discount to friends?"

"What happens if nobody claims that bicycle?"

"I'm not suggesting you disobey traffic laws, but my flight leaves in 90 minutes."

The Downside of Hinting: There are three potential drawbacks to hinting. First, people might not get the hint (not everyone's good at reading between the lines). Second, they might feel manipulated by the coyness and refuse to take the bait. Third, they might assume the hint indicates a low level of importance and easily dismiss it. If you overuse hints to communicate your needs, make requests more clearly and boldly with laser asks, or just as clearly if less boldly with lateral asks.

The Power Exception: Hints are not always as powerless as they seem. People in positions of authority may use them to soften commands. For example, a parent saying, "The dog crate needs cleaning" isn't making a general observation; they're telling Junior what to do without being explicit. In response to a writing assignment I'd completed, my then-boss emailed, "Is this your final draft?" Because I knew her communication style, I understood this to be a request for more work on the piece. I made the changes I figured she was hinting at and sent it back for her review. Her response? "Much improved. Thanks!" In the words of an Italian proverb, "Masters' hints are commands."

Same Ask, Three Ways

Laser ask: Can my brother join us on our Yosemite trip?
Lateral ask: Just floating the idea, but how would you feel if my brother came along on our Yosemite trip?
Hint: Did I tell you my brother wants to go with us to Yosemite?

Laser ask: Why'd you quit your job?
Lateral ask: I'm curious what went into your decision to quit your job.
Hint: You had very good reasons for quitting your job, I'll bet.

Laser ask: I want those ruby slippers.
Lateral ask: Would it be too forward of me to ask if I might possibly have those ruby slippers?
Hint: You might regret keeping those slippers, just sayin'.

In these last six chapters, we've explored the Desire-Belief–Skill foundation, the three interdependent components that serve as the core "operating system" of an ask. The balance of the book explores a wide range of topics and stories that ask essential questions, including:

What role does charm play, if any, in the success of an ask? What about flattery? Persistence? Audacity? Spontaneity?

How comfortable are you asking for help? What does it take to ask effectively for emotional support? For clarity? For feedback?

How might the way you ask sabotage your requests?

What in your life might change if you asked for the truth?

What kind of asks could enrich your current or hoped-for relationships?

All that and much more ahead.

Communication is about being effective,
not always about being proper.
—BO BENNETT, writer and speaker

CHAPTER EIGHT

WHAT INFLUENCES *YES*?

Charm is a way of getting the answer yes
without asking a clear question.
—ALBERT CAMUS

OUR SPECIES VALUES BEAUTY. WE EQUATE IT WITH success. We court it. We want it for ourselves. And, conscious of our bias or not, we reward it. In fact, the better looking a person is, the more likely they are to get the help they ask for.[1] They'll also get higher salaries, better performance evaluations, pay lower bail, and get more favorable judgements in trials.[2] However, if your looks don't cause people to lay out the red carpet or stammer in your presence, take heart. There's more to a successful ask than being good looking (or this book would end here). Sometimes all it takes is a little charm.

It's hard to define, but we know charm when under its spell. Something pulls us in—warmth, humor, shyness, or some endearing quirk. To be charmed is to be under a kind of "happy influence" and thus inclined to say yes.

My friend and former colleague David Boylan and I traveled often on business. Our time together gave me plenty of opportunities to observe his uncanny ability to charm hotel front desk clerks into giving him the best rooms. His disarming smile and pure enjoyment in being David was everything he needed to begin the wholesale seduction:

"Ivan, how's your day going, buddy? Great! Mine too. It's my first time in Park City. Did you grow up here? Beautiful area! Hey, do you happen to have a corner room for me with a nice mountain view?"

"Veronique? What a pretty name! Are you a singer? No? Well, you have a lovely speaking voice. I'm only here one night—what would it take to get the executive suite at the same rate?"

In my travels with David, I often felt embarrassed by what I judged to be his gabby glad-handing. Yet to my unending surprise desk clerks appeared to *enjoy* the banter and, more surprising still, granted his requests. As a counterreaction, I refused to schmooze. I stubbornly resolved to accept whatever room I was given. I thought, *How could these clerks be so gullible? Can't they see he's putting on the charm?*

I see it differently today. Sure, David's efforts may have been a bit obvious at times, but they did no harm. He's a person who genuinely likes people and takes interest in them. He recognized our front desk clerks as individuals, not just functionaries, and took time to connect with them. Even those who didn't oblige him couldn't help but crack smiles at his spirited salesmanship.

And the sonofabitch got the best rooms.

It may not be within everyone's ability to be charming (however you define it). But we're all capable of showing kindness and respect, the lifeblood of civility. As children, we're coached to "ask nicely."

A respectful, non-demanding request, we quickly learn, is not only polite but quite often the surest path to yes. That's the substance of the next story from a friend who asked for anonymity.

As a flight attendant, I receive all kinds of special requests from passengers, most of which I'm happy to fulfill. But as for who gets what, it's all in the presentation. On one flight, the pop star Miley Cyrus, then still a teen, was a passenger. A woman in coach waved me over to where she sat with her pre-teen daughter. In a very unpleasant, insistent tone she said, "*You need to* take my daughter over to meet Miley Cyrus."

Well, when someone makes demands like that it's an immediate turnoff. I told her, politely, that our policy discouraged such interactions with First Class passengers but that once we landed, she and her daughter could try to approach the singer in the terminal. She grumbled, but I held firm.

About thirty minutes later, while walking several rows down from the mother and daughter I heard a small voice say, "Excuse me." A girl, nine or ten years old, was shyly holding up a drawing of a girl with a big smile singing into a microphone. "Could you give this to Miley Cyrus for me?" she asked. "I'm her biggest fan." Her mother looked on encouragingly.

"Let me see what I can do," I said in a confidential tone and made my way to First Class.

I confided to Ms. Cyrus that her "biggest fan" had a drawing to give her, and I asked if I could bring the girl to meet her. "Absolutely!" she said. I went back and very quietly told the girl to meet me in the galley in a few minutes so as not to bring attention to me taking her up to First Class. When the girl came face-to-face with her idol she could hardly speak. Miley Cyrus made a big deal over the drawing, engaged the girl in a little conversation and gave her autograph. I snapped a photo of the two of them and sent it to her mother.

Had the other mother been gracious instead of demanding, I would have gladly given her daughter the same opportunity. But asking is all about the presentation!

On a recent flight to Kenya, when the flight attendant was clearing away our trays, my boyfriend asked her if he could have a second meal. I told him that I would never have thought to do that. And when she came back with his meal, I was, like, Huh! And he said, "It's because I'm kind." And it's true, he asked kindly!
—ADELE NANDAN, fundraising strategist and travel entrepreneur

The Liking Principle

As the last stories illustrate, people are more inclined to say yes to those they like. Dr. Robert Cialdini, an expert on the psychology of persuasion, calls this the liking principle. He has found that our opinions and requests are more likely to influence others if the receiver feels positively towards us. Physical attractiveness is one of the influences that animate the liking principle, as are similarity, unity, and compliments. But because we don't always have control over our level of hotness, let's focus on the last three.

Similarity: How Are We Alike?

We like those who are like us. Meeting people with whom we share similar backgrounds, attitudes, or interests can create various degrees of mutual liking. Even the most superficial similarities—clothing style, birth month, first name, pet ownership, favorite music or TV series—may be enough to evoke a mutual fondness. And that can make the parties more receptive to each other's ideas or requests.

Try it out yourself. Before you attempt to make a (long-shot) request of someone you don't know well or at all, chat a bit first. If you discover something in common, comment on the similarity—"Go Cleveland Browns!" or "I've got a kid in college, too" or "Hey—I, too, have peanut allergies!" Even if the similarity principle doesn't result in a successful request, you'll at least have had the pleasure of meeting a fellow Browns-cheering, tuition-paying, allergy sufferer (find a third and start a club!).

Here's a personal example. For the book, I asked to interview a few people from my alma mater, Illinois State University. I made sure to mention this similarity to them in my emails of introduction, right after "hello." And I can attest that the emails to my fellow Redbirds got a higher response rate than my non-college tries, and a few led to interviews.

Now, for me, meeting fellow ISU grads is fun but not personally meaningful. But some people feel an emotional connection to their schools. For them, having a common alma mater is not just a matter of similarity but a shared identity and sense of solidarity. And it's that difference in intensity that elevates those connections to the realm of the next principle, unity.

Unity: How Deep is Our Bond?

We like those with whom we share a sense of belonging, identity, purpose, or pride. Cialdini's unity principle holds that you'll have more influence with people (and they with you) of your same family, ethnicity, political or religious affiliation, military background, or other "tribal" connection. The mutual assumption of shared values and priorities carries a corresponding level of comfort and trust. Unity is also the glue in healthy organizations where people work cooperatively toward common goals. Belonging bonds us.

One April morning, Jeff Perry was first in a line of cars waiting at the service entrance of a Toyota dealership in Southwest Florida. "I don't have an appointment," he told the service rep, "but I could really use your help." (A direct personal request like that one is hard to ignore.)

Jeff explained that the van he was driving had begun making clunking noises on turns—the van that in two days would be transporting himself, his wife, their teenage son and three of his friends over 1,000 miles back from their vacation in nearby Siesta Key to their homes in southwestern Ohio. He told the rep he thought the problem was the axle and asked if someone could look at it.

The rep looked at Jeff. "I got ya," he said. "Just grab your registration and meet me inside."

Jeff cast an anxious look at the people in line behind him. "I said, 'Look, I've been in your position, I was a service writer at a Toyota dealership. I'm in no rush, take care of everyone else.' And he pretty much ignored what I said, showed me to the waiting room, and said, 'I'll get my best tech to work on it, he's been here 30 years.'"

About 20 minutes later, the master mechanic came out and told Jeff he couldn't replicate the noise he'd reported. Jeff hopped into the van and the two drove around until the clunking sound returned. While chatting, the men discovered that each hailed from Ohio.

Jeff returned to the waiting room. After another 20 minutes, the mechanic came out and told him the noise problem was related to minor wear in the upper strut mount, not the axle, and assured him it posed no safety risk for the long drive home. He handed Jeff the keys, and the service advisor who'd written the ticket announced, "No charge—it's on us." Jeff told me,

> I was just floored. I was expecting at least $150 in diagnostics and labor, if not $800-1000 for a new axle, which I was glad I didn't need. I handed him 40 bucks I had in my wallet and told him the least I could do was give them lunch on me. But the greatest part was the peace of mind I got for the drive back to Ohio.

Were the Toyota employees just nice guys who'd have done the same for anybody? Entirely possible. People are amazing. But, with human motivations as complex as they are, let's break down some possible points of influence in the story:

> Despite having no appointment, Jeff's "I could really use your help" was a personal appeal that evoked the rep's empathetic assurance, "I got ya."

> Jeff's attitude was respectful which, as it did for the flight attendant in the last story, makes people more willing to help.

> His chat with the mechanic about their shared Ohio roots (while literally being aligned, side by side, in the van, and trying to problem-solve together) checked the similarity box.

But my hunch is that a deeper bond, the unity principle, had the strongest impact. Jeff says he'd only mentioned his former Toyota position to let the service rep know he respected the appointment protocols, not to get preferential treatment. And yet, with that disclosure the service rep may have seen Jeff as "one of us"—a respected member of the team. And membership, as it's often said, has its perks.

Did you ever make a successful big ask of someone you didn't know well? Might the similarity or unity principles have factored favorably in the outcome? Were you aware of these influences at the time of the ask?

Use collective pronouns. In the workplace, the benefits of unity are obvious: a sense of shared purpose creates cohesion. So, how to make a request of a coworker from whom you expect resistance? Nothing beats "I" when speaking for yourself. But notice how the asker in the example below uses the collective pronouns *we, us,* and *our* to encourage a sense of employee solidarity with the listener.

> Zach, we're giving a sales presentation at Altus next month. The contract would be a major win for us, and your expertise will help prepare us for their toughest tech questions. Could we schedule time to put our heads together on this next week?

Now, if Zach is unmoved by the unity appeal, all is not lost. He might yet be persuaded by another influence lever in the request: the *compliment* about his expertise.

Compliments: Can You Feel the Love?

We like and are influenced by people who tell us something they like about us. Even those who pride themselves on not needing anybody's approval appreciate a genuine compliment. It's easy to develop a positive bias toward people who praise your skills, character, appearance, choices, or possessions (unless you're tired of hearing them go on and on about you!) Like similarity and unity, giving and receiving compliments fosters a spirit of agreement and goodwill.

And yet, unlike similarity and unity, compliments don't draw on shared backgrounds or identities. They're a way to connect with almost *anyone*. On the relationship front, Rachel Katz, the Disney-bound college student you met in Chapter 6, has advice for people using compliments to ask for dates. "Before I got in my relationship," she said, "I would say no a lot because people would say 'You're hot, you wanna go out with me?' Why would I say yes to that? That's just uncomfortable. 'You're hot' means 'you look good,' not 'I'd actually like to get to know you.'" Rachel hasn't forgotten, however, the good compliment she once heard as a prelude to an ask:

> I was at the gym with my friend and this guy came up to me and introduced himself and shook my hand. And I said, "Oh, hi!" He said, "I just want you to know I think you're really beautiful." I told him thanks, but that I had a boyfriend, and he said, "Ok," shook my friend's hand as well, and said to me, "I hope to see you around, at least."

Her admirer didn't get the date he wanted, but his personable, non-objectifying approach scored big with Rachel. "He seemed very genuine and nice," she said, "so it wasn't uncomfortable. Short and sweet is best for asking someone out, and it helps to have some charm and confidence." (Kudos to the guy for asking *face to face!*)

Prefacing a request with a compliment once worked beautifully for my friend Wendy Wise, who was directing a community musical. It seemed that no matter how respectfully she made requests of her sound operator, the young man reacted with exasperated sighs or snippy remarks. Everything was a problem for him. Wendy dreaded their interactions.

She approached him during a rehearsal one evening, bracing for snark, when inspiration struck. "Bryce, you did such a great job boosting the sound for Harper in act one," she began. "Her number never sounded better. Could you work the same magic for Alex in act two? He really needs your help."

Like a toad-turned-prince, he carried out her request without a grumble.

What accounted for his mysterious turnaround? My guess is that Wendy's congratulatory "Great job" was sincere and set the right tone. Her compliment, that by boosting the sound he'd enhanced the actor's performance, was specific, which made it genuine (unlike a general, "You're awesome!"). Her request—"Could you work the same magic"—was emphatic and flattering. And by adding "He really needs your help," she invited Bryce to be a hero.

Had tensions with Bryce continued beyond that conversation, Wendy would've needed to address their communication issues directly. But as a quick fix, a compliment worked. The show went on.

Beyond appeasing prickly sound operators, genuine compliments can build rapport, strengthen relationships, raise morale at work, and leave people feeling good about themselves. That's not exactly news, is it? But this may come as a surprise: studies show we like the person giving compliments even when we know the praise is *untrue* or that the giver *stands to gain from our approval*[3] ("Why, no, I've never been told I resemble Ryan Gosling! How much did you say you want to borrow?") We'll unwrap that next.

Flattery Will Get You Everywhere

Charm may be hard to pin down, but flattery is like the blinding flashbulbs of the paparazzi. It's in your face. Last summer I opened

an email announcing I'd been selected as one of the Most Influential
and Fascinating People in America or some such thing. I sat higher
in my chair. *Meeee?* I continued reading. "Just $1,500 assures your
place on this exclusive list." Damn. For one heady moment the
shameless flatterers nearly had me.

What effect, if any, does flattery have on a request? A 1996
study at Carnegie Mellon University (CMU) asked that question.
Student experimenters approached students on campus they didn't
know. Maintaining a neutral tone of voice and facial expression, the
experimenters asked the students to fill out a six-question survey
about the quality of life at CMU.

After participants completed the questionnaire, the experimenters flatly said, "Will you fill out this additional, optional five-page
questionnaire?" Five pages! Way too big of an ask, right? Nope. Both
male and female participants complied 40% of the time.

But wait, it gets better (or worse, depending on how you look
at it). When the request was preceded by the neutrally stated compliment, "You look like a really helpful person," compliance rose
dramatically to 90% and 100% for men and women, respectively.
At that point, you'll be happy to know, the experimenters explained
the study to the participants so that nobody got stuck filling out
the additional pages.[4] The study, among others like it, shows that
flattery is an effective persuasion lubricant and that most of us are
receptive to a little buttering-up. It's not that our BS meters aren't
working, it's that we're too flushed to notice the needle going wild.

The experimenters' assessment, "You look like a really helpful
person," is an example of *social labeling* applied to persuasion. The
"labeler" compliments the person on the very quality (helpfulness,
in this case) that the labeler hopes to draw out of the person *for
the labeler's own purposes.*

Social labeling operates on another of Cialdini's principles of
persuasion, consistency. When someone tells us "You're a thoughtful
person," or a reliable or fair one, the odds are good we'll want to

meet their high opinions of us. We'll act in ways consistent with the positive trait they've attributed to us (accurately or not), provided it matches our own character ideals.

If you're a parent or teacher, you may already use a form of labeling with children; not, perhaps, to flatter or favorably pre-dispose them to a future ask, but to empower them—"You are a person who is capable of achieving anything you set your mind to"—or to reinforce traits you've observed in them—"Well done! You're a very good problem-solver." What we tell children about themselves makes deep and lasting impressions. So, whenever you label, label with love.

Ask for Advice

Perhaps the most practical form of flattery, one that turns people to putty, is asking for advice. Who doesn't soften when asked to share their opinions or expertise? If sincere, the advice seeker is expressing their esteem for the advice giver. It's a double win; the giver has the pleasure of feeling smart and helpful while the asker gets the reward of their counsel or coaching. It's an easy ask:

> "I'd appreciate any tips you could share to help me improve my tennis backhand."

> "I'm struggling with an ethical question and would like to run it by you. Got a few minutes?"

> "I value your knowledge and experience in the industry and feel I might get a better sense of my own path if I could I ask you about some of the insights you've gained. Would you be willing to meet with me over coffee this week?"

One study showed that we elevate our perception of the person asking our advice. We think: *How smart of you to ask me! It's proof of your good judgment and competence!* But the study also showed that we'll negatively judge someone who asks our advice in an area in which we're *not* confident. We think: *Why on earth are you asking ME? It's proof of your poor judgment and incompetence!*[4]

Frankly, I'm surprised by the harshness of the latter finding. I'm always flattered when someone assumes I know stuff I don't. Like geography. Math. Or where I placed the TV remote.

I have been complimented many times and they always
embarrass me; I always feel that they have not said enough.
—MARK TWAIN

Do Givers Get More?

At this point you might be thinking, *I would never lean on my looks or use cheap, superficial tricks like charm or flattery to get what I want. And I'm not going to try to make someone like me by exploiting our similarities. Isn't there a way to get what I ask without employing a "strategy"?*

Yes. You can be a mensch, a Yiddish word for a good person. Someone who's kind, thoughtful, and, most of all, giving. A contributor to others' good. If people then feel inclined to reward your generous nature by consenting to your requests, it's a bonus. If they don't, there's no downside: you're still a mensch whose giving nature makes the world a better place.

Givers' rewards are internal. Studies have shown that people who give of themselves by helping others enjoy better physical and emotional health. Teens who help or volunteer are less vulnerable to depression. Seniors who give live longer and happier lives than those who don't give. For Winston Churchill, contribution was the source of true fulfillment: "We make a living by what we get; we make a life by what we give."

Are you a taker, matcher, or giver? In his bestseller *Give and Take: Why Helping Others Drives Our Success*, organizational psychologist Adam Grant explores three attitudes or preferences people have around giving, particularly at work. Takers tend to help others when it strategically benefits them to do so. Matchers put a premium on fairness and expect their help to be reciprocated by favors-in-kind. Givers accommodate others through acts of generosity, teamwork, and service, without the matcher's scorecard.

One of Grant's most surprising findings is that givers outperform takers even in traditionally aggressive arenas such as sales and negotiations. Far from being pushovers, givers receive more support, loyalty, and opportunities than those with less generous reciprocity styles. If someone working to fulfill their own ambitions has ever taken the time to give to you, and made your needs important, you know how strong the desire is to give back to them.

Asking for what you want, then, is only one ingredient for success in life; another is being willing to help others get what they want. You can do this by stepping up when asked for help, guidance, or input. Or by asking someone directly, "What do you need?" or "How can I help?" Givers contribute to others' good however they're able.

At work, you can share information, constructive feedback, best practices, credit for achievements, give earned compliments, or help people advance their careers.

In other orbits, you can listen with complete attention to a friend or loved one. Encourage someone to follow their dreams. Tell a person from your past about the difference they made in your life. Speak up for those who aren't heard. Pick up the tab. Leave positive online reviews. Volunteer. Donate to a cause you believe in. Reach out to someone who's isolated but doesn't know how to ask for company.

If you're a parent or caregiver, you may be used to giving without expecting reciprocity; one-sided giving is part of the job description. Outside those roles, however, it's not unreasonable to occasionally expect something back from the people to whom we freely give. Without some measure of reciprocity, we're liable to harden in resentment or collapse in burnout.

For Virginia Muzquiz, reciprocity is not just a good-faith practice but the key to business success. As CEO of Master Connectors, Inc., Virginia helps her clients build relationships with business referral partners. "One of the big challenges in giving and getting referrals," she said in our blog interview, "is over-giving and under-receiving. A lot of my clients come to me and say, 'I just give and give and give and nobody gives me anything back.' The problem is that they've been giving but they haven't been letting people know that they'd like something in return."

Virginia's solution? "Typically," she says, "if someone doesn't ask me, 'Well, what can I do for *you*,' then I simply say, 'Well, I have a request. Would it be ok if I asked you to do me a favor as well?' Nobody's ever going to say no to that."[5]

Asking a Community. *Rose Comadurán teaches at a Montessori school in Oregon.*

I have a philosophy that whatever it is you want, just say it and release it into the universe. Just say it and assume goodwill, that people want to help you. That's my assumption all the time, just as I assume there's no reason why anyone I interact with wouldn't like me. I also *give* all the time. If I can do something for someone, I almost never say no.

During the pandemic, I made a last-minute decision to apply to grad school and had to get all these recommendation letters. And that meant reaching out to former colleagues and mentors of mine with a pretty big ask, which was, "Hey, will you write me a recommendation letter, like, *today*, so I can apply to this program?"

And they did. But it's not like I cold-called random professors. Some asks require the deep rapport that can only come from having cultivated a strong community. If you just randomly start asking people for things without that rapport, you risk being seen as entitled or out of touch. If you're operating outside of community, you don't have a community to count on, and outsiders are trusted less. But when you ask people that know you really well because you've *nurtured* those relationships, they give you the benefit of the doubt.

We've looked at a range of factors that can influence the success of an ask, from being charming, to likeable, to getting because you give. But what do you do when your winning ways don't work? How do you turn no into yes? You don't give up—you persist. And that is the subject of our next chapter.

There is one word which may serve as a rule of practice
for all one's life—reciprocity.
—CONFUCIUS

CHAPTER NINE

WILL YOU PERSIST?

Energy and persistence conquer all things.
—BENJAMIN FRANKLIN

CHILDREN ARE MASTERS OF PERSISTENCE. THEIR
strategy is Zen-like in its simplicity: "Mighty rivers wear down
rock." The child just keeps asking and asking and asking until the
poor, miserable parent relents (which alone explains the enduring
strength of pony sales).

Yet children have something to teach us about persistence,
distinct from whining. What if we adults pursued our goals
with a child's optimism? What if we followed their example by
not giving up on the first try? What if we kept calling out, "Ice
cold lemonade!" even if the last 30 grumps strolled right past
our stand?

In some arenas, asking is a numbers game. Submit enough proposals, apply for enough jobs, ask enough people, and you're bound
to get a yes. But that takes belief in yourself and the willingness to
persist. Both are true of our next storyteller.

Before producing and editing for HBO/Warner Bros. Discovery and directing TV commercials, Matt Walsh Egan worked his way through film school creating video montages of people's family photos and home movies. When a customer had asked about his plans after college, Matt told him he wanted to pursue advertising. The customer turned out to be an account executive at advertising giant Ogilvy and Mather. He gave Matt his business card and told him to give him a call after he graduated.

A year went by. I graduated. Two weeks later I started calling the account exec to ask for an interview. Each time I'd get his voicemail and remind him where and when we'd met. I called him and other prospective agencies every week, and always at the same time, on Friday mornings.

Four months later, he finally called me back. He invited me to meet with him at Ogilvy & Mather. There he introduced me to the agency's head of production. She saw my work, loved it, gave me a list of people to call, and invited me to use her as a reference. Her name opened doors for me. I wound up having a choice of two great jobs and chose one, where I worked for five years.

When I asked her how I could ever repay her, she said, in the future, when you have the opportunity, help someone else find a job. Fortunately, I've been able to do that for people.

Making those phone calls every week was my way of asking persistently. I've been in the film production industry for over 20 years, and you don't get anywhere without it.

After a few weeks (let alone four months!) of unreturned messages, Matt Walsh Egan could've considered himself ghosted and given up. Instead, he persisted. Our next two storytellers showed similar determination.

Show Up Anyway. After resigning his commission from the Air Force during the Vietnam War, Robert O. Harder returned to his alma mater, the University of Minnesota, Duluth, for the winter quarter of 1971. Every day, he went to the University Employment Office to review the bulletin board listing upcoming on-campus job interviews. One day he saw a notice that got his attention.

My heart quickened when I saw Target Stores, headquartered in Minneapolis, was interviewing candidates for a new management training program, for one day only. (Target had only 27 stores at the time but had big plans.)

Moments later, I sagged. Every 15-minute time block had already been filled, from 8 a.m. to 5 p.m. I stared at the board for several minutes. And then I had a what-the-hell moment. There was a recession on, and entry-level jobs were in very high demand, to say nothing of a certain air of desperation among young men of my age. I pulled out my pen and wrote my name in between two 15-minute time blocks, sometime around 10 a.m.

The day came and I arrived about 9:30 a.m., explaining to the Target receptionist what I had done. "Out of the question," she responded. "Would you mind if I waited here in the reception room?" I asked. "Perhaps someone won't show."

"Go ahead," she said, "but you're wasting your time."

The hours ticked by. Noon came and the receptionist took pity and brought me a glass of water; I dared not leave for fear an opening would suddenly appear. From time to time the interviewer, Mr. McElroy, came out to wave in the next candidate.

About 2 p.m. he stopped to give me a hard look. I seized the chance, jumping up and hurriedly saying, "Mr. McElroy I really wish you'd give me a few minutes. I think I could really do the job for Target." He shook his head; there just wasn't time. "I'm very sorry." He quickly ushered in the next candidate.

At 5:20 p.m. he came out of his office, carrying his briefcase and looking very tired. I was the only one left in the office; the receptionist had gone for the day. He looked at me for a long moment, shook his head and sighed. "I can't believe you sat there all day." For a few moments he seemed to be mulling something over. Finally, he said, "Come on in, I can't walk away from that kind of perseverance."

We talked for a half hour, a very animated conversation concerning my military and family retailing background. A few days later, I learned I was the only person from that day's interviews to be invited down to Minneapolis for a second round of interviews. Subsequently, I was selected to be among the first class of 27 management trainees. I went on to a long career in chain retailing, finishing as Montgomery Ward's vice president of consumer electronics.

It's tempting to dismiss Robert O. Harder's story as irrelevant today. After all, digital job applications ensure that hopefuls don't write in their own appointments. But the timeless truth of his story is that initiative and persistence, no matter their form, stand out. Robert's interviewer had said, in 1971, "I can't walk away from that kind of perseverance." What are you willing to do to hear the same response from a decision maker today?

> If your ship doesn't come in, swim out to meet it.
> —JONATHAN WINTERS, comedian

Asking for the Family. I once complimented a neighbor on the garden she was planting in the courtyard of her building. She introduced herself as Trass Lyons. I noted a soft brogue and learned she was from Ireland, a country to which she has since returned. But before she packed her bags, she told me about her humanitarian work in which every advance made on others' behalf resulted from great effort and persistence.

In Chicago, I volunteered to teach English to refugee families. My most memorable assignment was a family from Burundi who had survived the Tutsi-Hutu war in that country. Their village was attacked by the Hutu, and their three little daughters, aged four, two, and one, were brutally murdered.

The traumatized parents fled to a refugee camp in Tanzania where they stayed for 12 years, during which time they had four more children. Life in the camp was not easy, and the family waited patiently to be resettled in any country that would accept them. They were anxious to start a new life.

I met them in 2005, when they had only recently arrived in the U.S. and were living in a dark, dreary, one-bedroom apartment. Really soul-destroying. The refugee organization had had difficulty finding accommodations for the large family, and they had limited funds available to subsidize the rent. I decided that I would scrape together some extra cash and help them rent a two-bedroom apartment.

I called many, many landlords. But when I explained the renters would be refugees with four children, the apartments suddenly were "no longer available."

One morning, I called yet another landlord in response to an ad. When I explained that I was calling on behalf of a family in crisis, he hesitated. In the background, I could hear he had little kids himself. He said he didn't want to rent to a family with children because of the wear and tear on the property. I pleaded with him to reconsider because the family desperately needed a decent place to live.

He took a breath.

"I'm Muslim," he said. "This is the month of Ramadan. One of the tenets of Islam is to do good for our fellow man. I really don't want to do this, but you've called me. You've asked me for this." And with that, he agreed to rent the apartment to them.

The mother held my hand and cried when she saw the apartment, much brighter than the other, with a white painted kitchen, curtains on the windows, and blue carpeting. The kids were excited, too. It didn't totally transform their lives, of course, but I could see in my subsequent visits that this landlord's compassionate decision had contributed significantly to the family's emotional well-being.

I have kept in touch with the family, and they are all doing well.

Countless calls. One yes. Six lives changed. Because one person persisted.

It always seems impossible until it's done.
—NELSON MANDELA

Is *No* Really the Last Word?

Have you ever accepted *no* as final, only to later find out that asking a few clarifying questions could've changed the outcome? Too often we take *no* at face value without asking the reasons for it—reasons that, if we were to understand them, could give us room to counter them. The examples below show that *no* can hide any number of unspoken qualifiers. Here's what the person might be thinking but not saying:

I don't know *how* to give you what you want.

I'm afraid I'd fail at giving you what you ask.

Not now, but maybe later.

I can't give you exactly what you want, but I know of alternatives.

I don't have the authority to approve that, but others do.

I could agree to some but not all of what you're asking.

I might say yes if you asked in a respectful way.

I don't understand how I'd benefit from giving you what you want.

Not until you give me what *I* want, and you'll need to ask me what that is.

I just don't have the energy to make another decision today.

No! Never! Nyet! Not as long as I'm alive and God's green earth is turning!

Of all the reasons for *no*, only the last one denotes an actual dead end. But failing to take a moment to inquire about those reasons is like quitting the race five feet before the finish. It's a missed opportunity.

In the worlds of selling and negotiation, hearing *no* is not grounds for giving up but a cue to ask more questions. "Probing questions" are questions that help the sales rep or negotiator understand people's needs, motivations, and preferences. If the offer or terms are declined, asking further probing questions enables the questioner to understand the reasons behind *no*. Thus informed, the questioner can look for alternative (and mutually agreeable) routes to *yes*.

You don't need to be in sales or at the negotiating table to ask probing questions. Here are a few helpful phrases:

"I want to be sure I understand. Could you tell me more about your hesitations regarding this?"

"What part of my request/proposal is causing you concern?"

"What would make my request/proposal more acceptable to you?"

"What would it take for you to say yes?"

"Who *can* help me and how can I reach them?"

"What would you do if you were in my situation?"

"What do I need to do (or what needs to happen) to resolve this?"

(Conditional request) "If you don't do *x*, would you do *y*?"

When you hear *no*, probe if appropriate. Naturally, there are limits. Repeatedly asking the same uninterested person for a date makes you a stalker, not "quietly determined" or "a tireless optimist." And if your neighbors decline to lend you a garden shovel, you'd be a jerk to ask, "Why not?" For other denied requests, however, it might behoove you to dig deeper. (And who doesn't enjoy a good behooving!)

No into Yes. Brian Vandenbroucke is a career entrepreneur whose resume includes professional actor, Chicago nightclub owner, founder of two successful marketing firms, and marketing consultant to clients in government, technology, energy, and publishing. Brian told me about the time he had to think fast to head off not just a *no,* but a *hell no!*

> A former client, "Ted," had a marketing concept he wanted me to pitch to his company, a multinational educational publisher. I'd been in marketing for 25 years then, and thought his concept was wrong for his company—not just wrong but excruciating, needle-in-the-eyes wrong. I tried to talk him out of it, but he held his ground. So, at his request I turned his terrible idea into a 40-page proposal complete with a shiny plastic cover with his company's logo on top.
>
> And I would be the messenger at the pitch meeting. The one they'd kill.
>
> All the top brass were there, the CEO, CFO, president, and everyone on down. As I presented the proposal, I could tell from the squinting, scowling, and squirming that this audience wasn't buying it. Ted's concept was going down in flames.
>
> About 15 minutes into this doomed presentation, it just became too painful to continue. Ted's company was not getting what they wanted. Not even close. I picked up the 40-page proposal … and tore it up.
>
> Ten stunned faces looked up at me (eleven including Ted's). I took a deep breath. "It doesn't matter what we created for you in this proposal," I said. "What do YOU want to do?"

Everybody visibly relaxed. And for the next couple hours the entire group brainstormed until we came up with a concept they loved and that met their business objectives. We got the job and it was a big success, although Ted never forgave me for my emergency intervention.

"In business you must always do what's right for the client," Brian said, "even if that means getting out of the way of your own ideas. And you do that early in the process by asking what they want and listening. The more you know, the fewer surprises."

One More Shot at It. Errol McLendon is a Chicago-based actor, director, storyteller, and two-time winner of the Moth StorySLAM, an open-mic story competition. He has appeared in numerous plays and films including Oliver Stone's *JFK*, in which he was seen as the mysterious Umbrella Man. Errol believes that we can learn a lot about persistence from people in the arts. "Actors or artists sometimes deal with rejections six times a week," he says. "We're constantly putting ourselves out there."

I went to an undergraduate school wanting to act but all they had was a Speech program. I came out of it wanting to go to the Dallas Theatre Center in Dallas, a working theatre that offered a graduate program in acting. I applied, got rejected. I wasn't too surprised—I had no acting experience and only four acting classes on my transcript. Tim Haynes, the registrar at the time, told me to go to New York or LA and start auditioning and acting and building up a resume, and that would be as important to them as a transcript.

I followed my fiancée to Atlanta because she had a job there, but I didn't get much acting work. After four years, I gave up and got a degree in computer science. I did really well in it, and soon accepted a job offer from Holiday Inn

International to be a computer programmer in Memphis, Tennessee.

It promised to be a great job. Great salary and benefits. Vacations. A company car. I put a deposit on an apartment in Memphis.

But I was miserable at the prospect because it meant giving up acting. I had to take just one more shot at it.

So, two weeks before I was to start the job, I called the Dallas Theatre Center. I was sure this was a wasted call, but I had to do it so I could put that part of my life to rest.

Tim was still the registrar. I said, "Is there any chance of getting in your program?"

He said, "We just had someone drop out. Send me your transcript and resume."

I told him my transcript and resume hadn't changed. Having to admit that felt embarrassing. I felt like I'd wasted four years.

He said, "Well, then, it doesn't sound like you meet the criteria for what we're looking for."

Determined not to waste yet more years, I said, "**What do I have to do to have a shot at this?**"

He said, "If you really want to, you can come in the next two days and audition and talk with the acceptance panel. But I can tell you we base admissions mainly on transcript and resume."

So, I drove from Cleveland, Mississippi to Dallas, Texas and auditioned the next day. It was *not* a great audition. But the whole drive back home I told myself, *At least I've made my shot. It's gonna go away, and then I'll start the new job in Memphis.*

When I got home, I got a phone call from Tim. I was in!

The program costs were a concern, so I called Tim back and said I wanted to discuss payment options. He said, "Oh, the guy who dropped out is on full scholarship. If we don't give it to you, we lose it—so *you're* on a full scholarship."

Sometimes fate taps you on the shoulder and sometimes it hits you like a brick! I don't know what made me ask that second time. It wasn't in my nature. I was a person who if I heard *no* was certain that life didn't want me to go in that direction. I was very ready to hear *no*—even anticipating it—but there was something that compelled me to ask if there was any way to get around this.

Months later, somebody who was on the panel told me my audition was just as I'd thought it was—pretty bad! But they said they accepted me based on my passion in the interview. I showed them that I was somebody who really wanted this, and that meant more to them than a resume credit or transcript.

I've had a lifetime of working in a career I'm passionate about. I've been a member of sketch comedy troupes, three theatre companies, have done film and TV, improv, and now storytelling. If you feel that fire, that passion, you've got to give it everything you can, or you'll always wonder if you let it go too easily.

Did you catch Errol McLendon's life-changing question, "What do I have to do to have a shot at this?" Pin that one to your sleeve. Stitch it on a pillow. Tattoo it if you must. But keep it close. As Errol said, "If you feel that fire, that passion, you've got to give it everything you can."

Another Way In. *Mac Smith is a theatre artist and production manager.*

At the school of the arts I attended, a visiting lighting designer was going to show a new lighting technology to one of the classes. I really wanted to see it, but freshmen weren't allowed access. I'm not very good at accepting that I'm not allowed to talk to someone, because I've always felt that raw humans should be able to talk to each other! So, at 6:00 a.m. I showed up at the classroom where the designer was setting up the equipment.

"Would you be willing to talk to me about what you're doing before you meet with the class?"

He said yes, accepted my help setting up, and then gave me a tutorial on the technology. I left at 9:00 a.m., when the class I hadn't been allowed into showed up to see the designer.

This is Mac Smith's second appearance in the book. You first met him in Chapter 3 as the two-year-old enthralled by a sock puppet. Although his blunt "I want that!" had initially embarrassed his mother, Kathe Mull, it became the turning point that convinced her to let him ask "even for the most extraordinary things."

Ask Again. *Alison Koeppel lives in Brooklyn Heights, New York.*

I called my mother's doctor's office to try to change a medication for which she was paying $100 per month. I asked, "Is there a less expensive medication she could take?" The receptionist said no. I called another day, got a different receptionist, and asked again. This time, the receptionist said to try Costco. My mother is now paying $10 a month for the same medication.

When No Means No

Sometimes, despite our most persistent efforts, *no* is final. The seal is airtight. The thing we want will not be ours, at least not in the way we'd hoped. Left empty-handed, all we can do, really, is thank the person for having considered our request and move on.

Avoid the temptation to apologize for having asked; an apology only obliges them to insist no apology is necessary. A friend turned you down? Consider that it may have been as hard for them to say no as it was for you to ask. Above all, never imply you should be rewarded for the braveness it took to ask. "Do you know how *hard* it was for me to ask you?" says they owe you consent, which is not an ask, and no, they don't!

But look at the bright side. You didn't passively sit on the sidelines wishing or worrying. You asked. Allow, too, for the very real possibility that the person simply couldn't give it. As the next storyteller discovered, the one you ask may be bound by limitations you don't understand.

Begging Him to Change. *Kevin Golden works for a Catholic nonprofit organization and is working to complete a master's in theology.*

My father was a great guy. And he had a lot of demons. He was an alcoholic and suffered greatly for it. When I was 14, I wrote him a letter. I pointed out the difference in how I saw him when he was sober and when he was drinking, and I asked him to stop. I was basically begging him. Please stop.

I left the letter where he kept his wallet and keys. He was always out the door before I left for school.

I felt a lot of fear, not being able to anticipate his reaction. I knew at that point in my life that addicts can get very angry when you call them on their issues. I didn't fear for my safety but for the possibility of an emotional confrontation.

The next day I found him on the front porch where he sat facing the street, smoking a cigarette. I asked him if he got my letter. "Yeah, I got it," he said. He didn't look at me. There was an awkward silence.

I went back into the house.

I was really disappointed in his reaction. He continued drinking. But writing him the letter, which I wrote from the heart, changed something in me. It increased my confidence. I wasn't as afraid of calling him on his addiction, which got worse and wound up killing him very young.

Many years later, at 27, I made the decision to abstain from alcohol. In a way, my abstention, personal growth, and ability to reflect on and process my father's life, has become part of his legacy.

> God, grant me the serenity to accept the things
> I cannot change, courage to change the things I can,
> and wisdom to know the difference.
> —SERENITY PRAYER

The Big Ask was my biggest ask and the result of my greatest persistence. I had a hardworking literary agent who believed in the book and for four years submitted proposals to hundreds of prospective publishers. Not a peep. The silence forced me to ask myself, *Am I going to let publishers decide whether my book lives or dies?*

Hello, self-publishing!

Ultimately, we are all responsible for our lives. It's up to each of us to determine the importance of our desires and dreams and what we'll do to make them happen. And it's for each to decide if *no* is the end or a nudge to keep focused, keep reaching, and keep asking. If you've made up your mind that you have no option but to go after what you want, *no* will not derail you whether you hear it five or five hundred times. Such was the extraordinary determination of the person in our next story, whom I had the great privilege to meet.

Looking for Adam

In her earliest memory of life in Poland, Ida was three years old when she witnessed a woman, mad with fear, jump from a building to her death to escape the Nazis. Germany surrendered three years later, in 1945, the year that Ida Maj learned she was Jewish, that her beloved Polish Catholic parents, Wilhem and Jozefa Maj, had adopted her at their own peril, and that the woman she'd seen take her own life was her birth mother, Ester Paluch.

Upon his release from captivity in Russia, her father, Leon Paluch, returned for Ida, who reclaimed the Paluch family name. The fates of Ida's older sister and twin brother, however, like those of obscenely vast numbers of Polish Jews, were unknown.

In 1957, Ida, her father, and stepmother started new lives in Israel. A search there for her lost siblings proved fruitless. Six years later, Ida married, gave birth to a daughter, and the three moved to the U.S. on an immigration visa, with help from her aunt in Chicago.

Soon after their arrival, Ida's aunt surprised her with something that took her breath away: a photograph of Ida's mother holding Ida and her twin brother, Adam; their older sister, Geinia, smiling brightly in back. Seeing their faces as if for the first time, Ida felt overwhelmed by sadness, curiosity, and a resurgence of hope.

She extended her search to the Red Cross, Social Security Administration, conferences for Hidden Child Survivors, and various agencies in Israel and Poland. Each failed inquiry brought her closer to despair.

Then one day, in 1995, Ida received a letter from a friend. It enclosed an article about a Holocaust survivor orphaned in Warsaw who didn't know his real identity. Ida compared the accompanying photo of the man to those she had of her father and paternal grandfather. The resemblance was undeniable. What's more, his story and timeframe matched hers.

Ida had found her twin.

With help from the reporter who interviewed Adam in Warsaw, Ida and Adam spoke to each other for the first time in 53 years, by phone. Ida felt giddy and faint. They cried together, brother and sister.

Their phone calls soon increased to twice a day. Within a few months, Ida flew to Poland. Their emotional reunion was covered by Polish and Israeli media and, upon Adam's subsequent visit to the U.S., a front-page story in the Chicago Tribune.

I recently sat with Ida Paluch Kersz, 83, at her kitchen table in Skokie, Illinois, once home to the largest population of Holocaust survivors in the U.S. "I didn't leave a stone unturned looking for our sister," she told me. "I believe that if she were alive, she would've come back. I have no answer for these things. It's very hard."

But she'd found Adam. I asked Ida what she considers her most pivotal ask in that momentous chapter of her life.

I met with my congressman in his office and asked him to write a letter to Immigration, to get my brother a temporary visa. But he said he wouldn't write the letter because Adam's birth certificate had a different last name [that of his foster parents], and that without proof that he was my brother getting a visa would be nearly impossible. I was very upset and started to cry.

Ida and Adam's dream of a shared life in the U.S. might have ended the moment the congressman said no. But someone else heard her ask that day.

The congressman's secretary, who was listening nearby, was very moved by my story. She introduced herself as Mrs. Stein and asked to see the photos I brought. She, too, saw the resemblance between Adam and our father and grandfather, and told me to send my story directly to Immigration along with copies of the photos.

Ida followed Mrs. Stein's advice. Just two weeks later (lightning speed for a bureaucracy) she received a letter from the U.S. Citizenship and Immigration Services. The agency accepted her claims and permitted her to sponsor her brother in the U.S. Though nothing could make up for their five decades apart, Ida and Adam lived together in Skokie from 1995 until his death in 2022.

"So many people had told me to give up hope of finding my brother," Ida said. "But I kept looking and kept asking. I could not let go."[1]

> Hope is the pillar that holds up the world.
> —PLINY THE ELDER

CHAPTER TEN

GOT CHUTZPAH?

> If you obey all the rules you miss all the fun.
> —KATHERINE HEPBURN, film actress

SOME HAVE AN INBORN TALENT FOR GETTING WHAT they want. Remember that smooth-talking classmate who got away with everything? The one who convinced teachers to make exceptions on his or her behalf and could wriggle out of situations that would've crushed anyone else? That student might not even have been particularly charming. But their *confidence* made them persuasive.

Confidence is the driving force of chutzpah, a zesty Yiddish word for exceptionally bold or brazen behaviors in the service of self-interest. Chutzpah takes nerve. When a person shows chutzpah, there's no middle ground; they either win others over colossally by their very audacity, or just as colossally offend.

Early in her career at National Public Radio, long before she became the executive producer and anchor of NPR's *Latino USA*, journalist Maria Hinojosa was asked by CNN to do a trial piece of reporting for them. "The executives loved what they saw," she writes in her memoir, *Once I Was You*, "but when CNN asked if I would fly down to Atlanta to meet with them, I was overwhelmed with anxiety. I was convinced I was going to fail, but what I didn't recognize was that they were the ones who had called me. I wasn't looking for a new job. They were looking to make a new hire and they wanted me." With encouragement from her husband, Maria agreed to meet with CNN.

> I went down to Atlanta in the first work suit I had ever bought and ate my fear. I asked all of the senior people I interviewed with why I should leave NPR to join them; in other words, what made CNN so special? Every one of them seemed shocked and then surprised, happily, that I had the chutzpah to ask powerful people that kind of a question with a self-assured attitude. They offered me the job, and I negotiated a four-day workweek and a salary increase.[1]

The same fortitude that pushed Pulitzer Prize winner Maria Hinojosa to "eat" her fear drove D.C. Anderson to his own five-star act of chutzpah. When he wasn't called back for a second audition for the Los Angeles production of *The Phantom of the Opera*, the actor and recording artist didn't ask why. He didn't beg for a second chance. Nor did he give up.

Instead, D.C. prepared a different audition song and showed up to the callbacks *uninvited*. Employing a bit of charm and fast-talk, he somehow convinced the audition monitor, whom he knew, that the casting team was expecting him. She announced him to the team.

D.C. strolled into the room as if he belonged there and handed his music selection to the accompanist. The casting director shot him the kind of wary, quizzical look one reserves, appropriately, for gatecrashers. "Uh ... do you have something new to show us, D.C.?" he asked.

"Yes, I do!" D.C. answered, beaming, and proceeded to wow the casting director and the team with his fresh material. The stunt paid off. D.C. was cast in the Los Angeles company for a four-and-a-half-year run, followed by two years in the Broadway company and 12 years on the road.

To be clear, D.C. Anderson's brash tactic was not an ask. But I've included it as a robust example of chutzpah, which in the right circumstances can give an asker the advantage. The audacious stories you're about to read feature people who asked for unconventional things or asked for ordinary things in unconventional ways. In each case, sheer chutzpah!

> Tact in audacity is knowing how far you can go
> without going too far.
> —JEAN COCTEAU, poet and playwright

Waiting Game. In the 40 years I've known Wayne Paprocki, he has not lost the high energy and humor he brings to his real estate training, coaching, and consulting business. Wayne is a Master Certified Negotiation Expert and State Director of the Real Estate Negotiation Institute. "I learned a long time ago," he said, "if you master your time, you master your life, and if you waste your time, you waste your life." In this story, Wayne realized his time wasn't well spent—and he needed to do something about it.

> I was trying to get a meeting with the head of a big company to do their sales training and kept getting no. I sent a note saying I was going to be in town on a day the following week and wanted to meet the president. The company replied saying they couldn't promise anything.

When I got there, the president's administrative assistant asked me if I had an appointment. I said no, but kind of schmoozed her a little and said that I had told the president I'd be there (which I had) and gave her my business card. She took it into the executive's office and returned a few moments later.

"He can't see you," she said. "He's got meetings."

"No problem," I assured her. "I can wait. I brought some work I can do." I figured he had to come out sometime, and I got busy working. By late afternoon, I had been there almost the whole day. The assistant threw me an anxious look.

"Really, sir, he can't see you."

"I understand, but would you do me a favor?" I asked. "It's getting late for both of us. I gave you my business card … would you go get it *back* from him? I've been here a long time and at the very least I just want my card back."

She looked at me like I was nuts and disappeared into the president's office. I don't know how their conversation went, but less than a minute later he opened the door, his face a mix of irritation, disbelief, and amusement. "You're waiting here all day *and want your card back?*" he shouted. "Most people would walk out with their tail between their legs. Get in here!"

In the discussion that followed, he concluded, "If you can train my salespeople to do what you just did here today, you're worth your weight in gold."

"I weigh a lot!" I said.

I got the contract.

Taking the Leap. *Sean Grennan is a playwright whose plays and musicals have been produced around the world.*

Over the years, friends and relatives always complimented my writing in casual correspondence, but outside of a little self-absorbed "journaling," I did nothing with it. One day, my wife, Kathy, and I heard that the local, prestigious Marriott Theatre had come up with an idea for a show they wanted to produce. They had subsequently commissioned, but then lost, a writer and were trying to decide on a next move.

On the way home Kathy and I started to talk about the show. Based only on the title, we started to come up with a plot. The next morning, we woke up still spinning on the idea. New plot twists, new characters, song ideas kept rushing out. So, we thought about it. How can we get from here to there? Finally, and uncharacteristically, we decided to *ask*—in this case, for a pitch meeting with the producer.

The actual phone call fell to me. Screwing up my low self-esteem to a rolling boil of nearly explosive adequacy, I called. The producer was a hard-nosed businessman. The theatre had the largest subscription base in the country, budgets in the millions of dollars, a national presence. When he asked, "Why should I give this job to you, people who have never written ANYTHING?", my naïve response was, "No one has ever written anything until they've written the first thing!" This was my first brush with pluck. Finally, he agreed to a pitch meeting.

Kathy and I worked feverishly on the presentation and sat down with him a week later. He laughed several times throughout the grueling hour (which was good, as we were writing a comedy). The producer agreed to take a chance on our idea. A series of meetings was set up, deadlines were planned, and we did the job.

In all modesty, it was a big success for them, nice reviews, and box office records, etc. It was soon picked up by the largest musical theatre publisher in the country and has been produced around the world. That ask changed the course of my life. If I hadn't taken the leap that day, a lot would have been different. And by that, I mean worse.

Don't Try This at Home! *David Sutor is a retired print and broadcast journalist in Evanston, Illinois.*

I had just pulled into the alley behind my home and saw two teenage boys walking nearby. I always take note of people in the alley at night, so as I pulled into my parking spot I looked around. But I'd lost sight of the boys.

I got out of the car and began walking to the building entrance when one of the teenagers I had seen called to me. I kept walking until one said, "Give us all you've got!" That's when I turned around and saw the kid on my right with a gun pointed at me.

I pulled out my wallet and gave them the cash inside it, seven dollars. I never carry much cash, though seven bucks was less than usual. The gunman frisked me. When they couldn't come up with anything else of value, they began to walk away with my cash and cell phone.

When his friend with the gun turned away, the other kid did something that shocked me. He handed me my seven dollars back. The amount, apparently, hadn't been worth the effort.

It then occurred to me that they might be just as disappointed in my old model cell phone, which unlike a smartphone could not be easily traded or sold. As they headed off, I walked in their direction and asked, "Can I have my cell phone back?"

Without hesitation, the one with the gun handed me my phone.

When I look back, I think what I did was kind of dumb. My daughter, Jennifer, called and said, "Dad, if ever this happens again DON'T ASK FOR YOUR CELLPHONE BACK! I'LL BUY YOU ONE!" She was right, of course; they could have put a bullet in me. However, I will say that if the one kid hadn't unexpectedly handed back my money, giving me the immediate sense that I wasn't about to be physically harmed, I might never have had the guts to ask for my cell phone.

A Rabid Sense of Justice. *Valerie Jones is president of Valerie M. Jones Associates, specializing in nonprofit fundraising and board development.*

I grew up French Canadian Catholic in Maine and went to Catholic school where, at that time, there were only altar boys, not altar girls. So, I asked the school for a debate between the girls and the boys about why girls should be allowed. My asking was full of chutzpah because I had then, at 12, a rabid sense of justice, as I do now. If it's not right, I'm going to do something to make it right.

The debate got approved at the school or parish level, which somehow got back to the bishop of the diocese of Maine, who wrote my mother (who had a column in the Catholic diocesan newspaper). And the bishop said, "Mrs. Jones, you need to control your daughter." And my mother, God bless her, wrote back and said, "Reverend, if the Catholic Church is scared of a 12-year-old girl, you have a much bigger problem than Valerie Jones!"

And the debate went on. We lost, of course (female altar servers weren't approved until 1994, a quarter century later). It would've been harder to ask if I'd had no encouragement, but I always knew my parents would have my back. I always had their support in being bold, in stretching.

Talking a Good Game. *Andrea Gotskind-Hamad is proprietor of a children's shoes and clothing boutique in Naperville, Illinois.*

In the '80s, I was a devoted basketball fan who avidly read the bible of the sport, Basketball Digest. I knew the magazine was published in a town nearby, so I called the office of its vice president. Though I phoned the VP many times, his secretary would never put me through to him. Still, I was determined to get through. I got in the habit of calling him every day, at a specific time.

After a month of calls that got nowhere, the secretary one day asked me to hold while she put the VP on the phone.

"Alright, I give up!" he said. "Who the hell are you?"

I said, "My name is Andrea Gotskind and I think I would be the perfect employee because I love basketball and would be best positioned doing public relations for you." (I actually had *zero* experience in professional writing or public relations!) He told me the magazine used an outside PR firm but as a concession offered to take a few minutes to give me a tour of the magazine next time I was in the neighborhood.

"Ok!," I said. "I can be there at 1:00 tomorrow—does that work for you?" It did.

I met with him, got the tour, and we sat down and talked basketball *for two hours.* He seemed very surprised and delighted to be having an in-depth conversation with me about the sport. "You have a real knowledge and love of basketball," he said, "and I'd like for you to be able to use that."

The next day he called and told me he had created a job for me as an in-house public relations liaison, a job that hadn't existed before.

I worked there for about a year. It didn't pay very much, but getting an inside look at the industry, meeting NBA players, and proofreading the pages of my favorite publication was a joy, and more than enough payoff for my persistence [and chutzpah!].

Shared passion for a sport or team can quickly activate the similarity and unity principles, creating instant rapport. In Andrea's case, the basketball bond was so strong that her new employer never asked for proof of her writing experience. Swish!

But is it Legal?

More than anything, Raven Anne Quigley (now Parr) wanted to be a healer. A career in massage therapy beckoned. Though she and her husband were employed, a mortgage and a child in high school made the $3,000 down payment for massage school challenging. Even so, she figured that with so strong a calling there had to be a way.

As a prominent member of the Elmhurst (Illinois) Chamber of Commerce, she had been to many dinner dances and fund-raisers where auctions and raffles were standard revenue builders. Contemplating the success of these events led her to what seemed an audacious idea—a raffle for herself. She did some research and learned that raffles were illegal unless the tickets were free or in support of a not-for-profit organization.

But it was not illegal to *give away tickets and ask for a donation*.

Raven Anne put together a tempting raffle package that would provide the winner one massage a month for a year. She printed 150 tickets that she would offer free or for a $20 donation. If all tickets received the suggested donations, she would net the needed $3,000.

As she prepared to announce her raffle at the next Chamber of Commerce breakfast, her confidence wavered. "They knew I wasn't a crackpot," she said, "but I felt vulnerable. Would my asking for something completely personal in a professional environment be deemed inappropriate? Basically, I was asking them, 'Please help me.'"

Raven Anne gave her pitch, and the Chamber got behind her.

Encouraged by the membership's backing, she went door to door at local businesses offering raffle tickets to owners and employees. "As I got more comfortable, I basically threw the doors open," she said. "I even went to the bowling alley and asked everyone there. I asked everywhere, asked everybody I could think of, and 'sold' every ticket. Not only did I receive the money to get into massage school, I created an enormous buzz around my becoming a massage therapist that I was eventually able to build into marketing my private practice. About five people were happy to have the free ticket, and as far as I was concerned, they were my proof that if the IRS ever called, the donations were just donations."

While working full-time, Raven Anne attended massage school and provided updates on her progress at Chamber meetings. When later in the year she completed her certification, she was made class valedictorian. "My proudest moment," she said, "was standing up at the Chamber breakfast and showing them my certificate and letting them know their support had not gone to waste."

To Raven Anne, a big ask so generously granted demanded a big thank you. In thanks for their support, she paid it forward with an offer to come to members' businesses and give free chair massages for employees during the Thanksgiving and Christmas holidays. She estimates that within one month she gave nearly 70 employee massages.

Despite her successful tuition-raising effort, there was a time when asking did not come easily for her. "I was raised to help yourself, to pull yourself up by your bootstraps; if you weren't self-reliant and self-sufficient, you weren't really successful or very worthy. So, I learned *not* to ask and to do things all by myself."

Raven Anne credits her campaign's success, in part, to skills learned in Pathways for Successful Living, in which she learned that obstacles can stimulate growth. "If my appointment calendar isn't as full as I'd like, I just call my clients and say, "Hey, I haven't seen you in a while, want to come in?"[2]

Creativity has got to have some edge to it, doesn't it?
—DAVID DROGA, CEO, Accenture Song

CHAPTER ELEVEN

HOW'S YOUR TIMING?

Faith—in life, in other people, and in oneself—
is the attitude of allowing the spontaneous to be
spontaneous, in its own way and in its own time.
—ALAN WATTS, philosopher

DO YOU RECALL FROM CHAPTER 1, WHEN ENTREPRENEUR
Michel Elings sensed his auspicious now-or-never moment at the
Apple conference? Instead of joining the mass exit, he followed an
impulse to change direction and approach the executives mingling
at the stage. And that impulse, which he could've just as easily
ignored or failed to notice, set his destiny in motion.

There are many asks that benefit from careful planning and
analysis. But some of the most inspired, life-affirming asks, the
kind with magic in them, happen in the moment. When you quietly sense the makings of an opportunity you didn't see coming, or
feel a sudden leap of curiosity or yearning, that's the time to ask.

You may not even consciously recognize the gift in front of you;
it's your intuition that nudges you to take the unscheduled route,

make the spontaneous phone call, or blurt the request or question that surprises even you. The stories in this chapter are about people who felt those nudges and followed their noses.

The Secret of Italian Beef

My friend Gail Trotter was grocery shopping in her newly adopted city of Santa Fe when she had a sudden whim to make a dish that she, a former Chicagoan, hadn't found in New Mexico: Chicago-style Italian beef. She prowled the aisles guessing at the ingredients she'd need to pull it off. (This was in the pre-smartphone Dark Ages). Giving in to a sudden what-the-heck attitude, she turned to a shopper nearby and asked, "Excuse me—do you know how to make Italian beef?

"Sure," he replied. "I was a chef at Italian Village Restaurant in Chicago for 15 years."

With that, he began pushing Gail's cart up and down the aisles, filling it with everything she'd need to make the *perfect* Chicago-style Italian Beef sandwich and offering his professional cooking tips. (Screenwriters, there's a great "meet cute" story for your next rom com. You're welcome!)

Now, the odds of Gail finding someone in Santa Fe with that knowledge, at that moment, were small. But rather than *assume* nobody could help she turned to a stranger placed there, evidently, by the culinary gods themselves. "You never know who you're talking to," says self-help author Barbara Sher in her TEDx talk in Prague. "We're all the center of enormous amounts of information and connection that we don't need and we don't think of unless somebody asks us."[1]

Door to Destiny

At 18, a few years before he would practice asking for his hoped-for salary in front of a mirror (as told in Chapter 5), Jeffrey Breslow was flunking out of Bradley University. One weekend, he went to visit friends at the University of Illinois (U of I). "My only *A* was in art in high school," he told me, "so the first place I went to at U of I was the new Fine and Applied Arts Building." There was amazement and reverence in his voice as he recalled the moment a spontaneous ask put him on an unexpected path.

> And I see a case with this extraordinary display. Students were given the same rectangular block of wood and allowed to make three cuts, glue it back together and sand and paint it with shiny automotive paint. There were eight or ten of them in stunning abstract shapes. It just blew me away. It was that beautiful.
>
> I turned around and there was a door halfway open with the name Ed Zagorski on it, who turned out to be chair of the Industrial Design program. I didn't even know what industrial design was. I knocked, went in, and said: "Can you tell me about industrial design?"
>
> And he did.
>
> After 20 minutes I said, "I need to be an industrial designer."
>
> Years later Ed admitted he had no recollection of talking to me that day. But for me it was a pivotal moment. I ended up going back to Bradley and *studying*, which took me from probation to the dean's list so that I could transfer to U of I and study with Ed.

Jeffrey Breslow went on to lead two highly profitable toy design studios, Marvin Glass & Associates and Big Monster Toys, LLC.

But the man best known for inventing and designing such best-selling games as Masterpiece, Ants in the Pants, and Bucket of Fun may have found even more fulfillment in his friendship with (the late) Ed Zagorski. "We were friends for 68 years," said Jeffrey. "He was my closest friend, my mentor. It was just extraordinary that I had somebody like that in my life."

Intuition will tell the thinking mind where to look next.
—JONAS SALK, developer of polio vaccine

Timely Text. *Lilly Harris lives in Portland, Oregon, where she works as a farmer and project manager.*

Several years ago, I was looking for work online and saw that a woman who managed the French restaurant where I'd worked 15 years earlier, was in an industry that I wanted to know more about. I texted her my interest. She replied that, *just that day* they had had a meeting about needing a new manager in one of the departments at her company and did I have any experience in warehousing and operations? It was perfectly aligned with my most recent experience as the director of operations for a small startup, so I was able to transition easily into that new role as operations manager.

Whose Harley? *Kieran Meeke is a journalist who has explored more than 100 countries, lived in eight, and currently resides in Kerry, Ireland.*

I was going into the Metro [British newspaper] office one day and there was a brand new, yellow Harley Davidson 850 Sportster parked right outside. I asked in the office, "Whose

Harley is that?" and found out it didn't belong to anyone; it had just been delivered for a test ride. But there was actually nobody on the features desk who had a motorbike license. So, I went and passed my license and so became the motoring correspondent.

A gorgeous $20,000 Harley V-Rod was the first motorbike I was asked to review after I got my license. I remember riding it across Tower Bridge and tourists were photographing me! So, asking, "Whose motorbike is that?" began a very interesting part of my career.[2]

Best Question Ever. *Eileen K. works for a biopharma company.*

I was the manager for a cardiac catheter lab at a community hospital and really wanted a change. I had just purchased a product for the lab, and on the spur of the moment asked the product rep, "Hey, is your company hiring?" She told me there was in fact a new position being created that required cardiology experience and gave me the names of the people to send my resume to. Four months later I was hired. The job has allowed me not only to do presentations and travel, which I love, but to complete my education, so that I now have a master's degree in nursing. It was the best question I ever asked.

A Profitable Pause. *Brian Vandenbroucke is a career entrepreneur.*

My new business partner and I were on a conference call to discuss our seminar proposal with a potential client. It was just a loose outline, a conversation starter. No numbers in it. And the conversation was going well. At one point my partner was about to quote our project fee, as we'd planned, when my intuition kicked in. I gestured for her to pause, and asked the client, "What have you got to spend?"

The client's amount *quintupled* what we were about to ask for. With that, Digital Equipment Corp. became our first major client, the one that put us in business.

Moved to Ask. *Patricia Hock, retired from a sales career, lives in Connecticut.*

The prospect of moving from my spacious two-bedroom condo to a compact one-bedroom in another town, was daunting. I had four rooms of furniture to downsize and only a few weeks to do it. I'm thinking, *How am I going to unload so much?* I suddenly got the idea to go to a local resale shop and just ask around.

I approached every customer in the shop and asked, "Are you looking for furniture?" Everyone said no except for one woman, who told me she'd just moved here with her family and needed furniture. I asked if she'd like to come over to my place and see what I was selling, and she said yes.

That afternoon, she came over with her husband. The two of them walked around looking at everything. Ten minutes later they joined me in the living room. Her husband stood there rocking on his heels, hands behind his back. He was very quiet for a few moments. And then he asked me, "How much for *everything?*"

I couldn't believe it. He literally wanted all of it. Not just the furniture but every plate, vase, and salt and pepper shaker. Even the ceiling fixtures. I gave him a good price and he accepted it (and, yes, the check cleared!). The day I moved out, he was there with trucks to clear out the place.

My initial thought to go to the resale shop and maybe sell some furniture, was *Why not?* And then this happened. What more could I have asked for?!

Don't Overthink It. *Elena E. is an accountant in Florida.*

A few summers ago, I responded to a woman's Facebook post about the [pre-war] conflict in Ukraine, where she and I were born and raised. I didn't know "Svetlana," but I commented on her post that her feelings about the situation resonated with my own. Later, I visited her page and saw that she lived in Alaska, a place I've always wanted to go. A couple of days later she posted a gorgeous photo of fresh caviar. I started thinking, *Caviar … Alaska … an interesting person … I'm going!*

I messaged my potential host. "Could I invite myself over to have some of that caviar?"

"Of course! When can you come?"

Within a couple of hours, we'd worked out the details. I'd be there for a week, including my birthday. I booked my airfare to Anchorage, and just in case she or her husband might have second thoughts, assured her that I had 24 hours to cancel it. "Don't overthink it," she said. "Everything happens for a reason, especially unusual and spontaneous things. This has all come about in a way that tells me it was supposed to happen."

Svetlana was right. Although she and I clashed a few times in our week together, Alaska was in every respect a deep spiritual experience for me. I fell in love with the beauty of the mountains and wilderness. We saw whales, moose, and eagles, caught and grilled salmon, and my special birthday pancake was "frosted" with caviar!

A Momentous Meeting. *Joshua Ellis is an ordained interspiritual minister and a former Broadway press agent.*

In 1981, before a performance of *Lena Horne: The Lady and Her Music,* Jaqueline Kennedy Onassis walks into the theatre with Mike Nichols. As the press agent for the show, I see this photo op and I'm salivating. Mrs. Onassis was as close to royalty as America ever had, so naturally I want to get a photo with her and Lena Horne after the show. But it was a big ask because of who she is and knowing I'm about to ask her to do what she famously doesn't like to do at all—pose for pictures. She was really press-averse.

So, I approach her, introduce myself, and say, "Could we possibly have a photo op with you and Miss Horne after the show? It'll take just five minutes."

At first, she charmingly deflected my request saying, "Oh, who would care about a picture with me and Lena Horne?" But I smile and give her a look that says, *We both know perfectly well you don't mean that.* And rather than ask her again, I simply say, "I'll meet you at your seat at the end of the performance and escort you backstage." She agrees to the photo, though I'm certain that it was not my power of persuasion that changed her mind but her respect for Lena Horne.

And then the evening gets even richer.

In the lobby I see Coretta Scott King, the widow of Reverend Martin Luther King Jr. And I know I have to get a photograph with them together. Now, I didn't know these women's relationship. Maybe they don't even want to be seen next to one another, let alone photographed together. You just don't know in that moment, so you proceed with caution.

And Mrs. King graciously agrees to do a photo with Lena and Mrs. Onassis.

Then, because I'd learned early on that people at this level don't like surprises—you have to tell them upfront—I go back to Mrs. Onassis and ask if it would be ok if Mrs. King joins us for the picture. And she agrees to it.

I alerted the media. It was the largest number of photographers I ever had cover an event. Backstage there were so many flashbulbs simultaneously going off that for two solid minutes there was continuous white light. Here were Jaqueline Kennedy Onassis and Coretta Scott King, arguably the two most famous widows of the twentieth century, there on the same night, as it happened, and I had asked each for their permission to pose for a photograph that turned out to capture a moment in history.[3]

Inexplicable Urge. *Sonia Choquette is the author of 27 books on intuitive development, personal growth, and transformational leadership.*

Several years ago, when on my way to Paris, flying from Chicago through Newark with my family, I found myself standing in line at the airport waiting to board our flight when, all of a sudden, I had an inexplicable urge to speak to the gate agent.

Following this urge without question, as I always do, and not knowing what it was about, I walked right up to her and spontaneously asked, "Is it possible to change our flight to another one?" I was surprised that I asked that question and didn't know why I did, but those words came flying out of my mouth and so I simply went with it. The agent looked at me as if I were crazy and said, "No way. Aren't you on this flight?"

"For the moment we are," I answered, "but I want to know if there is another flight we can take instead."

Again, she said, "No way. You mean today?" now certain that I was beyond crazy, and in fact truly weird.

I smiled and said, "Yes, today. Can you please just check? By the way, there are six of us."

Waiting for the signal to board the flight, she said rather impatiently, "I really have no time to do this right now. We are about to board."

Knowing I was pushing her every last button, I ignored her resistance and stayed in place. "I know, but until we do, please, just humor me and check," I said, once again. "While you do that, I'll pray."

She looked up, paused, but said nothing to that comment. Because I am a premier flyer and the flight was, in fact, not yet boarding, she had no choice but to accommodate me.

Shaking her head at me in complete irritation as she tapped on the keys of her computer, she said, "I'm absolutely certain there are no flights to Paris today, especially one with six open seats. Not through any airport in North America. You'll just have to take this one."

I wasn't about to budge. "Please," I persisted, still having no clue as to why I was doing this. "Just look a little harder."

"If I do find seats, they are surely going to cost you a fortune," she admonished, as though that might discourage me from making her continue this ridiculous search.

"No worries," I said. "Let's just see what you find."

Now, mind you, as I said, all the while I was not sure why I was asking her to do this, and neither did my family. We had our boarding passes in hand and were ready to go. It was a calm day and there was nothing out of place. No, it wasn't a logical impulse. I was simply acting on a vibe that strongly moved me, without any logical reason to back it up. I was trusting my vibes and because my family knows me so well, so were they.

Another stressful three minutes passed, the agent vigorously shaking her head in disapproval at me for the imposition and extra work I was making her do when suddenly her face brightened up. "I don't believe it. I just found six tickets to Paris direct. They were just released for the six o' clock flight, leaving from right here in Chicago. That is so weird. Now for the price." She continued, raising her eyebrows and whistling as though to emphasize it was going to be a lot.

Continuing to tap away at the computer, the captain of the flight suddenly came out from the jetway and walked up to her. Though he turned his back to me, he spoke loudly enough that I could hear him. "We have a mechanical," he said. "This plane and those people will not be going anywhere with us today, so you should let them know."

The agent looked at me incredulously. Tapping three more keys, she said, "I guess your flight is going to be *free*. I can't believe it." Facing the 200 people in line, she continued, "I don't know how you did it, but you are probably the only group getting to Paris today, now that this happened. Hurry, take your tickets and run."

And so we did. Dodging the uproar, we went to the restaurant, had a snack, bought some magazines, and were on our way two hours later. How did that happen? Did I sense the flight was going to cancel? Did I feel this might happen?

No, I didn't. I simply moved with the energy as it moved me, moment to moment. I spoke without thinking and trusted my vibes. The impulse was so subtle I wasn't even sure what I was doing or why. I simply did it.

The point is, don't wait for a telegram or Elvis to appear when it comes to trusting your vibes. When you receive a vibe, a gut feeling, or an inspiration, however subtle, act on it, without hesitation. If you do, all sorts of wonderful things will unfold in your favor.

Opportunities don't always announce their arrival. They reveal themselves through the whisper of intuition, the trigger of instinct, or the ask that forms on our lips before our mind has a say in it. Welcome these moments. When you do, you allow life to conspire on your behalf.

As soon as you trust yourself you will know how to live.
—JOHANN WOLFGANG VON GOETHE

CHAPTER TWELVE

NEED HELP?

Life is not a solo act, it's a huge collaboration.
—GEORGE TAKEI, actor

DOLLY PARTON ONCE TOLD ABC NEWS, "NOW, I'LL DO anything people ask me, but … when it comes to asking a favor from somebody, I'm just real backwards about that. It makes me feel like I'm hittin' on 'em."[1] The country superstar was joking, but her comment strikes a chord for many of us.

If it's within our power, most of us would rather not inconvenience anyone. Yet we often exaggerate our concerns. We imagine that any request for help or favors will create intolerable hassles for people, or that we'll look weak or inept and never recover our pride.

But let's look at this from the "askee's" perspective. Except for the demanding, high-maintenance, non-reciprocating people in your life (no need to name them out loud!), do you typically feel resentful when people ask you for help? Probably not. Why, then, would you assume they'd feel put out by helping *you*?

It's rewarding when we're uniquely able by virtue of our skills, knowledge, or resources to be of service—or even a hero—to someone who asks our help. Studies of the brain have shown that acting generously triggers the same reward pathways as sex and food[2] (tell *that* to the next person who grumbles at your ask!). In the rare instance that your request annoys someone, relax—in two minutes they'll forget you asked. Bottom line: if you, like most self-reliant people, worry that asking will make you a nuisance, take comfort. Real nuisances rarely have that worry.

In this chapter you'll meet people who asked for help, some bashfully, some boldly. But all of them asked and, as you might guess, *received*.

Piece by Piece. Eight-time Emmy award winner Jane Lynch credits a key moment in her artistic development to asking for help. Jane, who has hosted the TV game shows *The Weakest Link* and *Hollywood Game Night*, is perhaps best known for her comical and iconic characters in *Glee, The Marvelous Mrs. Maisel,* and *Only Murders in the Building*. A friend since our college days, she shared a time she asked for feedback and got much more than expected.

> I have historically never been a fan of asking people for anything. I don't like to put people out, I never wanted to appear that vulnerable to actually need any assistance, and I have this notion that I should be able to do everything for myself, by myself. But I recall a moment when I did ask for something and how strong the impact of receiving it was.
>
> Several years ago, before I had any measurable success in show business, I had an idea I should put together a one-person show by culling together monologues for characters I had been working on over the years in cabarets and sketch comedy stage shows. They were in a big notebook,

completely unorganized and had nothing to do with each other. I didn't have any faith that I could turn them into anything.

I asked an agent I greatly admired, Marla Kirban, to read them and give me her feedback. I was concerned, though, that the monologues would read "flat" on the page because they were written to be *heard*. But my greater fear was that she would see nothing of value in any of the pieces and dismiss them (and me) out of hand.

Other people's opinion of me at that time meant a heck of a lot more than my own opinion of me. So it was with a whole lot of courage that I approached her.

Not only was she happy to take a look at them, she suggested I act them out for her. She invited me to her home, and we sat on her patio as I acted out each piece. Afterwards, she took a long draw off her cigarette and proceeded to move the pieces around, giving them an order, a shape, an arc as well as a theme. Not only did she piece together what would become my one-person show, *Oh Sister, My Sister!*, she made it *mean* something. Something I had no idea was there.

Marla Kirban was willing to help me. And she helped me because I had the courage to ask her.

Broken Into, But Not Broken. Las Vegas-based fashion designer David Tupaz is the artistic force behind David Tupaz Couture, the first couture atelier in his city's history. The Philippines-born designer shows his work at every major Fashion Week in the U.S. and is the creative director of the international fashion and art magazine, Chic Compass. Every entrepreneur makes a million requests, but it was a crisis that forced David's biggest ask.

Early one morning, I arrived at my studio and realized the back door was open and there was a crack in the wood. The whole place was empty. Jewelry pieces, equipment, computers, all stolen. My collection of archive samples—15 years of work—gone. The only thing left were the clothes on the mannequins in the window.

There had been six wedding gowns in garment bags, on the rack, waiting for pickup. All were ordered a year before. The first dress was to be picked up in three weeks. I thought, *Oh my god, do I tell these women they can't have their wedding because their dresses were stolen?* The robbery wasn't their fault, or mine, but it was my responsibility regardless. I could not destroy the most important day of their life. I didn't even think about the loss of everything else, I was just so focused on those dresses.

While the detectives were all over the place looking for fingerprints, I was in a panic, on my phone, calling a friend, saying, "What am I going to do?" He asked, "Will you still be able to order the same material?" I said yes. He said, "Well, do that NOW!" That's when I started calling my friends around town. I called some of my designer friends, my manufacturing friends, for help. The good thing was that I had the patterns for the dresses.

I was able to divide up the six dresses with different designers and manufacturers. Six people were helping me recreate six dresses. And it's not just one person making one dress. There's a pattern maker, the person that cuts the fabric, the seamstress that puts the dress together, the people that sew the beads and sparkles onto the dresses, and the finishers, the people that steam it. A collaboration of five to six people per dress. It takes about a month and a half to create a dress, but they finished everything in just two and a half weeks.

Of course, there was a price tag because it was considered a rush job, but I didn't care! I was almost in tears when, one by one, they would call and say, "David come over and check this out." And I'd come over before they'd stitch the last piece of thread on the hem, and I'd see that it was exactly as I had done it, to perfection. When the brides tried them on, they never knew these weren't their original dresses. That's when I was able to breathe.

It's very seldom that I ask favors. I don't even ask favors from my own family. So, it was a very humbling experience. Not once did they have reservations when I asked. Their attitude was, *of course I'm going to help.* The fashion industry, the garment industry, is like a huge family. And we are a diverse family—Latin, Asian, Jewish, Persian. There's a genuine support, a genuine relationship. And everybody came together in my time of desperate need to save me. It felt like hearts were opened. The humanity of asking! I was so grateful.[3]

> When I was a boy and I would see scary things in the
> news, my mother would say to me, Look for the helpers.
> You will always find people who are helping.
> —FRED ROGERS, educator and children's TV host

Losing My Home. *Name Withheld by Request.*

It was at the height of the housing bubble. I was in the middle of a divorce, had bad financial troubles, was overextended on my mortgage and certain of losing my home. I kept trying to get government-sponsored home financial assistance but kept getting rejected even though I was exactly the kind of person the program was created for.

At some point, I just realized that I had to let somebody help me. That can be hard because we all like to be in control of our lives and think that *not* letting other people help us means that we're in control. But I also know that we all have different knowledge, skills, and gifts, and these won't be shared unless they're asked for.

Since it was a government program, I got the idea to ask for help from a government official, my Congressperson. I was assigned to a staff member who during my many visits went through the application process with me, dotting all the *i*'s and crossing the *t*'s. But even with her expert help, my loan modification request was denied. For the third time.

When my Congressperson learned of this, she did something I could never have expected. She personally called the bank and asked on my behalf. That call changed my life. I got the loan modification—$50,000 off what I'd owed on the mortgage, with a 2% interest rate that lowered my monthly bill by $900 per month. I was able to catch up on everything.

When you ask, sometimes what you get is just enough to see you through. And sometimes, even though you couldn't imagine how it would be possible, you get something even better than you thought you would. Throughout my life, I've learned to ask, relax, and have faith that things will work out. Somehow, they usually do.

A Televised Request. *Thomas Hilgardner runs a financial firm helping people recover money lost during foreclosures.*

One Christmas Eve, while my wife and I were staying at my father's house, our afternoon celebration was suddenly disrupted by my father's neighbors, who rushed over to tell us their house had been burglarized. Not only had clothes, phones, and jewelry been stolen but all the Christmas gifts for their two children. We immediately called the police.

Apart from the devastating timing of the crime, we knew that this low-income family's ability to recoup these financial losses would be extremely difficult. I wanted to find a way to inform the city about this family, because there are amazing people out there who if asked are willing and grateful to help out.

I called NBC Action News, told them what happened, and asked if they could ask their viewers for help. Within an hour they had a reporter and camera at the scene. They interviewed the family about the theft and closed with a direct appeal to viewers who might want to help.

Around midnight, people from the network showed up at their door and shocked the family with loads of wrapped presents, cash donations, and new bicycles for both kids. The parents invited us to their house Christmas morning and showed us the gifts. The efforts of strangers to help their family moved them (and us!) to tears. It was without question the best Christmas my family has ever had.

Tuxedo Trouble. *Barry Offitzer is a semi-retired television advertising sales manager living in Morristown, New Jersey and Lenox, Massachusetts.*

In town for a black-tie wedding at the Plaza, my wife and I spent a leisurely afternoon enjoying an unseasonably warm December day. When we got back to our room at a nearby hotel, I discovered that I had left my tuxedo shirt at home. I called down to the concierge and explained my situation.

"Hmm," she said. "Well, you can run out and buy a shirt."

"But the wedding is in a half-hour," I replied.

"Sorry, sir," she said. "I hope you make it. Good luck."

Running downstairs in search of a store, I passed through the lobby's revolving doors and noticed that the bellmen were wearing white shirts.

I went back in.

"Excuse me," I said to one who looked about my size. His name was Paul. "I've got a wedding in 25 minutes and no shirt. Can you help?"

He hesitated.

"What size are you?" he asked.

"Sixteen neck, 32 sleeve," I said.

He disappeared through a side door and came out minutes later holding a freshly laundered white shirt, on a hanger no less. I could have kissed him. Instead, I thanked him profusely and handed him $50.

After a late checkout the next morning, I found Paul to return the shirt and get my checked bags. He asked about the wedding, and I joked that we had looked great together. He began to walk away and then turned back.

"Thanks for showing my shirt a good time last night," he said.

I want to build a frequency counter, and I was wondering if you have any spare parts I could have.
—12-year-old Steve Jobs' call to Hewlett-Packard co-founder Bill Hewett (who gave Jobs the parts and a summer job at HP)

Ready for Opportunity. *Mari Weiss is a professional actor, voiceover artist, and teacher in Chicago.*

In 1991 I was broke, having spent my post college years doing wonderfully creative *non*-paying acting jobs. I'd been exploring voiceover work and had finally cobbled together a decent demo, but I wasn't getting much traction. I heard that Peggy Walter, a talent agent I knew who was always friendly to me, had taken a position at the ad agency DDB Needham, so I called her and asked her if she would take five minutes to listen to my demo and give me feedback.

Making that phone call was one of the most difficult things I'd ever done. I'd taken such pride in my self-sufficiency, asking for help felt like weakness. I was slow to realize that talent alone wasn't enough; I needed guidance, mentorship, a little help. Happily for me, Peggy agreed to meet.

When I arrived at her office, she had just a few minutes before she had to fly off to a meeting. But she very generously listened to my demo and gave me some feedback, and I was grateful.

As I left, she walked into a meeting where they were trying to find the next voice for a yogurt brand. And Peggy told them, "I just met with someone who could work well for this." Within a day I got a phone call to audition and as a result became—for the next three-and-a-half years—the voice of Yoplait Yogurt, a lucrative contract with multiple TV and radio spots. That campaign launched my voiceover career, opening many doors.

Did luck play a part? Yes. It was luck that I had met with Peggy right before that meeting. But just as important, I had asked for the opportunity, was prepared for it, and had the skillset to back it up.

Sometimes all you have to do is ask and it leads to your dreams coming true. Ask those questions. Just ask them. More often than you'd suspect, the answer you get is, "Sure."
—RANDY PAUSCH, author, *The Last Lecture*

Ask for Support

On the emotional front, help and support are not always the same. Except in times of crisis, you probably have more occasions to quietly ask for support than cry out for help. By "support" I mean the moral and emotional kind: the need to talk to someone about a troubling issue and know they care and understand you; someone who, by witnessing your burden without judgment, lightens it.

Lab-coated experts confirm that making intimate disclosures to a supportive listener can reduce our stress and anxiety, enhance closeness and intimacy, and restore our self-worth.[4] So, give yourself permission to ask for and receive support. And be specific about the kind of support you want. Are you asking only to be heard (which is also a chance to hear yourself) and then be on your way? Are you asking for counsel? Whatever your needs, be clear about them upfront.

Advice. "I'm at a crossroads in my career direction and am wondering if I could talk to you about it. I'd welcome any insight or guidance you might have to offer."

Feedback. "I'm committed to becoming a better parent (partner, boss, employee, etc.) but it's hard to be objective about my own behavior. What am I doing right? And what is something I could improve that might be hard for you to say but important that I hear?"

Perspective. "I've got to have an honest conversation with Luis, but I'm afraid I'll say something I regret. It would help me to talk it through. Would you be my sounding board?"

Venting. "I had a rough morning with the kids. Can you spare a few minutes while I get it off my chest?"

Validation/reassurance. "At the risk of sounding weird, it would mean the world to me right now if you would look me in the eyes and tell me I'm a good person. Would you do that for me?"

Verbal support isn't the only option. You can ask a friend for a hug, to join you for a movie, or to sweat it out together on the pickleball court. But if you want a conversation, be intentional about it. Set up a time and place in which your listener can give you their full attention. And consider these best-to-worst options:

Face to Face. Have the conversation in person, if possible. Silence your phone and put it away. Sherry Turkle, author of *Reclaiming Conversation: The Power of Talk in a Digital Age,* reports that "Eighty-nine percent of Americans say that during their last social interaction, they took out a phone, and 82 percent said that it deteriorated the conversation they were in."[5] If your listener tries to split their attention between you and their phone, find a friendly way to ask them set it aside (ideally, turned off) until the conversation ends. If they're unwilling to do that, limit the conversation to small talk. Don't attempt to speak from the heart to someone who's unwilling or unable to give you their undivided attention.

Phone. A phone call is the next best way to receive meaningful support. Over the phone, your listener has an opportunity to hear the nuance of your inflections, note where you pause, comment on what you seem to *not* be saying, and give *you* a sense, from their tone of voice, of how the conversation affects them. And yet, if the sounds of a TV, keyboard taps, or vacuum cleaner indicate they're multitasking while "listening" to you, you're not really being heard. In that case, you may need to reschedule or ask, "I'd feel more connected with you if I know I have your full attention for the next 10 minutes or so. Would you mind unplugging until then?"

Texting. Texting is ideal for quick exchanges and letting people know we're thinking about them. But it can't make us feel seen, certainly, nor heard except in the most superficial sense. Texting offers a screen of invisibility. It encourages self-editing, brevity, and emojis as substitutes for embodied self-expression. Plus, words without a voice are easy to misinterpret. This leaves both parties open to misunderstandings, which can be especially painful when one is vulnerable and wants support.

Are you worthy of receiving support, asked for or not? Are you worthy of another person's undivided attention? Of expressing yourself and having the opportunity to clarify your feelings? If you answered "no" to any of those questions, the next question to ask is "Why not?"

When you need it, there's nothing so comforting or encouraging as being thoughtfully heard. Give yourself permission to bask awhile in the warmth of human understanding. If you can't get that from those you count on for support, consult a therapist or seek out counseling services in your community, church, school, or workplace.

A Coded Question. *Bridget Piekarz is recently retired from 40 years in publishing and bookselling.*

Like all small children, my son loved to test me. He had a habit around ages four and five of posing a series of escalating questions on some thorny topic, wanting to find out what the line would be and where it would be drawn.

Example: "Mom, what would happen to me if Dad was dead, and you were in jail?"

"Oh, honey, that would not happen. Dad is healthy and I wouldn't ever do anything that would put me in jail."

"But what if he was dead and you were in jail for something?"

We went back-and-forth in this manner until I finally realized what he was looking for: reassurance. I said if that happened Grandma would take care of him like she does now while we work. He was perfectly happy in the knowledge he would be taken care of and never asked again.

I felt it shelter to speak to you.
—EMILY DICKINSON in a personal letter, 1878

Ask for a Mentor

Asking for help or support without shame or apology is a giant step in personal and professional growth. But sometimes we need guidance beyond immediate challenges, especially at work. We need someone willing to share their wisdom and experience, to help us avoid pitfalls and pursue possibilities. "To know the road ahead," goes the Chinese proverb, "ask those coming back."

"I certainly wouldn't be where I am if people hadn't been willing to mentor me," said Rocki Howard, whose background in talent acquisition leadership led her to found Diversiology.IO, a platform designed to create more inclusive workplaces. "Mentors have been some of the greatest relationships I've had, because they saw something in me, saw that I was willing to listen, and felt they had something to give."

Yahoo Finance recently profiled Rocki among its Top 100 HERoes Women Executive Role Models. Having been both mentor and mentee in a 20+year career that spans banking, manufacturing, retail, pharmaceutical, and insurance, she has advice for those seeking mentors.

Asking, "Will you be my mentor" is pretty audacious unless

there's a basis for the relationship. Know what you're asking for in a mentor. A lot of people want a mentor to be someone to bounce ideas off of or make them feel good about themselves. But that's not always what gets you to the next level.

Some people want mentors that are also going to be sponsors and create opportunity for them. It's great when a mentor can be a sponsor, but they don't always go hand in hand. Or someone might just want someone to talk to once a quarter because they find them inspirational, or they're looking for a truthteller (we all need truthtellers). But each of these is a different kind of relationship.

As a mentor, I always try to ask a set of questions back. Why did you ask *me*? What is the connection that you see? What is it that you need help and support with? How are you planning on getting there? What are you willing to contribute? What is your expectation of what you're going to get out of the relationship? Is there a professional values alignment between us?

Some relationships slide almost imperceptibly into mentorships. Without a clear agreement or mention of the word *mentor*, we come to realize that the person we've occasionally asked for guidance has taken on a more influential role. But if you don't have that "accidental mentor," follow Rocki Howard's advice and formally ask for one. We all do better with someone in our court.

The only way mentoring works is that you've got to find somebody and grab hold of them; they're not looking for you.
—JEFFREY BRESLOW, author, sculptor, and toy designer

Help! I Don't Understand!

It was sneaky, I'll admit it. But it served a useful purpose.

For many years I led customer engagement and presentation seminars for companies exhibiting at trade shows. At one point in the program I'd firmly advise the audience not to use *UA's* when talking with prospects. This typically got blank or quizzical looks. I'd go on to mention UA's two or three times before the bravest in the group would ask, to everyone's relief, "What's a UA?"

"Unknown Acronyms."

Like I said, sneaky. But it made the point that if they, too, used jargon with their prospective customers, those prospects could be reluctant to ask for clarification and sales opportunities would be lost. And it followed that if these exhibitors heard prospects say something *they* didn't understand, they were to ask about it. Far from seeming stupid, they would come across as interested and professional: "Before I give you a demo, Marvin, what do you mean when you say you're 'K5'ing' your company's '3VTM' model? I want to be sure I understand."

Up to this point, *The Big Ask* has focused mostly on making courageous requests for assistance, permission, or opportunities. But "help me understand" can take similar courage. Who among us hasn't had brushes with rogophobia, the fear of asking questions? If I ask for the clarity I need, will I sound stupid? What if everybody knows the answer but me? What if my question is taken as a challenge that I didn't intend?

But silenced curiosity has consequences. A reluctance to ask for clarity at work or school can result in poor performance, if not something more serious. Elizabeth Even, now a nurse in the emergency department at Chicago's Northwestern Memorial Hospital, recalled a time at another hospital when a question became an intervention.

I had a doctor who ordered a fluid bolus for a patient who had an irregular, rapid heart rate. And it didn't make any sense to me because their heart was already stressed, so why would we make it work harder with all this fluid? I was fairly new at the time, and I remember asking the doctor, "I don't know, is this fluid going to help this problem? I'm not sure."

And the doctor, who was also new, looked at me and said, I don't know—I thought *you* knew." And so, we figured out then that both of us were new and needed to talk to someone who knew the answer, which we did. [The procedure] might have gone fine, or it might've caused more stress on the patient's heart or caused a decline for the patient. In anything, if you're not sure, ask.[6]

"Not sure? Ask!" is universally good advice. But as we discussed earlier in the book, asking is shaded by our psychology. *Was I supported or shamed for asking as a kid? Have I developed the self-esteem to advocate for my own needs? Would revealing my ignorance threaten my self-image or professional reputation?*

Asking questions often means having to knock the ego off its throne and admit we don't know something. It can be a test of whether we feel secure enough in ourselves or our leadership, to trust that seeking another's expertise or perspective will not make us smaller.

Dr. Michelle L. Buck is clinical professor of leadership at Kellogg School of Management at Northwestern University. Her students are MBAs, graduate students, and executives, whom she describes as having a lot of work and life experience. "And still," she says, "it's just human that people, for a lot of reasons, are sometimes nervous and reluctant to ask questions. So, I've changed the questions I ask."

I used to explain the assignments and then ask, "Are there any questions?" And there were *not* any questions, so I'd think, *Great, I did a good job explaining!*

Well, when the assignments were turned in, the expectations were apparently *not* clear to some students.

I now tend to say, "What questions do you have?" which intentionally presupposes that they *have* questions. "Where can I be more clear? What examples can I give?" Not everyone raises their hand, but I'm more likely to get some questions.

I think the most important question in any learning environment, particularly at the level of adult or executive learning, is the question "So what?" At the outset of my classes, I tell them, "If the relevance of anything I'm saying to your work and life and leadership is not clear, I'm counting on you to say, "So what?" And some of them take me up on that, which is great.

Through perspective-taking and remembering my own experiences as a student, I've changed the questions I ask and tried to create the conditions in which others are more likely to ask. That is the way that I approach leadership. In this case of asking or speaking up, I believe leaders are people who create the conditions that enable and empower the kind of behavior they hope to inspire in others.

Ask for Clarity

Not everyone is lucky to have a teacher or boss who goes out of their way to make it "safe" to ask. Maybe you, too, are among those Dr. Buck describes as "just human" and therefore reluctant to ask questions. If so, I offer the following questions to lessen the fear of seeming incompetent at work, school, or anywhere—while getting the clarification you need. (These are the kinds of questions I asked hundreds of content experts in various industries while writing their marketing and training media.)

Ask for simplicity. "This isn't my area of expertise. Could you put it in layman's terms?" or "What do you see as your most important point?"

Ask for examples. "Would you give an example of how that might play out?" or "How would that theory look in practice?"

Ask for a definition. "Just so I'm clear, how are you defining x?" or "When I hear x, to me it means x and y. Is that how you're defining it too?"

Ask for a picture. "I'm more of a visual learner. Could you literally draw a picture or diagram for me?" (which may need to be followed by "I see your graph, but could you break down what each piece means?").

Ask for a demo. "Would you show me how it works?" or "Mind if I video you going through each step?"

Ask for a role-play. "Would you role-play with me the kind of (behavior, dialogue, process, etc.) you're recommending?"

Ask for priority. "How would you prioritize the assignments you've just given me?" or "It would help me to know what you consider to be priority actions, and why, so we're on the same page."

Ask about the hurdles. "When *you* were first learning x, what seemed most confusing or challenging?" or "What are the biggest misconceptions people have about x?"

Pose a problem scenario. "How could I apply your solution in a situation like this _____?" (It's a fair question, but if they're a teacher they may encourage you to think for yourself by asking what you would do.)

State what you do understand. "I understand *a* and *b,* but I think I'm missing the connection between *b* and *c.* Could you fill in those blanks for me?"

"Own" the knowledge gap. "Pardon me if this was mentioned earlier, but (question)" or "I may have missed this detail in your instructions, but (question)."

Ask to confirm accuracy. "Here's what I heard you saying (summarize); does that track?" or "So, my take-aways are (summarize); is that accurate?"

Like "What's a UA?", the questions we ask are often those that others have too. And if they're not, so what? There's no shame in asking. There's always a fresh point of discovery for each of us. Unknowing must precede knowing. It may feel foolish in the moment to ask, but considering the consequences of ignorance, it's foolish *not* to ask.

I notice that my higher performing students aren't afraid to speak up, ask questions, and ask for help more than the struggling students do. Students somehow think it's wrong to ask for help, but I'm always promoting self-advocacy and telling them that asking for help is one of the most important things you can learn in school.
—CATHERINE BROWNSTONE-STILLWELL,
sixth-grade science and social studies teacher

The One with All the Answers

I thought it would be fun and fitting to close the chapter with a story from someone you don't know but will recognize … one who, contrary to our help-through-clarity theme of the last few pages didn't ask for answers but provided them. In fact, she answered more questions than anyone on the planet, at any time in human history, and with astounding speed and accuracy. (Hint: She made her debut on the Apple iPhone 4S.)

Here's Susan Bennett, better known as the original voice of "Siri" in North America, with the story of a request that changed everything for her.

> It took me two years before I "came out" to the public as the voice of Siri. My attitude was, I do auditions and do the work and love my work and move on to something else. I had never really intended to be famous. Up to the point that Siri was created, IVR [interactive voice response] recordings were basically anonymous.
>
> But when that voice is in this little computerized phone and has a persona and a personality, suddenly people are talking to "you" many, many times a day, sometimes hundreds of times a day, and so they get used to the sound of your voice. Sounds great, right? But I felt that my voice would be so ubiquitous and so well known that I wouldn't have opportunities to get other voice work.
>
> And another thing, too. In one episode of *The Big Bang Theory*, they were talking to Siri and when "Siri" shows up, she's this gorgeous, voluptuous redhead … and *I'm* just this little 60-plus woman! And I'm thinking, *Hmmm, I just don't know if I can handle all this.* But my husband and my son were both pestering me about it and said, "You are missing out on a unique opportunity. You've just got to forget about all that."

My biggest issue has always been fear, and I think it's because I was raised by very cautious, fearful people. But they were born in 1912. They lived through a flu pandemic, two world wars, and a major depression, so it makes sense. I grew up around that attitude of *Protect yourself. Be careful.* And, of course, for a performer, that's not necessarily great advice because we have to put ourselves out there and take chances.

Now, I have been very fortunate in my life, and don't recall having to ask for all that much. But my biggest ask was asking my son to help me figure out how to make being the voice of Siri work for me. I had finally decided to reveal myself, but I wasn't sure how to go about it. He really came through for me.

He was living in Los Angeles at the time, and I didn't know anyone there. I asked him to do a little networking for me and find some people to help me promote my voice. Through a friend, he found an agency, Vox Inc. With Vox's help I did a lot of TV appearances—CNN, *To Tell the Truth*, *The Queen Latifah Show*, radio and podcast interviews, etc.

Having Vox behind me gave me a lot of confidence, but I'm still surprised when people are thrilled to meet "Siri." It's always kind of felt like a happy accident. But they'd never have known the voice was mine if I hadn't decided to take a chance, put myself out there, and ask my son for help.[7]

In the spirit of the ask that changed everything for Susan Bennett, voice of the original virtual assistant, I asked ChatGPT to generate a short poem about asking for help. An eyeblink later, this:

> In asking, fears dissolve like mist,
> As souls, once strangers, coexist.
> And in the act of seeking aid,
> A deeper, truer bond is made.

CHAPTER THIRTEEN

WANT FEEDBACK?

There is always space for improvement,
no matter how long you've been in the business.
—OSCAR DE LA HOYA, holder of 11 world boxing titles

"A FEW YEARS AGO, TOM BROKAW INTERVIEWED ME FOR a piece on Facebook," writes Sheryl Sandberg in her bestseller *Lean In*. "Tom is a magnificent interviewer, and I felt that I stumbled through some of my answers. After we wrapped, I asked him how I could have done better. He seemed surprised by my question, so I asked him again. He then told me that in his entire career, I was only the second person to ask him for feedback."

What stops us from asking for honest assessments of our performance, behavior, or ideas? Once again, the answer is fear. Fear of appearing unsure or obliging people to find something nice to say. Fear of their disapproval or handing them the power to influence us. Fear of hearing something we'll disagree with or that slams us with doubt. Fear of ... oh, you get the idea. If fears were dollars, we'd all be millionaires.

But the best, most helpful feedback is more than "thumbs up-thumbs down." It's a gift of insight, a glimpse of the strengths and weaknesses that may be hiding in our blind spots. In whatever ways we wish to learn and grow, perceptive, honest feedback speeds our progress.

Think of the various orbits in which you work and live. What aspects of your impact are you curious about? Whose feedback could help you become a better employee, leader, student, parent, or romantic partner? Although we'll focus mostly on the world of work, you can apply these feedback guidelines anywhere you want to understand your impact. We'll follow that discussion with a look at what happens when leaders, too, ask—not only for feedback, but for the wisdom of those they lead.

Take Charge

In *Thanks for the Feedback*, authors Douglas Stone and Sheila Heen report that asking for feedback at work "has been linked to higher job satisfaction, greater creativity on the job, faster adaptation in a new organization or role, and lower turnover." Just as encouraging, they find that pointedly asking for *negative* feedback with a question like, "What's one thing you see me doing, or failing to do, that you think I should change (or is getting in my own way)?" can result in higher performance ratings.[1] After all, who but a humble, confident, conscientious, flexible, and motivated person would ask such a question?

Requesting feedback puts you in charge of your own growth and development. If you're already a feedback-seeker, you know it's wiser to ask for it than assume that hearing nothing means you're doing fine. And it's far more empowering to ask than "wait to be told." In fact, you might wait for a very long time, because those responsible to give feedback may take pains to avoid it. A New York

University study found that people felt anxious whether giving or getting feedback, but when feedback was *asked for*, both the giver and receiver felt more comfortable. We're also likely to listen more carefully and act on feedback we've requested.[2]

Incidentally, a team of researchers found that people who were asked for "feedback" mostly offered judgements (likes and dislikes) whereas those asked for "advice" gave more input about possible actions the feedback seekers could take in the future.[3] Whatever you choose to call it, here's how to make the process more productive.

Ask the right people. Based on the kind of feedback you want, who is qualified to give it? Are there people in other departments, or of different ranks, whose perspectives could be helpful? Could the perspectives of novices or outsiders be informative in some way? Tell them why *their* feedback (as opposed to Joe Blow's) would be helpful to you.

Ask at the right time. If asking for feedback about past presentations, meetings, or other events, ask within a day or two of their completion. The further you get from the event the less people will remember about it. Want feedback on something in development, such as a proposal or project? Ask for it while you still have time to make changes. Those whose feedback you invite early might even turn into collaborators or champions who expand the visibility of your efforts.

Prime yourself. The unpredictability of feedback can put us on edge. Make a pact with yourself to stay calm and curious regardless of what you hear. Decide that you won't interrupt, attack, or "freeze out" the person if you disagree with their assessment. Shift into neutral. Relax your jaw. Let your tongue drop from the roof of your mouth. Soften your gaze. Unfold your arms. Ask and listen with an open mind.

State your need clearly. Unless you're scoping out a general impression, such as "How am I doing so far?" or "What did you think of my email to Mom?", be specific about the feedback you want and why you want it. Example: "My goal is to get into management, which means showing I can think strategically. Based on my input in the meeting this morning, how would you assess me as a strategic thinker?"

Make it safe for them. Help reluctant feedback givers by modeling the kind of candor you want from them. Open with a self-critique. Example: "I recently became aware of a blind spot, my tendency to complain without regard for the impact on everyone else, which I'm now committed to change. I value your honesty and am curious to know what other aspects of my communication I could tweak or overhaul to make me easier to work with." Another way to make it safe for them is to express genuine appreciation for their feedback regardless of what you hear.

Ask open questions. Closed (yes/no) questions discourage elaboration. Invite detailed responses by asking open questions, such as:
  "What advice do you have for me regarding ___?"
  "What are your suggestions for how I can improve ___?"
  "What do you see as my strengths in ___?"
  "What could I have done differently or better in ___?"
  "How am I meeting/not meeting expectations in ___?"
  "What is the target and how close am I to hitting it?"
  "Where do I stand in relation to others' performance?"

Ask for clarification. Are their comments too general? Ask for specifics.
  "You say my portfolio is 'promising but not quite there.' Would you say more about what it needs?"
  "Can you help me understand my low score for 'engagement'?"

"Could you give me *examples* of when I haven't followed through on my commitments?"

"I admit to feeling shocked hearing that, but can you help me understand what's created the impression that I shift the blame to others?"

"I'm glad you think my designs are 'amazing'—what is it that makes them amazing for you?"

Limit the scope. What if they start sharing opinions about additional areas for your improvement? Unless you're dealing with a boss, tell them you want to focus, for now, only on the feedback you asked for. The asker sets the parameters.

Neutralize the jab. Personal put-downs don't belong in feedback. But if you hear them, keep listening. Despite the rough remarks, are they making valid points? Ignore the jab and "act as if" the feedback is impersonal and constructive.

> *Giver:* Half the time you just sit there *totally useless* while the rest of us figure out the logistics.
>
> *Receiver:* You're wanting me to take a more active role in logistics.
>
> *Giver:* Yes.

In close relationships, however, you may want to explore, not ignore the emotions behind a jab. Show that you're willing to get to the heart of the matter, which may be deeper than the issue they initially present.

> *Receiver:* I can hear your frustration, Travis. Is there more you want to tell me about that?

Ask for coaching. Some improvements won't happen without help. "Learn as you go" is fine if you have the time and the risks are few, but coaching—whether a one-off conversation with the boss or support from an expert—is the most efficient route to performing at the level you desire. Ask for it!

Summarize and plan. Briefly summarize the feedback you heard and say what you'll do to act on it. Brian Little, vice president and global head of corporate human resources for Intel, suggests …

> One of the things I do very intentionally is write their feedback down on a pad of paper because it shows the feedback was important to me. It's both an acknowledgement and a thank-you. And when I'm *really* on my game, I type up my notes and send a note back to them saying, "This is what we talked about, I really appreciate it—is there anything else you'd like to add?" And every now and then they're like, "Wow, that was great—yes, here are a few more things." Once you develop that loop, your performance increases dramatically in the areas you're trying to improve.

Respectfully disagree. If you disagree with the assessment and aren't obligated to act on it, consider "I'm not completely sold on your evaluation, but I appreciate you sharing it with me." Or keep your response noncommittal, such as "You have a point, thank you" or simply "Thanks for the feedback." But before you discount their opinion, allow for some "Know Yourself" reflection to see if your ego isn't trying to shield itself from valid criticism.

Check your motives. At work, home, or anywhere, seeking feedback *too often* on your behavior or performance can be a red flag for people-pleasing, a way of asking, *How can I change so that you'll like/love/approve of me?* Don't give others the power to determine your self-worth. If you grew up playing the peacekeeper, downplaying or denying your needs in the hope of easing conflict, this red flag deserves your attention.

How would it feel to take the initiative and ask, not wait for feedback? How might asking for feedback change the way others perceive you? And what might you gain by asking and acting on their feedback?

> Take the attitude of a student, never be too big to ask
> questions, never know too much to learn something new.
> —MAYA ANGELOU, author, poet, activist

Ask the Customer. *Cynthia Barnes is an entrepreneur and founder of the National Association of Women Sales Professionals.*

One of the ways for us to show up as our best selves is to elicit the feedback of other people. What can I do to improve? And you don't want those people to say, "Oh, you're fine." No. You're looking for the constructive feedback.

So, after that first interaction you want to follow up in two days, two weeks, and two months—that's the magic formula. So, two days after the product is delivered, I ask, "How's it going? What about the experience of buying do we (or I) do well? For the next time, what can I improve on?"

Two weeks after that: "So, you've had a chance to use the service. What do you like about it? If you could change anything, if I brought you to our product development team, what would you change?" And they might say what that would be. [Then I would say] "Thank you so much. I wrote those things down and I'm going to take it back to our team to see what we can do about that."

Two months in: "How are things going? What do you like, what can we improve on?" Never what you 'dislike,' but "What can we improve on?"

They're shocked that I actually pick up the phone and call and ask. Because I care. I don't send a survey. *I* want to know. So, because we have that relationship it makes them feel comfortable enough to say, "You know, Cynthia, I really like this and this and wish we could do [something else] differently."

I *want* that feedback.[4]

What Did You See in Him? *Errol McLendon is a Chicago-based actor, director, and storyteller.*

I've acted and directed, so I understand the courage of asking a director for feedback as well as the respect of a director giving an honest answer. If as an actor I don't get cast, I'll call the director and leave a voicemail saying exactly what I'm looking for: "I know you've cast someone else in the role. It's one I would've loved to have played, and I appreciate you giving me some time to show you what I'd do in that role. Because I'm committed to polishing my audition techniques, would you be willing to share with me what it was that you saw in the actor you cast that you didn't see in me?"

The answer can be brutal, but I always take what they say and assess whether it's applicable or not. If the director doesn't return the call, I leave it at that.

Passed up for a job or promotion? Ask for feedback or advice that might help you become a stronger candidate next time. Even if you privately disagree with their assessment, you'll have shown a willingness to listen and learn that puts you in a positive light.

Ask for Feedback from Those You Lead

The most effective leaders ask for feedback up, down, and across their organizations. In a study of over 50,000 executives, those who asked for feedback *the least* were rated at the 15th percentile in overall leadership effectiveness, whereas those who diligently asked for feedback ranked at the 86th percentile.[5]

Leaders like these, who make seeking feedback routine, would score high on curiosity, humility, and flexibility. Leaders who lack these qualities, or who rarely ask for feedback, may get only guarded comments topped with pretty bows. After all, why should their direct reports risk reprisals when they have mortgages and college loans? If the leader hasn't earned their trust, it's "Great idea!" and "You're doing just fine, boss!"

If you hold a position of power, how can you gain people's trust to give you honest feedback?

You can commit to become curious, humble, and flexible.

You can follow the "Make it safe for them" guidelines in this chapter, including self-critique and appreciation for those who give you feedback.

Encourage candor and listen openly to even your harshest critics.

Strive to make continuous learning a prime value in your leadership, so that you not only get better at asking for feedback but using what you learn to flourish as a person and a leader.

By seeking feedback and embracing growth, you have the potential to not only transform yourself but inspire meaningful change in others.

Ask, Don't Tell

Asking for and acting on performance feedback makes leaders better. And so does asking for employees' insights, ideas, and concerns. According to Dr. Michelle L. Buck, clinical professor of leadership at Kellogg School of Management at Northwestern University, there are at least two benefits when leaders ask questions of their workers.

> One is that they're likely to get information that they don't have access to, because the workers are the ones who are closest to the client or the product or service, and the leaders will be enlightened by the information they gain. The second benefit is that no matter what the answers are, there's a significant motivational boost when people feel that they're being asked and that their opinion counts.

Leaders who engage employees stay on top of what's going on in the organization and in the minds of the people who make it run. And those people feel validated and more invested. This dynamic is more than a "nice idea"—it's been shown to reduce turnover and safety incidents and increase productivity and profitability.[6] But according to G. Dan Lumpkin, many leaders fail to ask for, or seriously consider, employee input. Dan is a Certified Management Consultant (CMC) and president of Lumpkin & Associates, a management consulting firm in Fairhope, Alabama. Some who move into positions of leadership, he said, believe their primary job is to tell employees what to think and do, rather than ask for their ideas and collaboration.

"People get so used to telling as they come up the ranks," he said. "But in a lot of tell-oriented cultures, many [employees] are afraid to ask or even to speak up. They feel like they're being told, 'If we want your opinion, we'll beat it out of you—otherwise shut up.'"

The consequences are predictable. Dr. Buck warns that when employees "feel their opinion does not count, they sometimes give up trying to offer it, they become disengaged, and sometimes they quit." And that should concern employers, because silenced workers may not volunteer ideas that could benefit the business or even save it from ruin. (It was this reluctance to speak up that factored into the worst airline disaster in history, in which a KLM crew, trained to defer to authority, failed to forcefully voice their concerns about their captain's misguided orders. See https://tinyurl.com/2bvk7tjr.)

But, just like asking for performance feedback, it's up to leaders to not only ask for employees' input but make it safe for them to do so without fear of ridicule or reprisals. Dan Lumpkin explains the key to engagement:

> The best leaders are the ones who take a breath and ask questions. Asking is the #1 skill that I teach the top executives that I coach. It's about listening more than you speak, asking instead of telling. Because the very nature of questioning is, I get to hear how you're thinking. It's the ability to not just ask but listen, verbally and nonverbally, to participate in the dialogue to make the person feel heard and understood. Leadership is about earning the right to lead people and become merchants of hope. It's leaders like that, who ask more than tell, who can help others become better individuals and, therefore, better employees.[7]

Ask Everybody. *Bridget Piekarz is recently retired from 40 years in publishing and bookselling.*

My last employer was the best example of an ask-me-anything culture. Every few years they had different steering committees, groups handpicked from all different parts of the company, people who'd worked here six months or 30 years. And we were asked to start thinking about what's not being done here. What would be cool to do? And, hey, *What if?* Nothing was off the table. There were things that came out of that that became part of the corporate culture.

The last two years of the pandemic, our CEO and the president of our division both held monthly town meetings and asked us, What do *you* want to hear from us? Do you have any ideas you'd like to propose? What can we do differently? It was the healthiest corporate culture I could ever have imagined.

Ask the Students. *Mark Elliott is a private voice teacher and faculty member at The Theatre School at DePaul University.*

As someone who is resistant to being told what to do, I find it much more effective to ask questions and let the students' answers guide our work. When one of them has finished a song or an exercise, the first question I ask is, "How did you do?" I want to encourage them to honor their own opinion before overlaying anyone else's, including mine.

I tell them that the only fair way to answer my question, "How did you do?", is to remember what they set out to do and then measure how close they came to that goal. Asking for their assessment helps them clarify their intention for the next attempt. Soon, meeting their goal not only becomes possible but routine.

Ask the Patients. *Dr. Janyce Agruss is a nurse practitioner and faculty member at Rush University College of Nursing.*

As an educator and a practicing health care provider, it's important to me that I have a discourse with my students, patients, and colleagues. Before responding to their questions, I'll frequently first ask their opinion about what *they* think, because I respect them, want to empower them, and make them feel we are a team.

For example, people who don't like taking cholesterol medications often ask, "Do I really have to take it?" My first response is to ask them about their hesitation—"What's concerning you?"—and listen. Then, rather than just tell them to take the medication, I might ask, "Well, what do you think about your numbers?" or "What will happen if you don't take the medication?" It's empowering when the answers come from them instead of me.

Lastly, could Ask, Don't Tell be effective in parenting? Might helping kids find their own answers and solutions instill in them a greater sense of autonomy and accountability? Yes. And sometimes in surprising ways. Bruce Feiler, author of several bestsellers including *The Secrets of Happy Families*, writes that instead of dictating the rewards for good behavior or the consequences for bad, he and his wife ask their children to come up with their own. "Far from being lax," he wryly notes, "our girls turn out to be little Stalins. We constantly have to dial them back."[8]

Where do you have opportunities as a boss, teacher, parent, friend or family member to get better results by asking, not telling? In what situations might you benefit from collaborating, not commanding? Who, if asked to come up with their own solutions, might come running to you less often?

In these troubled times, we don't need more command and control; we need better means to engage everyone's intelligence in solving challenges and crises as they arise.
—MARGARET J. WHEATLEY, writer and educator

CHAPTER FOURTEEN

ASKING FOR TROUBLE?

... we carry our worst enemies within us.
—CHARLES SPURGEON, English Baptist preacher

NONE OF US PLANS TO TAKE AN AXE TO OUR ASK. But we do it anyway. Absent the skills covered in Chapter 6, we might approach the decision maker with the wrong attitude, ignore their interests, or veil our request in vagueness. But the surest way to turn our wishes to splinters is by asking in ways that make people too resentful to say yes.

Whenever we ask from a place of unchecked frustration, anger, or judgement, we risk destroying two things: the goodwill of those we ask and the chances of getting what we want. In short, we're asking for trouble. In this chapter, we'll explore how we sabotage our desires by asking carelessly, or by believing we've asked when we haven't asked at all.

Harry Holds It In

Amelia is having coffee with her brother Harry on the first day of her five-day visit. Harry suggests activities she might enjoy during her stay, including a movie night and various outings with his two children. Almost as an afterthought, he mentions that he's bowling with his league tonight. Amelia proposes to take the kids out for pizza while Harry enjoys his bowling night.

Harry frowns. "Do whatever you want," he snaps.

Amelia is stung. And confused. "Did I say something wrong?"

"Nope."

She tries again. "I'm sorry, Harry, is it about the pizza? Because I can treat the kids to something healthier ..."

"The kids love pizza," he says, forcing a smile, then abruptly changes the subject.

Ok, psychics, why is Harry in a snit? What is he failing to ask or express? If we could telepathically hear his thoughts, they might sound something like:

> *I really wanted Amelia to hang out with me tonight, watch me bowl, and meet the guys. I didn't ask her because I didn't want her to feel pressured, and yet, if she said no I'd feel angry, and I don't like confrontation. But I also feel like if she really cared about me, she would've wanted to show me a little support tonight, without my having to ask. Maybe she'll get the hint.*

Harry could've directly communicated his wants. He could've asked, "Come watch me bowl tonight?" or asserted "I'd love for you to come along." Instead, he made a cutting remark to punish his sister for not reading his mind and then denied having done so—a classic "hit and run." Amelia's visit is off to a rocky start.

Harry's behavior is an act of passive aggression, an indirect expression of hostility. A common example is the silent treatment, in which we leave others to figure out our unspoken wants and feelings and then pounce on them when they don't attempt to guess or guess incorrectly (think of a trip-wired room: one wrong move and *snap!*). It's a self-defeating maneuver that leaves both parties feeling on edge and resentful.

The choice to sit on our ask may be rooted in the kinds of old, barnacled beliefs we looked at in Chapters 3–5: *Who am I to ask? Asking is selfish. People don't care about what I feel or want. I'm not going to get what I want anyway, so why bother asking? I shouldn't have to ask; my needs and wants should be obvious,* etc. But if we believe we're unworthy or "above" asking, or feel it's unsafe,* we won't ask. Instead, we'll do our best to suppress those needs or try to manipulate others into giving us what we want, like Harry did.

If you don't ask for what you want, don't expect to get it, and don't blame others for not giving what you don't ask for. Ask yourself:

What if others really don't know what I'm wanting or feeling?

What if their failure to read my needs is not a lack of regard for me but evidence that I need to speak up for myself?

How is my choice to withhold expressing what I want a form of self-sabotage that ensures my frustration and reinforces my feeling of victimhood or core belief that *I'm always disappointed?*

What would it take for me to ask directly for what I feel, want, need, or expect? And how would I feel about myself by doing that?

For those in abusive relationships at home or work, the choice to not speak up about wants and feelings may be a survival strategy. If this applies to you, consider seeking professional help. See Resources.

Like any new behavior, becoming more assertive takes study and practice.* If you're not used to being upfront about your wants, you'll feel self-conscious, at first, and may not "ask well." Anxiety around asking can result in requests that sound demanding instead of assertive—"I would like your help staining the fence PLEASE!"—or that end with apologies—"…if that's ok with you." Start by asking for small things and be patient with yourself. You'll soon get better at it.

What's the Unspoken Ask?

Needs expressed in off-putting ways are likely to go unmet—or at the very least trigger resistance. The examples in the left column are not requests but emotionally charged reactions. (The first one is *phrased* as a request, but its guilt-inducing "poor-me/shame-on-you" tone is coercive.) The right column shows what each desire could sound like as either a request or assertive statement. Note the respect for self and others that comes through in the right column.

INSTEAD OF …	ASK OR ASSERT …
Shaming: I know you have better things to do, but maybe you could spare a few minutes to come visit me in the hospital? I'll pay for your parking.	I would love to see you while I'm laid up here. Any chance you could stop by sometime this week?
Scolding: The *previous* tenants were always courteous enough to remove their lint from the dryer screens.	We've all got into the habit of scraping the lint screens so they're clean for the next person. Could I ask you to do the same?

---

*For recommended reading on assertive communication see Resources.

INSTEAD OF ...	ASK OR ASSERT ...
Sniping: Must be nice to just sit there while I do all the work.	I could use your help. Give me a hand?
Snapping: Do not interrupt me while I'm busy, do you understand?	I need an hour to focus on my project. Let's talk after that.
Slamming: Does publicly correcting my grammar make you feel superior?	When you corrected my grammar in front of the team today, I felt embarrassed and angry because it made me look foolish.
Silent Treatment: "_____."	Normally your humor cheers me up, Mike, but it hurt when you called me "old man." Can we agree to keep that one off limits?
Whining: Why'd they seat us so close to the kitchen? It's so noisy here. This table wobbles. The AC's blowing right on us. Just our rotten luck.	We'd like a different table, please.
Panicking: Ohmygod! I'm only one person! I can't lead the webinar and handle the ten-thousand technical issues that might come up!	If I focus on leading the webinar, would you be able to troubleshoot any technical glitches that come up?

When you catch yourself about to react in ways you'd cringe about later, take a few deep breaths. Focus on what you really want in that moment. Ask yourself:

- What is my true desire, need, or expectation right now?

- Will I communicate it as a request or an assertive statement?

- How will I convey it in a way that respects myself *and* the person I'm asking?

Assertion messages. The example of the person upset about the public correction of their grammar (right column) is a three-part assertion message:

1. Factually describe the negative behavior (without inferring a motive or blasting their character): "When you corrected my grammar in front of the team today ..."

2. Tell how their action made you feel: "I felt embarrassed and angry ..."

3. Describe the effect on you or others: "... because it made me look foolish."

In the best cases, the person will acknowledge they understand the negative impact of their behavior and commit to not repeating it. But if they're silent, add a fourth step:

4. Ask for change: "If you feel the need to correct my grammar, I ask that you speak with me in private."

After your request, be silent. Pull back from any impulse to repeat or over-explain it. If you get no response, ask for one: "Do I have your agreement?", "Your response is important to me", "Will you do that for me?", etc.

Asking or Nagging?

Asking doesn't guarantee getting. People may say no directly. Or they may say it indirectly by saying yes and then doing nothing. Some might say yes and sabotage your request by fulfilling it badly, or broodingly, to discourage you from asking again.

It's frustrating when someone consistently snubs your requests. The mounting frustration can turn you into a badgering nag or a timebomb. Are you the problem? Is it them? How might you both be contributing to the situation?

Although nagging is a universal behavior, I asked New York-based psychotherapist Rachel Sussman about its effects on couples. A writer and nationally recognized relationship expert, Rachel has appeared on the Today Show, Good Morning America, and CNN, and has been featured in publications including *The New York Times* and *The Wall Street Journal*. "Over time," she said, "nagging wears down the bond between a couple. They don't feel heard, respected, or understood. They get a chip on their shoulders, which can produce more fights."

> In the relationship space, some people are so uncomfortable asking, and sometimes they don't even realize they're not asking. What I often do with my individual clients is coach them on how to speak to a partner about something they're uncomfortable or not happy with in the relationship. A lot of times, people make the mistake of not asking the right way. Maybe they're doing it in a way that puts the person down, that shames them. So, what I often do with my clients is help coach them on how to ask for what they need, but in a way that's solution-focused.
>
> Take for example some of the things that men and women nag each other about. Let's say the husband never cleans up after himself and the wife often wakes up to a

kitchen that's a disaster. And she'll say, "How many times have I told you, if you leave dirty dishes out, we're gonna get bugs!" When you shame someone, nothing good comes from it. And the next thing you know, it's a big fight.

So, what's the alternative?

> I might encourage them to say something like, "Hey, can I talk to you about something? It's so important to me to have an organized, clean home, and I think there are many benefits for both of us to keep things clean and organized. It would mean everything to me if you could partner with me and we could talk about what that means to both of us. And if there's some things that you need me to do differently, I'm happy to do that as well."
>
> The way I often put it, is to try to let your partner see the vision of how things can be, and that there's something for both of you to benefit by what you are asking for.

I asked Rachel what a win-win example might sound like.

> Let's use the same couple. The win-win is that the husband finally hears her explain why it's important to her, and he says, "I get it now—I can try harder." And she feels heard and validated, and says, "Thank you so much. Is there anything that *I* can do?"
>
> And he says, "Well, yeah, as long as you're bringing it up, you know, in the morning you never make enough coffee, and I always have to make coffee a second time. If you could just make a little more coffee in the morning, that would save me a good 10 minutes." And then they both do this for each other, maybe as a favor, and they feel cared for. And they feel heard. And the relationship gets better.[1]

Rachel said that some of her clients admit, after a breakup or divorce, that there was a certain area in which they never got their needs met. "And it comes down to they didn't ask for it, or didn't know how to ask, or tried to ask and were turned down and didn't have the confidence to end the relationship."

Not asking for what we want can send the message that we don't trust our partner's willingness or ability to come through for us. When they sense our low expectations, they meet them, and the bond weakens. But the mutual (and patient) work of clearly communicating needs and expectations can bring back the pulse not only in romance but in business, family, and other connections. (For help in communicating with children, I highly recommend *How to Talk So Kids Will Listen & Listen So Kids Will Talk* by Adele Faber & Elaine Mazlish.)

In what relationships would you and others benefit from communicating clear needs and transparent asks?

Danger: Criticisms Disguised as Questions

Why asks for reasons. The question may spring from innocent curiosity, such as a child asking, "Why are there cows?" Less endearingly, *why* is disapproval: "Why did you say that?" "Why are you doing that?" "Why are you like that?" *Why* makes us feel criticized and judged. Looking down the barrel of a weaponized *why* means we won't be answering the question so much as *answering to* the person asking it.

Here's a three-part formula that might look familiar. (My how-to format is purely tongue in cheek.)

1. To make a fault-finding remark about your listener, pose it as a question that you're "just curious" about:

"Why do you wear your hair like that?"
"Why don't you try to be more of a team player?"
"Why *that* tattoo?"

2. When your listener reacts negatively, act surprised. "Why are you so sensitive? I only asked a question!"

3. When they erupt at that comment, put on a sad face and say, "This is why I can't say *anything* to you."

Tip: To achieve full mastery, begin the interaction with the baiting question, "Can I ask you something?" Continue to Steps 1–3.

Danger: Requests that Presume Consent

I was at dinner with friends when the host's five-year-old son asked, "Could I have another piece of cake probably?" We all laughed but had to admire the way he embedded the answer in the question, like a sales rep's "presumptive close" that frames the deal as already done. But apart from kids and salespeople, asking in ways that presume consent is maddening. The message of a presumptive ask is, "I'm sure it would be no big deal for you to be of service to me."

"You wouldn't mind if the kids stay with you this weekend, right?"

"You can practically design logos in your sleep, so I figure you could maybe whip one out for me at, you know, the family rate?"

"Could you just swing by and pick up me up for the offsite meeting tomorrow—I'm less than three miles from you."

Even if we expect a yes, an ask that presumes consent can offend. If the offended person says yes anyway, then they'll be *resentfully* watching our kids, designing our logos, and picking us up. No, thanks!

Danger: Leading the Witness

Wouldn't you agree that this question I'm asking is intended only to get you to nod your head? I'm directing you to the answer I want, *aren't I?* And you probably find it a little irritating, *don't you?* These are leading questions, similar in impact to the presumptive requests we just discussed.

Leading questions are not "bad," they are the effective tools of the trade for teachers: "Children, we must pay attention in class, mustn't we?"; salespeople: "It makes sense to save money, doesn't it?"; trial attorneys: "In fact, you never came home that night, did you!"; and caring friends: "Wouldn't it be safer to drive *away* from the tsunami?" In each case, the speaker is prompting the listener to respond with the yes (or no, in the case of the trial attorney) the speaker wants to hear.

But in some contexts, leading questions can seem controlling or condescending. Nobody who's trying to sort out complicated feelings wants to hear, "Wouldn't it be better to end the relationship?" And "After all, you don't want to fail, do you?" will poison even the best advice. Oxen may be agreeable to being led by the nose, but people, not so much.

Danger: Accusing Before Asking

We've all done it: righteously accused somebody only to discover their innocence in the matter. Suddenly we feel ridiculous standing there in our angry suit of armor, broadsword raised. Face scalded with embarrassment, we apologize in a small voice and creep away, chainmail clanking noisily.

When we believe we've been wronged, it's not easy to calmly pull out our little detective's notepad and methodically investigate the facts. And yet, it takes much less time to ask for their side of the story than repair a relationship damaged by wrongful accusations. Itching to accuse? Take a breath. Get curious. State what's troubling you. Then be silent or invite their response.

> "There's something I'm hoping you can clear up for me. Here's what I heard ..."

> "The cash balance didn't match your report. Know where the error might be?"

> "Do you know who's leaving cigarette butts in the yard?"

> "I noticed you rolling your eyes when I was talking at lunch. Was it in response to something I said?"

There's no guarantee you'll get honest answers. But by giving them the benefit of the doubt you'll be modeling the respect you expect from them. The next three storytellers have some insight into this.

The Respectful Rep. *Name Withheld by Request.*

When I was the director of customer service for a manufacturing company, we had about 32 customer service reps and 120 sales reps. Invariably with a company of its size, a sales rep would call every day about a problem a customer had complained to them about. Just as predictably, the salespeople would take the customer's word and assume the customer service rep had made a mistake.

But one sales rep was an exception. He would call me and say, "I visited the customer, and this is what they told me happened. Will you talk to your customer service rep, find out as much as you can about what transpired and let me know?"

He was the only one who asked for all the details rather than accused, and I think the respect he earned went a long way in his career. He moved from a district sales manager to regional sales manager to vice president of sales, and for over 20 years was president and CEO. His non-accusatory approach made a big impression on me, setting the example as to how I handled myself with others.

Truth in the Middle. *Kathryn Hutchinson, a former high school teacher, is an award-winning poet and editor-in-chief of a poetry journal.*

A question I loved hearing from parents at conferences was: "What can we do at home to help our child succeed in your class?" In an ideal world, a parent would not automatically believe that what their child says about a teacher or class is true. The parent would want to understand the teacher's perspective, asking and listening with an open mind rather than being defensive for the child's sake.

This isn't to say there aren't poor teachers or that teachers never make mistakes. But too often parents come into a conflict-resolution situation assuming their child did nothing wrong, and that it's all the teacher's fault. The truth is usually somewhere in the middle, and asking to find a compromise or solution with the child's best interests in mind is the best outcome.

A Delicate Ask. *Elizabeth Even is a nurse in the emergency department at Northwestern Memorial Hospital, in Chicago.*

I wouldn't question someone on a surgical procedure because I'm not a surgeon. But I would question a medication order or something if my experience has proven it might not be a good idea. I might say something like, "I have a quick question about this," or "Can you educate me on this?" I kind of play dumb sometimes, like, "Isn't that for this?" Or "I've never seen that done that way, can you tell me about that?" I try to phrase it in a way that's not adversarial. It's "Teach me," rather than to make them wrong.[2]

Don't Be an Askhole

When does asking cross the line and become rude, obnoxious, or otherwise inappropriate? When does an ask make you an askhole? Top 10:

1. Asking for what you wouldn't do for others.

2. Treating the person with respect only when asking them for something.

3. Asking about things that are none of your business. "Wow, how much did that ring set you back?" or "So, what's the medical procedure you're having?"

4. Tacking zingers onto otherwise respectful requests. "Would you clean the grill today—*or do I have to do it myself?*" or "Would you join us for the committee meeting—*for once?*"

5. Starting the request with a pressure tactic. "We're family, and family should have always help each other out, am I right?" or "Remember when I did you that favor?"

6. Asking questions that undermine people's confidence or accomplishments. "Are you sure you're the kind of man she wants?" or "How did you manage to get that promotion?"

7. Asking questions to engage people who don't want your attention. "Hey, baby, why don't you smile?"

8. Inquiring about someone's ethnicity by asking, "What are you?" or "Where do you come from?"

9. Asking someone with different political views, "Why do you hate our country?"

10. Always asking others to do what you're capable of doing yourself. "Would you change the printer cartridge? I'm so bad with technology!"

If you find yourself doing any of these things, STOP—you're being an askhole!

Did You Really Just Ask Me That? Biased Questions

We all have biases, those assumptions about, and preferences for or against, a particular culture, race, gender, age, belief, religion, socioeconomic class, etc. Research shows that we remain unaware of our biases until they are pointed out to us. If you're like most, you've casually said or asked something that your listener then informed you had left them feeling slighted or marginalized.

James Catchpole, author of *What Happened to You?*, based on his experiences of having one leg, said, "The problem wasn't me, the problem was the intrusive questions, the simple rule that you don't ask personal questions of a stranger, which is somehow not being applied to people with disabilities."[3] Dealing with unwanted questions is something our next lineup of storytellers have in common with James Catchpole, though each in different ways.

Please Don't Ask That. *Dr. Sonja Kelly is vice president of research and learning for Women's World Banking.*

There's this new layer of bias that I've experienced as a mother that is so stunning to me. For example, the question, at a conference, "Who is taking care of your kids while you're here?" I don't like that question because it's very gendered, and I don't hear it being asked of my male colleagues. The underlying implication is that a woman who works outside of her home finds it difficult to take care of her children.

Why Do You Ask That? *Rocki Howard, a former chief diversity officer, is founder of Diversiology.IO.*

I try to go through the world assuming positive intent. But when we're asked a question that makes us feel uncomfortable, we have the right to ask questions back to ascertain the intent. If I had a big afro and someone asked to touch my hair, I might say, without being snarky, "That's an unusual request. I'm just curious—why would you want to do that?"

There was a time in my life when I wore dreadlocks. And people would ask me questions, like, did I wash my hair, was it clean, etcetera. And those were cross-cultural questions.

Sometimes people ask questions out of an authentic need to understand, but sometimes it's like, "Oh, you have locks, so your hair must be dirty." A lot of times your gut will tell you their intent.

There's a question I've been asked as a Black woman that I feel most people wouldn't have been asked, and I've been asked it more than once: "Do your children have the same father?" Because I have four children. I've been asked that question by a complete stranger where I just looked at them and said, "You know what, I'm going to choose to not answer that question." Because, exactly what are they trying to get to? What difference would my answer make? I want the person to question themselves a little bit, like, "Why am I asking this?"[4]

Assumed Competence. *Jim Lew is a former teacher, psychotherapist, trainer, and public speaker.*

Biased questions happen all the time. I was a theatre major, yet so many friends would say, "Would you come over and look at my Mac computer?" And I'd say, "Why do you ask me that? I don't know more about computers than the average consumer. Is it because I'm Asian?" And they'd go, "Well …" and stumble around. That's a common phenomenon in my life. Asians have some negative stereotypes, but I don't take the brunt of it like my Black or brown friends do.[5]

Undermining Question. *Sonya Perez-Lauterbach is a leadership coach and speaker.*

I went into the CEO's office and told him about a program I was developing. I presented all the reasons it was good for our organization and our donor base, the various markets it would bring in, and that I really wanted to run it. And the first question he asked me was, "What was your GPA in college?"

It completely threw me off and put me on the defensive.

The question I wish I'd asked him was, "Can you explain how that is relevant to the work at hand?" Because, by asking me for that qualification he seemed to be imposing the kind of arbitrary hurdle that I, as a woman and Latina, had experienced before. No matter how ridiculous the question, it does impact one's confidence, sense of belonging, and willingness to pursue opportunities in the future.

Truth is, I'll never know his motives for asking that or whether he asked everyone who pitched ideas for their GPA. But I wish he'd had the curiosity to ask me instead about what I'd done with the program so far, how we could best utilize it, or what I would bring to the role. A respectful conversation like that would have allowed me to stay in the confidence of what I was bringing to the organization and better understand what he wanted or expected in the people he promoted, without me feeling undermined.

It was once pointed out that my asking people about their distinctive last names just after meeting them—"What nationality is Bellodarvishton?"—made some uncomfortable. It hadn't occurred to me that my friendly icebreaker could make people question if I were hostile to their ethnicity or wonder why I'd singled out their differentness. As one interested in people, I'm still inclined to ask about names and origins, but I've learned to wait until we've established some rapport first.

It's distressing to discover the unintended negative effects of our questions and remarks. But we can opt to see it as a favor—one that makes us more aware of our impact and opportunities to bridge the gaps between each other.

Asking or Demanding?

In asking hundreds of people about their asking experiences, a few confused asking with demanding. One man prefaced his story with "I always insist on the best and get it," and then proudly told me how easily he bullies (my word, not his) service industry workers into getting what he wants. The conversation left me wondering, *Is anyone happy to see this guy when he enters a room?* But folks like him, whose coercive stories I did not include, convinced me that pointing out the difference between asking and demanding is worth the ink.

An ask seeks help, consent, or cooperation yet respects the right of the respondent to reply as they wish. If the answer is no, the asker knows they're free to try another way, or at another time, or ask someone more inclined to say yes. So, an ask is not a demand. A demand is a claim on something we believe we're entitled to (hopefully, legitimately so) and therefore feel compelled to express ourselves with more force. Like Matt Walsh Egan did. Here's his story.

> I was severely overworked and underpaid at the production house where I worked as an assistant editor. Many nights, it was not unusual for me to work until 1 a.m. So, when my annual review came around, I'd done the math and was prepared to make my case for a 25% raise.
>
> The general manager and two of the partners sat across from me. I showed them, clearly and concisely, that I'd accounted for all my time, the projects I was working on, the budgets, and how my salary factored into my hourly rate. I had the right numbers and they knew it. When I asked for the increase and they said it was "insane," trying to bait me to back down, I wasn't fazed. I didn't use emotional language. I knew my work was high quality and knew my worth in the marketplace.

I was always very polite in the job. Eager to learn. Never say no. But there I was putting my foot down, fighting for myself. I thought they might give me only half of what I asked for, but I knew they wouldn't fire me. I was doing a good job, and the clients liked me.

I got the raise—25%—*and* a paid-week-off to finish unpacking in the one-bedroom apartment I'd just moved into. I learned that day never to hesitate to ask for what I'm worth.

Matt Walsh Egan is the same person who, in Chapter 9, called an ad agency every week for four months before getting a promised meeting. Both stories are good reminders that some goals need the fuel of determination. A respectful show of resolve can move others to take our requests more seriously without turning them into adversaries.

Asking or Provoking?

Just as a demand is not an ask, neither is its escalated form, the ultimatum. An ultimatum says *Do this or else.* Here we see the spouse who threatens divorce if the partner continues to refuse help for a gambling addiction; the employee who vows to report a colleague's harassment if it doesn't stop immediately; the customer service rep who warns, "If you keep shouting and calling me names, I will end this call." When inviolable boundaries are crossed, ultimatums earn their moment.

Right timing is critical here. It's unfair, for example, to surprise a "first offender" with consequences when they may not even be sure what they've done or had a chance to correct it. And as a hardball tactic in negotiations, the one who says "Take it or leave it" too soon loses face if they wind up backing down from that position. (Studies of negotiations show that if the ultimatum is made with anger or frustration, only half as many offers are accepted.[6])

So, what would incite a person to punch prematurely? Several possibilities. They might distrust their own ability to ask effectively or the other's willingness to listen. They might fear appearing weak. Or perhaps they're habitually "wired for combat," approaching even minor conflicts with fists balled up expecting, and getting, a fight. A mix of these motives was clearly at work in a story from my own life.

While refinishing an old maple table, my friend "Charlotte" ran out of tung oil, a wood finishing product. When she went to her local hardware store and couldn't find the same brand, an employee told her that any tung oil could be used to finish the job. She chose one and took it home, only to discover that the oils did *not* mix. The table's lustrous finish became a sticky, blotchy mess. It would need to be redone from scratch.

She believed the hardware store was at fault for giving her bad advice and wanted them to cover the costs of having the table refinished by a professional.

Charlotte asked me to accompany her to the store, both for moral support and the not unreasonable belief, sadly, that her request might be taken more seriously if she were with a man in the mostly male environment. I figured her chances of the store paying for pro refinishing were small but that they might offer her some free products or discounts.

She asked for the manager, who greeted us cordially. He listened with a concerned expression as Charlotte began to calmly tell her story. As she neared her ask, however, she became agitated. Her words rat-a-tatted like machine guns. I was relieved when she finally got to the point.

"So, I think it would be fair if the store pays for my table to be professionally refinished."

But then, before the manager could respond, Charlotte added, fatally, "And if we can't work this out, I have an attorney who will get involved."

The manager's jaw dropped as fast as mine did. Blindsided by the unprovoked threat, he shot back, "FINE! CALL YOUR ATTORNEY!" and stormed off.

Charlotte's obstacle was not the manager but herself. Her panicky thoughts, *You'll deny my request and I'll feel powerless and angry,* escalated into *I'll stick it to you before you can stick it to me!* ... though the manager had done nothing but listen attentively. She had virtually backed him into a corner, an act that detonated any deal she'd hoped for. She walked away with nothing. To her credit, she knew she mishandled the whole thing and gave no thought to legal action.

In a few brief moments, I had witnessed my friend's fears turn a reasonable ask into an insulting ultimatum. Except in response to extremes, demands and ultimatums should be the *last* step to get what we want. Premature, they're disastrous. Ask first.

> You cannot antagonize and influence at the same time.
> —JOHN KNOX, Scottish clergyman

CHAPTER FIFTEEN

WANT TO CONNECT WITH PEOPLE?

The greatest compliment that was ever paid me was when one
asked me what I thought and attended to my answer.
—HENRY DAVID THOREAU

ON *LATE NIGHT WITH SETH MYERS*, GUEST MAYA RUDOLPH
reminisced with the host about their mutual experience on *Saturday
Night Live* with a famous socialite-heiress. "No one could really get
Paris Hilton, our host, to engage in any personal conversations,"
says Rudolph in the interview. "And [Seth Myers] said, 'The first
person she asks a personal question I'll give a hundred bucks.'"[1]

Nobody got the hundred bucks.

This chapter is about the overlooked power of asking personal
questions to connect with people. By "personal questions," I mean
everything from superficial icebreakers—"How long have you lived
in Mayberry?"—to high-disclosure probes: "How do you feel that
near-death experience changed you?" By "connect," I mean finding

common ground, mutual understanding, or some degree of intimacy. And by "people" I mean anybody—prospective romantic partners, friends, family members, clients, co-workers, and even strangers, those folks Mom warned us not to talk to.

My friend Ben Hollis understands how personal questions connect us. The winner of eight regional Emmy Awards for creating and producing shows including *Wild Chicago* and *Ben Loves Chicago*, Ben now hosts a live (non-broadcast) show in which he interviews random individuals in corporate and community audiences starting with the question, "What's it like to be you?" (it's also the name of the show). From there, the conversation goes anywhere and everywhere.

"It's a joy to see people light up when I'm asking them personal questions," Ben said. "They come to life. My take is that it's been a long time or maybe never that they've been asked about their experiences and insights."

I'm struck by Ben's assessment, "a long time or maybe never." Perhaps failing to engage others through personal questions, as Seth Myers was betting on, is not unique to socialite heiresses? Some people are so incurious about others that if by some magic they had the opportunity to ask ONE QUESTION of, say, the builders of Stonehenge, would ask, "Know what my idiot boss said to me this morning?" And that's a problem. Because if it's only chatbots or product surveys asking us about ourselves, we're failing each other.

We're certainly not obliged to uncover everyone's life story. But without even a mild interest in our fellow earthly travelers, conversations get reduced to waiting our turn to talk (if we're conversing at all). And that leaves us with little understanding of each other, little connection, and fewer opportunities to develop empathy. If people call you "deep" because you ask about things other than their Netflix recommendations, you know how rare personal inquiry can be.

Tell Me What It Is. *Allan Biggar is a former managing director (London) of the global public relations and communications firm Burson-Marsteller.*

There was a young lady who worked for me. We were doing a professional review, and she was going through all the predictable answers to things. And I just instinctively felt, this isn't where she wants to be. I asked her, "What do you want to do?" She was literally taken aback by my question; her whole body moved back, and she was flustered and speechless.

I said, "Tell me what it is."

She told me she was intimidated because I was her boss, and she thought I was going to fire her. I asked her to trust me to answer the question. And she did. She was profoundly unhappy in the support-admin world and wanted to be client-facing.

She went on to an extremely successful career as a senior communications director in a very large company and credits that simple intervention—when somebody actually asked her what she wanted—as the opportunity to move to something else.[2]

Allan Biggar's curiosity sparked a question that resulted in more than a momentary connection; it changed a career. And yet, as our next story shows, even small talk can have a big impact.

Candy Man. *Andrea Gotskind-Hamad is proprietor of a children's shoes and clothing boutique in Naperville, Illinois.*

Entering a chocolate store, I saw a man buying eight giant bags of boxed candy and jokingly asked him, "How badly did you screw up?" He told me with a smile that he'd just had his last chemo treatment, and the candy was for all the nurses and doctors who had saved his life and treated him so well. I helped him carry the bags to his car as he told me more of his story. He sent me off with a lovely hug. Back in the store the clerk gave me a big bag of candy for helping him. Instant karma indeed! My advice: engage warm, kind folks like this man, for it can truly change your day.

Andrea Gotskind-Hamad could've walked into the store, scrolled through her phone, and ignored the stranger buying half the inventory in front of her. But curiosity drove her to ask him a funny offhand question. His answer not only brought her joy but surely doubled his own. We may never know the impact of our briefest interactions with those we meet. But sometimes, if we're lucky, we do.

If you want to have an interesting conversation, be interested. If you want to meet interesting people, be interested in the people you meet—their lives, their history, their story. Where are they from? How did they get there? What have they learned? By practicing the art of being interested, the majority of people become fascinating teachers; nearly everyone has an interesting story to tell.
—JIM COLLINS, author, *Built to Last and Good to Great*

Dumping the Script

A good conversation can take us into unknown territory— unexplored topics, fresh observations, unexpected insights. It's an area Kevin Sessums knows well. He is an author and journalist best known for his in-depth profiles of Beyoncé, Tom Cruise, Barbra

Streisand, Matthew McConaughey and other celebrities for publications including *Vanity Fair, Playboy,* and *Interview*. He's also
the author of two *New York Times* bestsellers, *Mississippi Sissy* and
I Left It on the Mountain, and writes the Substack column SES/
SUMS IT UP. I asked Kevin about his approach to interviews.

> I never look at an interview as an interview. I look at it as a
> conversation and I just listen. I listen actively. I don't have
> a formal set of questions. Every interview I've ever done I
> surprised myself with the questions I asked because I don't
> know what the person's going to say. People don't talk about
> anything they don't want to talk about, so you have to really
> listen to them and realize, oh, *this* is what they want to talk
> about. And you begin to ask them questions you had no
> idea you were going to ask about, because it's a conversation.

When is the last time you, like Kevin Sessums, were *surprised*
by the questions you asked in a conversation? When did you find
yourself asking questions to discover something new about the
person (as opposed to sticking to the safety of your favorite topics)?
Asking questions that invite personal disclosure is like casting a
fishing line into a river; you never know what might come up. And
if there's rapport, the other party might cast a few questions in *your*
direction. In my book, that's an ideal conversation.

At 26, fishing of this nature took me into deep waters. Every
Sunday, for one year, I sat in a circle with 10 others as we strived to
examine our belief systems, authentically express ourselves, resolve
conflicts, and listen with open minds. Week by week, we learned
to trust each other with our greatest vulnerabilities. The 200-hour
Facilitator Training Program was run by the Oasis Center[3] on
Chicago's north side, likened at the time to the Esalen Institute
for the breadth and depth of its personal growth curriculum. My
biggest "aha" from that powerfully bonding experience was that

we all have an inner life, quite often a rich and complex one, and it is only when we trust we'll be thoughtfully heard that we feel safe to express it.

That said, we don't need to sit on floor pillows and probe the souls of others to connect with them. But we can do something just as selfless: we can give them our undivided attention. If it doesn't come naturally to you, challenge yourself to give your full listening presence to people. Pick up on something they've said and ask open-ended questions (who, what, where, when, how, why) that encourage them to reveal a little more of who they are and what they're about.

"How did it feel to get that news?"
"Why did you decide to go it alone?"
"What's it like to have that responsibility?"
"What's important to you about achieving that?"
"What helped you get through that rough time?"
"What surprised you most about the experience?"
"At what point did your perspective change on that?"
"What attracted you to that (person, hobby, sport, place, etc.)?"

As a society we're becoming more cut off from each other, and more insular. But one small way to spring the lids on our isolation pods is to become curious about people. Set the intention to be more present with them (ideally in-person). Ask questions and engage them. Give yourself to your time together. As a handmade Christmas card from an old friend and her family once encouraged, "Be a light on the tree, not just an ornament!"

Seduction 101: Tell me More

Do you recall Dr. Robert Cialdini's findings, that we like people to whom we're similar, or with whom we feel a sense of unity, or who compliment us? Another factor that influences liking and helps us connect, is asking personal questions (a form of compliment in itself). People like us more when we ask them about themselves,[4] even if being liked by them may be unimportant to us.

But if you want to supercharge the connection and totally rock their world, here's the secret: ask follow-up questions. Few of us expect to be asked one question, let alone several. It can be startling to find ourselves the subject of interest, whether the listener is someone we've just met or known for years. Who isn't thrilled when a conversation partner invites us to "Tell me more"? Is it any surprise the French *coeur* (heart) is at the very center of *encouragement*?

If you're not naturally curious about others, make a point of asking follow-up questions. As you talk with someone, face-to-face or by phone, tell yourself you're going to ask at least three questions based on the thread of the conversation. This intention primes you to stay focused in the moment, to pay attention. You're strengthening your ability to concentrate—a skill in short supply in the digital age that you can use anywhere.

Ask a question related to the topic—"You say you never planned to become a paramedic. How'd you get into that line of work?" As they respond, listen for something you could ask them to expand on or clarify—"So, what's an example of the new medical techniques you mentioned?" Do that two or three more times in the conversation, without turning it into an interview or interrogation. Studies indicate the person will like you more. Why? Because you're responsive. You're interested. You're finding them worthwhile.

The benefit to you? In addition to exercising your capacity to be fully present, you might discover something interesting you didn't know about them, or something you have in common (similarity principle) if not a deeper bond (unity principle) than had you asked only one question, or none. And if they're curious and socially on the ball, they might ask questions to learn about you. If they don't, don't take it personally. Many people are so hungry to be heard, or socially insecure, or self-absorbed, that it doesn't occur to them to ask questions in return; the engagement is strictly one-way. And yet, nice as it is to be asked, you don't need their questions to share something about yourself.

What of more ambitious intentions? It's easier to turn someone into a client or referral partner if they like you. And they'll like you more if you fire a few follow-up questions—a *must* in job interviews. The candidate who comes prepared with questions and listens and asks follow-ups has an edge over those who sit passively waiting for the next question.

And here's a hot tip for love-seeking singles: regardless of gender, "people who ask a higher proportion of follow-up questions have increased date success."[5] Psychotherapist Rachel Sussman, introduced previously, observes this dynamic often in her practice.

When one of my clients tells me what they didn't like about a date, what they all say is that their date talked about themselves the entire time and didn't ask anything about them. Some people who only talk about themselves on dates may just be nervous, and for that reason I might advise my clients to give that person another chance. But if they give them another chance and the person *still* talks about themselves the whole time, I'm like, never see that person again.

What they *do* like, though, is when their date was a great listener, or asked really good follow-up questions, or remembered something said earlier in the date, or the second date, and said, "Hey, how was that trip you went on?" or "How was that big work meeting that you were preparing for?" That's always an excellent sign.[6]

Talking only about oneself isn't just poison on dates; it's a conversation killer everywhere. As a friend of mine said of a long-winded in-law, "All I have to do is ask "How are you?" and I'm done for the evening!" If you catch yourself dominating a conversation, take a breath and give the floor to others. Listen and ask a few follow-up questions.

In close relationships, asking personal questions builds intimacy. Most of us seek genuine understanding and connection with our friends and romantic partners. And yet, over time we stop asking the questions leading to mutual discovery we asked at the start. We begin to assume more than we ask, which can lead to a gradual disconnection. If one person is asking about the other but not being asked in return, he or she may grow to feel undervalued, if not invisible in the relationship.

For couples, Richard Schwartz, associate professor of psychiatry at Harvard Medical School, gives this advice: "What keeps love alive is being able to recognize that you don't really know your partner perfectly and still being curious and still be exploring. Which means, in addition to being sure you have enough time and involvement with each other ... making sure you have enough separateness that you can be an object of curiosity for the other person."[7]

Our love shines through in the quality of our attention. Sometimes, all it takes is asking the person we know so well, "How's that book you're reading?" or "How was your day?"—and then listening as if nothing else matters.

Attentiveness shows respect in business conversations; heightens attractiveness in dating; keeps intimacy alive in relationships; lets our children know they're worth our time; and roots us in the present moment in a chronically distracted world.

Attention is the rarest and purest form of generosity.
—SIMONE WEIL, philosopher

Calming Influence. *Charity Cox-Hayden has served in various nursing leadership roles including chief nursing officer and director of surgical services.*

A nurse called me to help her with a patient who was having a procedure that required him to lie still. But the patient was incredibly tense. He also had a cognitive disability. The nurse probably just wanted me to help hold him still. But instead, I went around to the front of the bed, got on my hands and knees because the bed was so low, held onto his hands, and had a personal conversation with him. I didn't ask him about his pain level or whether he was warm or cold because the nurse had already taken care of that. My opportunity was to talk with him on a personal level, where he was from, what he did in life, and just listen. And he quieted down. The doctor was able to perform the procedure and later thanked me.[8]

For a distressed patient, Charity Cox-Hayden's questions were a balm and a bridge. That the man had a cognitive disability doesn't minimize the power of her actions. For any of us, even the smallest gestures of interest and empathy can be good medicine.

Safe to Ask. Jeffrey Saver is a musical director and conductor on Broadway, Off-Broadway, and in regional theatres. His credits include the Kander and Ebb hits *Chicago* and *Kiss of the Spider Woman*, and Stephen Sondheim's *Merrily We Roll Along*, *Sweeney Todd*, *Into the Woods*, and *Sunday in the Park with George*. On the topic of asking personal questions, he shared this story.

When you work with people you admire but never thought you'd have the opportunity to work with, you find out just how human, how vulnerable they are.

One night in 1991, at the Arena Stage in Washington D.C., I was sitting with Stephen Sondheim as he gave me notes after a performance of his and George Furth's show *Merrily We Roll Along*. I was the music director/conductor. There was nobody there in the back of the theatre but us and it was quiet.

When he'd finished giving his notes, he asked me about my family, and I started talking about my parents a bit, that I was excited they were coming to see the show. I didn't know anything about his personal life at that point. He started asking me more probing questions about my parents and said, "It sounds like you have a great relationship with your mom."

And I said, "Yes, I have great relationships with both my parents. Do you have a good relationship with your mom?"

At that point he was facing straight ahead, not looking at me, and said, "My mother was in the hospital for an operation several years ago. And just before she went into surgery, she said to me, 'The only mistake I ever made'—Sondheim turned his head to face me—'was having you.'"

I wanted to disappear. I wanted to sink down into Middle Earth! I felt like I had asked the worst possible question. Also, I couldn't even take in the information. What kind of parent would say that to their own child? I somehow changed the subject and then walked him back to his hotel.

Upon arriving back in New York, I immediately called [composer] John Kander and told him about that conversation. And he said, "You asked him WHAT? *Everybody* knows that story about his mother, and that he had a f'd-up childhood!" Well, I didn't know.

Sometimes asking questions takes courage, and I suppose to have that courage you have to feel it's safe to communicate. You've got to trust that the person senses that your interest in them is genuine and that the choice to respond is always theirs. [9]

One of the most beautiful qualities of true friendship
is to understand and to be understood.
—SENECA

Mending a Broken Connection: Asking Forgiveness

If asking personal questions creates deeper connections, asking forgiveness mends broken ones. A heartfelt, face-to-face apology (or at the very least, one spoken over the phone) is not just an expression of remorse. It's also a plea to reconnect, redeem ourselves, and restore harmony with those we've wronged.

A true apology calls on our humility, empathy, and commitment to make amends.[10] Whether you're the one apologizing or forgiving, you know how freeing it is move forward in peace. The potential for mutual healing is significant. Forgiveness has the power to settle souls.

John Qualls is the CEO and president of Purpose HQ, an Indiana-based talent optimization company. I met John as a fellow presenter at a motivational conference in Terra Haute. A few days after the event, he told me his story of reaching back through time to ask forgiveness.

> At 15, I hung out with the wrong people, made some bad choices, and got a girl who I was dating pregnant. While I was scared to death and denying I was involved, she went through that process alone.
>
> She gave the child up for adoption. My lowest moment was when she sent me a picture of the baby. I felt ashamed that I wasn't strong enough to accept that responsibility. Determined to get a new start, I graduated early from high school, joined the Marine Corps, served in the Gulf War, and eventually got married.

By the time I was 36, I was the father of our three children. One day I got a call from the birth mother of the baby she'd put up for adoption. She said that our child, now a young woman, wanted to meet us.

We met with her at a hotel downtown. Showing her where we grew up, and where she was conceived and born, was surreal for us, but it answered a lot of unanswered questions for her as well. Her adoptive father had passed away and she seemed adrift in understanding who she was. It was uplifting to see her reaction to the places and stories about how she came to be.

In the 21 years that had passed since our high school crisis, I had never asked the birth mother for forgiveness. But shortly after the visit with our daughter, I poured out my heart to her. I apologized for the decisions I'd made and for the ramifications on her life. I told her how incredibly brave I felt she had been to do the right thing, that I was profoundly sorry.

"I forgive you," she said. "We were kids doing adult things."

Up to that point in my life, I had been successful but not satisfied. I was always out to prove myself because I had felt like an imposter. But when I asked and received the forgiveness of my wife, the birth mother, and, ultimately, myself, I had put the last remnant of that shame behind me.

While the relationship with my daughter has had challenges, I remain supportive in her life, maintaining a connection within healthy boundaries. I understand that healing takes time. And being available, even at a distance, has made a difference.

We are all connected to everyone and everything in the universe. Therefore, everything one does as an individual affects the whole.
—SERGE KAHILI KING, director, Huna International

Asking for the Truth

Next to forgiveness, one of the most difficult things to ask for is the truth. A truth unveiled has the power to level or liberate us, to connect or divide us, and everything in between.

While out for a walk in a quiet wooded area one morning, a friend of mine was startled out of her reverie by a clear, calm voice: *Ask James if he's having an affair.* She said the voice that came out of nowhere had an almost physical presence, as if beside or behind her, but she knew it had spoken from a place within herself. That evening she asked James, her husband of 16 years, the question she'd never consciously considered but had been so mysteriously prompted to ask. He answered *yes.*

Very often we already know, at some level, the truth of things. But asking offers the only chance for confirmation, the only hope for peace. If someone holds the key to something you long to know—or *must* know to set things right—set aside the weight of speculation. Ask. The unburdening may be mutual.

What Happened? *Name Withheld by Request.*

For three months during my senior year in high school I was hidden away in a convent. My mother, acting on the advice of a priest, had sent me there, determined to keep her unwed daughter's pregnancy a secret. Besides my parents and older brother, Brian, nobody was told the truth about my time away, not even my six younger siblings. The story they were given was that I was in Baltimore taking care of a sick aunt.

Under the care of the nuns, I delivered a son who at my mother's insistence was quickly put up for adoption. When I returned home, I found that Brian, then 18, had moved out of the house. What I couldn't have anticipated then, however, was the length of his absence.

There was little contact. Brian didn't come to any of the family events. The story I got from the family was, "Oh, he's gotten all wrapped up in a new church group and doesn't want to be bothered by us."

I carried on with my life, went to college, and that kept me occupied. Once in a great while, he would briefly reappear. We attended each other's weddings but had no quality time together; we were just each other's guests. He had children; I had children. Our separate lives went on. A good chunk of my adult life went by without seeing him.

By my early 40s, I was becoming increasingly troubled by the estrangement. As the two oldest children, Brian and I had always been close growing up. We had had a bond. I missed him.

One day I wrote him a letter that basically asked, "What happened?"

I got his answer a few weeks later, in a phone call. Nothing could have prepared me for what he told me. While I was at the convent, he said, someone at my high school had guessed I was away because I was pregnant. Our mother was furious and immediately blamed Brian for telling, though he vehemently denied it. She then did the unthinkable. She told Brian that if she found out that anyone was told about the pregnancy, she would say that he had raped me and was the father of my child.

The ugliness of the lie and the viciousness of the threat upset him terribly, and he moved out of the house. He began detaching himself from the rest of the family, including me, the unwitting source of his trauma.

My asking, and his telling me the truth, was the turning point in our relationship. It was very healing. Since that conversation he has made an effort to come to every family event that he can. We've even had some hugs along the way, which we hadn't had. We will never be what we were, but I feel we've had closure.

Our mother has had Alzheimer's for several years, so confronting her about this isn't an option. And my brother and I agreed not to tell our siblings the reason for his previous absences. If any of them want to know, they'll have to care enough to do what I did. They'll have to ask him.[11]

Peace, if possible, but truth at any rate.
—ABRAHAM LINCOLN

CHAPTER SIXTEEN

WHAT ARE YOU WAITING FOR?

Our doubts are traitors,
And make us lose the good we oft might win
By fearing to attempt.
—WILLIAM SHAKESPEARE

AT THE CLOSE OF EACH CONVERSATION I ASKED THE storytellers, "What is something you regret not having asked?" In sharing their "if only's," they've given us a timely and priceless gift: the opportunity to ask ourselves, *What can I ask now to avoid regretting my silence later?*

I happened to be one of the early members of a company I worked for, and I did not ask about equity in the company. I learned later that I could probably have bought into it and had ownership, but I never thought to ask about it. At the

time, it would've felt risky to ask, and that's why I didn't. It felt like, Who are you? You're just a nurse, you shouldn't be asking that kind of question.
—*Charity Cox-Hayden*

I was invited to become a member of a comedy troupe, which meant I'd be in every show. But a quiet voice within me didn't feel right committing to it. What I really wanted was to ask if I could do their shows *without* joining the company. But I wanted it so badly I didn't have the courage to ask that, because I just assumed they'd say no. So, I became a member. Soon afterward, the company was sued. Cost me a couple thousand to get out of it.
—*Errol McLendon*

When I was in college and ready to graduate, I had a horrible student teaching experience that made me feel I wasn't worthy of becoming a teacher. My supervising teacher was hypercritical of everything I did. And so, I decided not to teach.I worked in a different field for eight years before finally leaving to again pursue a teaching career. But I really regret not talking to my education professors at the time and asking for help through that internal struggle. Because if I had taught right out of college, I'd have 25 years of teaching and be retired right now!
—*Catherine Brownstone-Stillwell*

I ran track in college and had an exceptional college experience at my alma mater. But because I felt I was a good student and athlete, I'd really wanted to go to an Ivy League School or a West Coast athletic school instead. Yet I didn't have it in my head to clearly ask and make that happen. I was waiting for *them* to select me versus reaching out to Cornell

or UCLA or USC, to talk to them about getting me there. If I'd read [sales expert] Zig Ziglar back then, I'd have known that the worst thing the schools could've told me was no. But I didn't give them the chance to tell me because I didn't feel I earned it or deserved it, and I self-talked my way out of making those asks.
—*Brian Little*

At 24, I was handed an extraordinary opportunity. As a senior assistant editor at a Chicago production house, I'd crafted a 90-second network promo for our ad agency's top client, Disney. The senior creatives at the agency screened my promo for a top commercial director—a legend in the industry—who they wanted to direct it. After watching it, the director told the agency, "This is amazing! I want to meet this editor!" It was the opportunity of a lifetime, a chance to ask to work for him. But fear held me back. I worried that if he declined, word would spread to my employer that I was job-hunting, and I'd be fired. So, I didn't ask. And I still regret it.
—*Matt Walsh Egan*

I regret not asking for more guidance about student loans and financial planning in college. I had a private loan but didn't realize the impact that would later have for me. I was so engulfed in the idea of just getting to school and trying to do things myself, that I didn't even think to ask for the one-on-one consultation I needed.
—*Corey Washington*

My father was a very closed-in person, always careful and always sad. He never drank alcohol because he was afraid that he would talk about his secrets. I ask myself why I

didn't ask him about his childhood or how he grew up. It was many years later that I learned he was married and had a child before marrying my mother.
—*Ida Paluch Kersz*

My mother died very young, when I and my children were also very young. I wish I'd have asked her more questions about things: What was it like for you when we were younger? What was it like being the middle child? What do you remember about your 20s? Tell me about *you*.
—*Dr. Janyce Agruss*

I was 21 when my grandfather died suddenly. He taught me how to drive and fish and I expected he'd be around for a while. But I should've asked him early on: How did you have the guts to leave your family and everybody in Russia? How bad was it?
—*Jeffrey Breslow*

[There was a rider on a black stallion] in Aleppo, just before the civil war. It's one of my big regrets that I didn't ask if I could ride that horse … By the time it even occurred to me to ask, they had galloped off into the night. But, oh, I still feel it as such a missed opportunity. To paraphrase the old saying: you only regret the things you didn't ask.[1]
—*Kieran Meeke*

Four years ago, a friend sent me a terrifying little meme that made me think about my life very differently. It said, "Definition of hell: in the moment before you die, the person you are with the life you've lived meets the person you could've become with the life you could've lived." I put difficult questions on myself as often as I can to get deeper

into me and get rid of the layers of what blocks me. But I regret earlier on not having turned the questions that I asked other people on myself, and what I wanted in my own life. Questions like, "Am I using my time in the most valuable way for me?" I spent a lot of time on things that were successful but didn't make me happy. But I get the joke now!
—*John Cummins*

* * *

In *Oliver Twist*, an ask serves up the story's first pivotal moment. Standing up to the brutal stares of the workhouse officials, young Oliver raises his bowl of gruel to ask, "Please, sir, I want some more" (echoes of my airline peanuts request). The punishment is harsh and swift. But Oliver's ask ultimately catapults him far beyond the frigid workhouse into the warmth of his true home and family. Had our young hero not braved the ask he'd have remained in his prison, eyeing the world through narrow, sunless windows.

Most of us are looking through narrow windows—frames of perception that distort our beliefs about what is possible. We assume life is only as it appears through the glass. We see the present through the pane of the past, believing the way it has been is the way it will be always. As Voltaire spun it, we're like the silkworm mistaking the confines of its tiny web for the limits of the universe.

But simply acknowledging that we don't have the whole picture frees us from the delusion that we do. When you understand that you're seeing through filters, you can begin to challenge your assumptions about what is true and possible. The window widens; you become more curious and engaged. Once-hard boundaries blur. Options increase. And as that space expands, asking—for anything—becomes a matter of choice, not courage.

Make it your practice to ask:

- Focus on what you want, not on what you don't want.

- Examine your rules about asking and receiving and change those that no longer fit.

- Decide you're worthy of the ask or do what you must to become worthy of it.

- Challenge your beliefs about what is possible: ask What if?

- Assume possibility.

- If you're not confident about asking, Act as If you are.

- Follow the Big Ask Plan to ask effectively and flexibly.

- Persist.

- Risk an audacious ask.

- Ask spontaneously (before you talk yourself out of it).

- Be a giver (it feels great, and others may reciprocate).

- Ask for help without apology.

- Make clarity more important than your fear of asking for it.

- Ask, don't wait for feedback.

- Don't be an askhole.

- Ask others about themselves—and let the people you love know you're listening.

Are you ready to unlock the possibilities in your life? Are you ready to move your thoughts and feet in the direction of your dreams?

Are you ready to ask?

A BIG ASK FROM THE AUTHOR

NOW THAT WE'VE COMPLETED OUR BIG ASK JOURNEY together, I have a few things to ask of you …

- *(Laser ask)* Would you take a few minutes to share your positive reactions to *The Big Ask* on social media and post reviews on Amazon, Goodreads, etc.?

- *(Laser ask)* Who in your life needs encouragement to ask for what they want? Will you tell them about the book?

- *(What If?)* How would it feel to see your big ask story featured in my blog and/or future editions of this book? https://bigaskbook.com/ask-story-submission-guidelines/

- *(Conditional ask)* Will you register at https://bigaskbook.com/ *if* I promise to send you notices of my latest blog posts and book-related updates?

Thank You!

ABOUT THE AUTHOR

PAUL QUINN writes The Big Ask Blog and speaks to audiences on asking as a tool for personal and professional development. As a presentation coach, he assists a wide range of leaders in preparing and delivering talks and keynotes that move their stakeholders to action.

Paul wrote hundreds of multimedia marketing and training materials, many award-winning, for Encyclopedia Britannica, PepsiCo, United Way, Allstate Insurance, Sears, Kraft Foods, Abbot Labs, Junior Achievement, Bosch Automotive, and other clients. As head of client coaching for Unipro Marketing Services, Inc., then the second largest tradeshow marketing company in North America, he led seminars on customer engagement and presentation skills, domestically and abroad, for clients including Xerox, Panasonic, Unisys, Maritz, Amdocs, and Sabreliner Aviation.

A graduate of Illinois State University (Theatre), Paul studied improvisation with Don DePollo at Chicago's Second City and appeared in TV commercials, corporate training videos, and local sketch comedy shows. He received practitioner certification in Neuro-Linguistic Programming from the NLP Institute of Chicago.

www.bigaskbook.com
https://www.linkedin.com/in/paul-quinn-bigaskbook/
Facebook (PaulQuinnAuthor)

ACKNOWLEDGMENTS

I AM GRATEFUL TO THE STORYTELLERS WHO MET WITH me over coffee, by phone, and on video conferencing to share their stories and insights. You are the bright and hopeful heart of this book. My appreciation to the friends who provided feedback on the completed manuscript: Meribeth Kisner-Griffin, Kathryn Hutchinson, Hadley Jaeger, Kate Jordan, and Jenny Suzumoto; and to those who shared their responses to the early sample chapters: Benjamin Dahlbeck, Jan Harris, Evelyn Hopkins, Judy Kowal, Jeffrey Perry, Gail Trotter, and Mari Weiss. Big thanks to my mother, Jackie Denney, for her forever support and encouragement, and to the Chicago Botanic Garden for being the most serenely spectacular place a writer could ever hope to go to clear his head and find inspiration.

PERMISSIONS

Sonia Choquette's story (titled here, Inexplicable Urge) appeared in her Good Vibes newsletter (July 2010) and is reprinted with her permission.

Maria Hinojosa's story, excerpted from her book, *Once I Was You: A Memoir of Love and Hate in a Torn America*, is reprinted with her permission.

John Livesay's story (titled here, Just Imagine) is used with his permission.

Barry Offitzer's story, Tuxedo Trouble, appeared with the same title in The New York Times' Metropolitan Diary (March 31, 2024) and is reprinted with his permission.

RESOURCES

SOME OF THE CONTENT IN *THE BIG ASK* REFERENCES suicide, alcoholism, and domestic violence. If you or someone you care about needs information, resources, or someone to talk to, here are a few services that could help:

National Suicide Prevention Hotline
The lifeline provides 24/7, free, and confidential emotional support to people in suicidal crisis or distress.

1-800-273-TALK (8255)

https://suicidepreventionlifeline.org/

Substance Abuse and Mental Health Services Administration (SAMHSA) National Helpline
A free, confidential, 24/7 treatment referral and information service for individuals and families facing mental and/or substance abuse disorders.

1-800-662-HELP (4357)

https://samhsa.gov/find-help/national-helpline

The National Domestic Violence Hotline

A free, confidential hotline available 24/7 for anybody who is experiencing domestic violence. Their website includes safety tools for those in abusive relationships.

1-800-799-SAFE (7233)

https://thehotline.org/

Recommended Reading on Empowerment/ Assertive Communication

Presence: Bringing Your Boldest Self to Your Biggest Challenges by Amy Cuddy (Little, Brown, Spark) 2015

Crucial Conversations: Tools for Talking When Stakes Are High by Kerry Patterson, Joseph Grenny, Ron McMillan, Al Switzler (McGraw Hill) 2012

Fierce Conversations: Achieving Success at Work & in Life, One Conversation at a Time by Susan Scott (Berkley Publishing Group) 2002

Trust Your Vibes: Secret Tools for Six-Sensory Living by Sonia Choquette (Hay House, Inc.) 2004

REFERENCES

Chapter 1: Why Ask?

1. Vanessa Bohns, *You Have More Influence Than You Think: How We Underestimate Our Power of Persuasion, And Why It Matters* (New York: W.W. Norton & Company, Inc. 2021), 54-55.

2. Jena McGregor, "Asking for a Bigger Starting Salary Pays Off Most of the Time: Survey," *Forbes,* April 25, 2023, https://perma.cc/S42H -JEPW.

3. Jerold Panas, *Asking: A 59-Minute Guide to Everything Board Members, Volunteers, and Staff Must Know to Secure the Gift,* (Medfield, MA: Emerson & Church Publishers, 2007), 24.

4. Michael T. Nietzel, "Students Who Meet with High School Counselor Much More Likely to Receive Financial Aid for College," *Forbes,* February 1, 2023, https://perma.cc/KBY4-L5AM.

5. Vanessa K. Bohns, *You Have More Influence Than You Think: How We Underestimate Our Power of Persuasion, And Why It Matters* (New York: W.W. Norton & Company, Inc, 2021), 67.

6. Heidi Grant, *Reinforcements: How to Get People to Help You,* (Brighton, Massachusetts: *Harvard Business Review* Press, 2018), 41.

7. Dr. Robert Cialdini, *Influence, New and Expanded: The Psychology of Persuasion* (New York: Collins Business Essentials, 2007).

8. Candice DeLong, *Special Agent: My Life on the Front Lines as a Woman in the FBI* (New York: Hyperion Books, 2001).

9. Axel Danielson and Maximilien Van Aertryck, "Ten Meter Tower," 2016 (17 minutes), https://www.youtube.com/watch?v=5QMlIjSnt_E&t=134s.

10. Paul Quinn, "Prove You Can Do This: Russell Leander's Story," *Big Ask Blog,* April 8, 2022, https://bigaskbook.com/2022/04/prove-you -can-do-this/.

11. Paul Quinn, "His 'Asks' Led to Apple Acquisition," *Big Ask Blog,* June 21, 2022, https://perma.cc/7D3W-KTYF.

Chapter 2: What Do You Want?

1. Paul Quinn, "100+ Countries and the Power of an Ask: A Chat with Kieran Meeke," *Big Ask Blog,* May 24, 2022, https://perma.cc/MP95 -EUQV.

2. Paul Quinn, "Dinosaurs in the Shark Tank: Don and Val's Big Ask," *Big Ask Blog* September 14, 2022, https://perma.cc/8ZNX-66E8.

3. Paul Quinn, "Why Today's Great Leaders 'Ask Don't Tell,'" *Big Ask Blog,* March 17, 2022, https://perma.cc/PA3Y-49TB.

4. Paul Quinn, "Asking for Shoes: Intel's Brian Little," *Big Ask Blog,* July 26, 2023, https://bigaskbook.com/2023/07/asking-for-shoes-intels -brian-little/.

Chapter 3: Is It Ok to Ask?

1. Paul Quinn, "Hate to Ask: Jim Lew on Cultural Attitudes About Speaking Up," *Big Ask Blog*, May 17, 2022, https://tinyurl.com /yx74xn26.

2. Dr. Deborah Tannen, "The Power of Talk: Who Gets Heard and Why," *Harvard Business Review*, September-October 1985, https: //hbr.org/1995/09/the-power-of-talk-who-gets-heard-and-why.

3. Ibid.

4. Nancy Colier, "A Woman's Right to Have Needs: The Next Revolution," *Psychology Today*, October 8, 2018, https://www.psychologytoday.com/ intl/blog/inviting-a-monkey-to-tea/201810/a-womans-right-to-have -needs-the-next-revolution.

5. Paul Quinn, "Ask the CEO: The Power of Asking at Burson-Marsteller UK," *Big Ask Blog*, April 11, 2022, https://tinyurl.com/5n77shx3.

Chapter 4: Are You Worthy of the Ask?

1. "Billy Joel Q&A: Can I Play on 'New York State of Mind?' (Vanderbilt 2013)," https://www.youtube.com/watch?v=zxLjtx8wukQ.

2. Tara Sofia Mohr, "Why Women Don't Apply for Jobs Unless They're 100% Qualified," *Harvard Business Review*, August 25, 2014, www.hbr.org/2014/08/why-women-dont-apply-for-jobs -unless-theyre-100-qualified.

3. Janet T Phan, "Apply to a Job, Even If You Don't Meet All Criteria," *Harvard Business Review*, July 20, 2022, https://hbr.org/2022/07/apply -to-a-job-even-if-you-dont-meet-all-criteria.

4. Paul Quinn, "Dinosaurs in the Shark Tank: Don and Val's Big Ask," *Big Ask Blog*, September 14, 2022, https://perma.cc/8ZNX-66E8.

5. Paul Quinn, "Cynthia Barnes: Becoming 2x Confident, 2x Strong," *Big Ask Blog*, July 8, 2022, https://tinyurl.com/5e4fnzbm.

Chapter 5: Is *Yes* Possible?

1. Kai Strittmatter, *We Have Been Harmonized: Life in China's Surveillance State* (Boston, MA: Mariner Books, 2021) 116.

2. Fran Simone, Ph.D, "Negative Self-talk: Don't Let It Overwhelm You," *Psychology Today*, December 4, 2017, https://www.psychologytoday.com/us/ blog/family-affair/201712/negative-self-talk-dont-let-it-overwhelm-you.

3. "Anthony Hopkins on Believe Believe Believe in Yourself," https://www .youtube.com/watch?v=mLuiruce9qE.

4. Paul Quinn, "Want It? Affirm It!" *Big Ask Blog*, October 29, 2024, https://tinyurl.com/2an77sj4. See also "Want It? Imagine It!", *Big Ask Blog*, October 31, 2024, https://tinyurl.com/2s8ejjff.

5. Chan Hellman, "The Science and Power of Hope," TEDxOklahoma City, May 2021, 0:17-0:24, https://www.youtube.com/watch?v =qt0fRSx5Kl4&t=222s.

Chapter 6: How Effectively Do You Ask?

1. Paul Quinn, "Dinosaurs in the Shark Tank: Don and Val's Big Ask," *Big Ask Blog*, September 14, 2022, https://perma.cc/8ZNX-66E8.

2. Mary Wells Lawrence, *A Big Life in Advertising*, (New York: Alfred A. Knopf, 2002), 146.

3. "Get on the Bus; First-Time Voters Get a Ride to the Polls," Green Dot Public Schools, June 30, 2016, https://blog.greendot.org /get-on-the-bus-first-time-voters-get-a-ride-to-the-polls/.

4. "Raise the Titanic fundraiser," https://givebutter.com/Nu4Gev/adriansaker.

5. SB Algoe, LE Kurtz, NM Hilaire, "Putting the 'You' in 'Thank You': Examining Other-Praising Behavior as the Active Relational Ingredient in Expressed Gratitude," Soc Psychol Personal Sci. 2016 Sep;7(7):658 -666. doi: 10.1177/1948550616651681. Epub 2016 Jun 7. PMID: 27570582; PMCID: PMC4988174. https://www.ncbi.nlm.nih.gov /pmc/articles/PMC4988174/.

6. Vanessa Bohns, "A Face-to-face Request is 34 Times More Successful Than an Email," *Harvard Business Review*, April 11, 2017, https://hbr.org/2017 /04/a-face-to-face-request-is-34-times-more-successful-than-an-email.

Chapter 7: Laser, Lateral, or Hint?

1. Lewis Howe, "What's the Chance is the Secret Line to Make Things Happen," https://www.youtube.com/shorts/iacnB2wxpeU.

2. Paul Quinn, "Are You a Victim of the Hedging Epidemic?", *Medium*, September 26, 2018, https://perma.cc/4PMK-DKJR.

Chapter 8: What Influences *Yes*?

1. Dr. Robert Cialdini, *Influence, New and Expanded: The Psychology of Persuasion* (New York: Collins Business Essentials, 2007).

2. AC Little, BC Jones, LM DeBruine, "Facial Attractiveness: Evolutionary Based Research." Philos Trans R Soc Lond B Biol Sci. 2011 Jun 12;366(1571):1638-59. doi: 10.1098/rstb.2010.0404. PMID: 21536551; PMCID: PMC3130383, https://pmc.ncbi.nlm.nih.gov /articles/PMC3130383/.

3. Jill Goodall; Irma Ilustre; Catherine Marquis; Nicholas Nicolella; Joline Sikaitis, (2018). "Effects of Flattery in Obtaining Compliance," Carnegie Mellon University, Journal contribution, https://doi .org/10.1184/R1/6712625.v1.

4. A.W. Brooks, F. Gino, and M.E. Schweitzer, "Smart People Ask for (My) Advice: Seeking Advice Boosts Perceptions of Confidence," Management Science 61, no. 6, June 2015, 1421–1435, https://www.hbs.edu/faculty/Pages/item.aspx?num=47824.

5. Paul Quinn, "Ask and Expand Your Network: Secrets of the Referral Diva®," *Big Ask Blog*, May 2, 2022, https://perma.cc/5A8Z-Z99R.

Chapter 9: Will You Persist?
1. Paul Quinn, "Holocaust Memory: The Ask That Changed Everything," *Big Ask Blog*, March 30, 2023, https://perma.cc/4FZH-YGNV.

Chapter 10: Got Chutzpah?
1. Maria Hinojosa, *Once I Was You: A Memoir* (New York: Atria Publishing Group, 2021) 161-162.

2. Paul Quinn, "An Ask Was Her Ticket to Success," *Big Ask Blog*, March 18, 2022, https://bigaskbook.com/2022/03/an-ask-was-her-ticket-to-success/.

Chapter 11: How's Your Timing?
1. Barbara Sher, "Isolation is the Dream-Killer, Not Your Attitude," TedXPrague," 2016, 14:46, https://www.youtube.com/watch?v=H2rG4Dg6xyI.

2. Paul Quinn, "100+ Countries and the Power of an Ask: A Chat with Kieran Meeke," *Big Ask Blog*, May 24, 2022, https://perma.cc/MP95-EUQV.

3. Paul Quinn, "Asking Big on Broadway: Joshua Ellis Remembers," *Big Ask Blog*, February 20, 2024, https://perma.cc/F25Z-CA8L.

Chapter 12: Need Help?
1. Dolly Parton, ABC News, November 27, 2023, https://abcnews.go.com/GMA/Culture/dolly-parton-talks-assembling-avengers-group-rockstar-collaborators/story?id=104618851.

2. Sam Kean, Mariel Carr, Rigoberto Hernandez, "When Generosity Turns Pathological," Distillations Magazine (Science History Institute Museum & Library), March 26, 2024, https://www.sciencehistory.org/stories/disappearing-pod/when-generosity-turns-pathological/.

3. Paul Quinn, "Inspired Journey: Fashion's David Tupaz," *Big Ask Blog*, June 13, 2022, https://bigaskbook.com/2022/06/inspired -journey-fashions-david-tupaz/.

4. Annabell Ho, Jeff Hancock, and Adam S. Miner, "Psychological, Relational, and Emotional Effects of Self-disclosure After Conversations with a Chatbot," *Journal of Communication*, Volume 68, Issue 4, August 2018, Pages 712–733, https://doi.org/10.1093/joc/jqy026.

5. Jill Suttie, "How Smartphones Are Killing Conversation," *Greater Good Magazine*, December 7, 2015, https://perma.cc/7ZQF-5BBU.

6. Paul Quinn, "When ER Nurses Ask, Patient Outcomes Improve," *Big Ask Blog*, June 7, 2022, https://bigaskbook.com/2022/06/nurses -who-ask-questions-improve-patient-outcomes/.

7. Paul Quinn, "Becoming Siri: Susan Bennett's Story," *Big Ask Blog*, August 2, 2023, https://tinyurl.com/359khaaw.

Chapter 13: Want Feedback?

1. Douglas Stone and Sheila Heen, *Thanks for the Feedback: The Science and Art of Receiving Feedback Well* (New York: Penguin Books, 2014) 9.

2. Dr. Heidi Grant, "Asked for Vs. Unasked for Feedback," https://vimeo .com/291804051.

3. Jaewon Yoon, Hayley Blunden, Ariella Kristal, and Ashley Whillans, "Why Asking for Advice is More Effective Than Asking for Feedback," *Harvard Business Review*, Sept. 20, 2019, https://hbr.org/2019/09 /why-asking-for-advice-is-more-effective-than-asking-for-feedback

4. Paul Quinn, "Cynthia Barnes: Becoming 2x Confident, 2x Strong," *Big Ask Blog*, July 8, 2022, https://tinyurl.com/5e4fnzbm.

5. Jack Zenger and Joseph Folkman, "A Leadership Tip That Just Works: Ask for Feedback," https://zengerfolkman.com/articles/a-leadership -tip-that-just-works-ask-for-feedback/.

6. University of Oregon, Human Resources. https://hr.uoregon.edu/sites /default/files/at_work_my_opinions_count_GallupQ07.pdf.

7. Paul Quinn, "Why Today's Great Leaders 'Ask Don't Tell,'" *Big Ask Blog,* March 17, 2022, https://perma.cc/PA3Y-49TB.

8. Bruce Feiler, "Should Kids Pick Their Own Punishments?", *The New York Times*, April 4, 2013, https://www.nytimes.com/roomfordebate /2013/04/04/should-kids-pick-their-own-punishments-9.

Chapter 14: Asking for Trouble?

1. Paul Quinn, "Is it Hard to Ask the One You Love?", *Big Ask Blog*, August 8, 2023, https://bigaskbook.com/2023/08/ask-the-one-you-love/.

2. Paul Quinn, "When ER Nurses Ask, Patient Outcomes Improve," *Big Ask Blog*, June 7, 2022, https://bigaskbook.com/2022/06 /nurses-who-ask-questions-improve-patient-outcomes/.

3. Tiziana Dearing and Emiko Tamagawa, "What Happened to You' Teaches Kids and Parents How to Address Limb Differences," WBUR.org, May 2, 2023, https://www.wbur.org/hereandnow /2023/05/02/what-happened-to-you-book.

4. Paul Quinn, "How Our Questions Reveal Bias: A Conversation with Rocki Howard," *Big Ask Blog*, May 9, 2022, https://tinyurl.com/3yk63adp.

5. Paul Quinn, "Hate to Ask: Jim Lew on Cultural Attitudes About Speaking Up," *Big Ask Blog*, May 17, 2022, https://tinyurl.com/yx74xn26.

6. Stuart Diamond, Getting More: How to Negotiate to Achieve Your Goals in the Real World (New York: Crown Business) 138. For a related study see Marina Krakovsky, "When Threats Are Better Than Anger," Insights by Stanford Business, April 25, 2012, https://www .gsb.stanford.edu/insights/when-threats-are-better-anger.

Chapter 15: Want to Connect with People?

1. Late Night with Seth Myers, "Maya Rudolph Reveals the Bet Seth Made About Paris Hilton," https://www.youtube.com/watch?v =tgQCz6se80s, 6:17.

2. Paul Quinn, "Ask the CEO: The Power of Asking at Burson-Marsteller UK," *Big Ask Blog,* April 11, 2022, https://tinyurl.com/5n77shx3.

3. The Oasis Center was founded, in Chicago, in 1968 and closed in the late 1990s. Its advisory board included Getstalt therapy founder Fritz Perls and renowned family therapist Virginia Satir. See "Midlife at the Oasis." Chicago Tribune, August 12, 1993, https://www.chicagotribune .com/1993/08/12/midlife-at-the-oasis/.

4. K. Huang, M. Yeomans, A. W. Brooks, J. Minson, & F. Gino. (2017), "It Doesn't Hurt to Ask: Question-asking Increases Liking," *Journal of Personality and Social Psychology*, 2017, Vol. 113, No. 3, 430-452, https: //perma.cc/MQX9-XWUB.

5. Ibid.

6. Paul Quinn, "Is It Hard to Ask the One You Love?", *Big Ask Blog*, August 8, 2023, https://bigaskbook.com/2023/08/ask-the-one -you-love/.

7. Alvin Powell, "When Love and Science Double Date," *The Harvard Gazette*, February 13, 2018, https://tinyurl.com/mr2wf6pc.

8. Paul Quinn, "Safe to Ask? A Chat with a Chief Nursing Officer," *Big Ask Blog*, September 30, 2022, https://tinyurl.com/4cstms7a.

9. The personal conversation Jeffrey Saver and Stephen Sondheim began that night was the first of many the two would enjoy in a friendship that flourished until Sondheim's passing in 2021.

10. Paul Quinn, "Asking Forgiveness: Is Your Apology Empty or Effective?" *Big Ask Blog*, February 11, 2025, https://tinyurl.com/4xc5dh58.

11. Paul Quinn, "Asking for Truth: The Mystery of an Estranged Brother," *Big Ask Blog*, May 4, 2022, https://tinyurl.com/yxwcnhxp.

Chapter 16: What Are You Waiting For?
1. Paul Quinn, "100+ Countries and the Power of an Ask: A Chat with Kieran Meeke," *Big Ask Blog*, May 24, 2022, https://perma.cc/ MP95-EUQV.

PEOPLE INDEX

www.ingramcontent.com/pod-product-compliance
Lightning Source LLC
Chambersburg PA
CBHW021706120626
46545CB00004B/1422